HENRY FIELDING
AUTHORSHIP AND AUTHORITY

Studies in Eighteenth- and Nineteenth-Century Literature

General Editors

Andrew Sanders, Reader in English, Birkbeck College London
David Nokes, Reader in English, King's College London

Published titles

Forms of Speech in Victorian Fiction Raymond Chapman
Henry Fielding: Authorship and Authority Ian A. Bell

HENRY FIELDING
AUTHORSHIP AND AUTHORITY

Ian A. Bell

LONDON AND NEW YORK

Longman Group UK Limited,
Longman House, Burnt Mill,
Harlow, Essex CM20 2JE, England
and Associated Companies throughout the world.

*Published in the United States of America
by Longman Publishing, New York*

© Longman Group UK Limited 1994

First published 1994

ISBN 0 582 08162 9 CSD
ISBN 0 582 08163 7 PPR

British Library Cataloguing-in-Publication Data

A catalogue record for this book is
available from the British Library

Library of Congress Cataloging-in-Publication Data

Bell, Ian A.
    Henry Fielding : authorship and authority / Ian A. Bell.
      p. cm. -- (Studies in eighteenth- and nineteenth-century
literature)
    Includes bibliographical references (p.) and index.
    1. Fielding, Henry, 1707–1754--Criticism and interpretation.
    2. Authors and readers--England--History--18th century.
    3. Authorship--History--18th Century.   4. Authority in literature.
    I. Title. II. Series
PR3458.A9B44   1994
823'.5--dc20   93–34653
                                                        CIP

Set by 7VV in 10pt Goudy Oldstyle
Produced by Longman Singapore Publishers (Pte) Ltd.
Printed in Singapore

Contents

Contents

Acknowledgements

I want to thank a number of people for their help in writing this book. Longman and my editor, David Nokes of King's College London, have been constantly patient and encouraging, and their suggestions have invariably been helpful. My colleagues at Aberystwyth – Brean Hammond and David Shuttleton – should be mentioned by name on virtually every page of the text for the ideas they have stimulated in informal and undirected discussion of eighteenth-century writing, and, of course, many of my students have contributed energy and enthusiasm over recent years. Joan Crawford and June Baxter helped immensely with secretarial matters, and the staff of the Hugh Owen Library also assisted ably. As ever, my main debt lies with my immediate family, who have put up with me tolerantly during the whole period of writing.

Ian A. Bell
University of Wales, Aberystwyth

Chronology

1707	22 April: HF born at Sharpham Park, near Glastonbury, in the county of Somerset, son of Colonel Edmund Fielding and Sarah Fielding (née Gould).
1709	HF lives on family farm at East Stour, Dorset (–1719).
1718	14 April: death of HF's mother, Sarah Fielding.
1719	HF's father remarries; HF sent off to Eton to begin education (–1724).
1728	30 January: HF's first published work appears, *The Masquerade, a Poem* – a satirical poem 'By Lemuel Gulliver'. 16 February: production of first play by HF, *Love in Several Masques* at Drury Lane, published 23 February. 16 March: HF matriculates as student of classics, University of Leyden, Holland.
1729	By the end of April, HF discontinues studies at Leyden and moves to London.
1730–7	HF active as dramatist, author of popular comedies and burlesques performed mainly at the Haymarket theatre or Drury Lane, including *The Author's Farce* (1730), *Rape upon Rape* (1730), *Tom Thumb* (1730), *The Modern Husband* (1732), *The Miser* (1733), *Don Quixote in England* (1734), *Pasquin* (1736), *The Historical Register for the Year 1736* (1737).
1734	28 November: HF elopes with and marries Charlotte Cradock.
1737	June: passage through Parliament of Walpole's Theatrical Licensing Act effectively impedes HF's theatrical output. 1 November: HF takes up study of the law at the Middle Temple.
1739	15 November (–June 1741): HF edits *The Champion; or, British Mercury.*
1740	20 June: HF called to the bar.

1741   2 April: *An Apology for the Life of Mrs. Shamela Andrews.*

1742   22 February: *The History of the Adventures of Joseph Andrews, and of his Friend Mr. Abraham Adams.*

1743   12 April: *Miscellanies* (3 vols), including *The Life of Mr. Jonathan Wild the Great* and *A Journey from This World to the Next.*

1744   13 July: publication of second edition of Sarah Fielding's novel *The Adventures of David Simple*, to which HF contributed.
November: death of Charlotte Cradock.

1745   5 November (–17 June 1746): edits *The True Patriot: and the History of Our Own Times.*

1747   27 November: marries Mary Daniel, who had served as a maid to Charlotte Cradock Fielding.
5 December (–5 November 1748): edits *The Jacobite's Journal.*

1748   25 October: empowered as magistrate for district of Westminster, London.

1749   January: HF takes up his commission as magistrate for County of Middlesex.
3–10 February: *The History of Tom Jones, a Foundling.*

1751   19 January: *An Enquiry into the Causes of the Late Increase of Robbers.*
19 December: *Amelia.*

1752   4 January (–25 November): edits *The Covent-Garden Journal.*
13 April: *Examples of the Interposition of Providence in the Detection and Punishment of Murder.*

1753   29 January: *A Proposal for Making an Effectual Provision for the Poor.*

1754   April: illness leads to resignation from magistracy.
26 June–7 August: for reasons of health, HF undertakes a difficult voyage to Lisbon, during which *The Journal of a Voyage to Lisbon* is written.
8 October: HF dies at Junquiera, near Lisbon.

Abbreviations

The following abbreviations are used throughout the text in sources of extracts of Fielding's work:

CGJ   *The Covent-Garden Journal*
Charge   *A Charge Delivered to the Grand Jury*
JA   *The History of the Adventures of Joseph Andrews, and of his Friend Mr. Abraham Adams*
Journal   *The Journal of a Voyage to Lisbon*
Journey   *A Journey from This World to the Next*
JW   *The Life of Mr. Jonathan Wild the Great*
Misc   *Miscellanies*
Shamela   *An Apology for the Life of Mrs. Shamela Andrews*
TJ   *The History of Tom Jones, A Foundling*

CHAPTER 1
Author! Author!

The death of the author?

AUTHOR. A laughing Stock. It means likewise a poor Fellow, and in general an Object of Contempt. [1]

As institution, the author is dead: his civil status, his biographical person have disappeared; dispossessed, they no longer exercise over his work the formidable paternity whose account literary history, teaching, and public opinion had the responsibility of establishing and renewing; but in the text, in a way, I *desire* the author: I need his figure (which is neither his representation nor his projection), as he needs mine. [2]

To undertake a critical study of an author nowadays seems an oddly paradoxical and anachronistic activity. The chronology which begins this book – so confidently charting the life of an individual uncontentiously identified as Henry Fielding – may turn out to be the last moment of certainty within it. After years of heated debate within literary criticism, the role and status of the author have been extensively reappraised, and the more traditional scholarly attitudes of respect or reverence for a historical personality recoverable from a body of writing have been put under pressure. The notion that texts are the unmediated vehicles for authorial expression no longer seems as unproblematic as once it did, and the corresponding account of the readership as passive consumers now seems archaic. But no simple ideas have as yet emerged to replace these 'common-sense' beliefs. Consequently, it is necessary to offer some preliminary remarks about the nature of the index entry labelled 'Fielding, Henry' under discussion in the ensuing pages.

Of course, anxieties about the status of the author are not only the result of recent theory, and parallels can easily be found within the acknowledged corpus of eighteenth-century writing. The first quotation above, from Fielding's 'A Modern Glossary', articulates contemporary scorn for authors, a recurrent source of concern for so many eighteenth-century writers struggling to cope with their change of status within the developing market economy. The paradox is that as writers became more visible and more prominent in eighteenth-century Britain, with the spread of literacy and the growth of publishing, the social status of the author was radically diminished. As we shall see, Fielding's novels, like so many of Pope's poems, contain within themselves heated and constant chattering about the role of the author and the competence of the reader. The issue here is one of social standing and cultural authority at a moment of radical social change, and it will emerge forcefully as the argument unfolds throughout this book. However, there remains the vexed and more fundamental question of the epistemological status of the author (of whatever period) for literary critics, and that, too, needs some attention.

To what extent is the named author to be seen as the source of meaning and authority in a literary text? The authorial presence, however represented, has traditionally been taken as central to literary criticism and remains prominently inscribed in the language of academic specialisation – 'I'm working on Fielding' – as well as in a whole range of diverse social practices, from library catalogues to TV chat shows. But even though we may still have difficulty in avoiding the language of authorship, any consensus about the author as a literary producer and as a recoverable personality has long since broken down. In recent years, amid intense discussion of the problems of defining the proper subject for literary criticism, and often fervid reassessment of the attendant methodological complications, we have seen the once secure and cohesive 'author' appear and disappear from view with the speed and bewildering dexterity of a conjuror's rabbit: now you see him, now you don't.

As a result of this pervasive crisis of confidence in the received practices of literary study, it is perhaps no longer as easy or as natural as once it must have seemed to assemble a critical monograph around the unifying figure of an established and well-known writer, even one as visible and prominent in contemporary culture as Fielding was. On this subject, as on so many others, the flamboyant questions posed by Roland Barthes are always an exciting and stimulating point of departure, forcing us to confront our most deep-seated critical assumptions and perhaps to reconsider the appropriateness of our inherited and intuitive interpretive procedures.

In the second passage quoted above, from *The Pleasure of the Text* (1973), Barthes moves away from the more rigorous structuralist economy of his earlier work, most dramatically announced in 'The Death of the Author' (1968), towards a partial reinstatement of recognisable authorial presence. In his earlier work, Barthes provocatively and deliberately overstated his case in such a way as to make the 'author' a wholly redundant piece of critical terminology for literary critics. The legitimate business of such commentators was, he claimed, to desist from arid or fanciful speculation about the human or biographical origins of individual pieces of writing. Instead, the critic should dispassionately articulate the internal narrative grammar of texts, after the fashion of Vladimir Propp or A.J. Greimas, or show how the particular text under examination realised an inter-connection of identifiable codes, signs and meanings. Barthes himself famously offered exemplary specimens of these procedures applied to the popular James Bond novel *Goldfinger* in his essay 'Introduction to the Structural Analysis of Narratives' (1966) and, in an even more systematic and extensive way, he produced an extensive taxonomy of the narrative and semiotic devices to be found in Balzac's story *Sarrasine* in *S/Z* (1970).

In his more eclectic post-structuralist essays, however, Barthes decisively breaks with the constraining inheritance of formalism, leaving such detailed and exhaustive technical analysis behind. In its place he offers an altogether more mystical and suggestive account of the reading process and of writing. While still challenging and seeking to discredit the prevailing bourgeois notion of the self-determining individual human subject, Barthes subsequently emphasises the importance of hedonism in reading, of what he calls *jouissance*, the joyful possession of reader by text and text by reader – that rare moment when the reader and the thing being read come together. In an odd way, then, the author returns from a period of enforced exile, not as a recoverable historical personage, but as some kind of experiential presence, an aphrodisiac component of the reading process, no more (and no less) alive than a personal pronoun.

Although the way Barthes addresses the problem of authorship is especially provocative, it would obviously be wrong (as well as flagrantly paradoxical) wholly to personalise the issue. Barthes may act as a useful focal point, but he is by no means the only recent commentator to address the problem of articulating the presence or absence of the author in ways relevant to (and sometimes disconcerting for) the present study. Since the 1960s, there has been a decisive move away from traditionally understood biographical study in many areas of intellectual pursuit, hastened and encouraged by the development of semiotics and the increasing prominence of psycho-analytic approaches to texts, all of which tend to destabilise and disperse the identifiable single controlling 'author' for any utterance. Semiotic approaches have concentrated on the communicative practices within texts, and psychoanalytic strategies have been more concerned with the 'unconscious' elements of writing than the deliberate expressiveness of any author. Developed theories of authorship have consequently become problematics, intricate and complex materialist negotiations of ideology, commodity, history and subjectivity, as in the later work of Barthes himself, in Julia Kristeva, or, at its most systematic, in the writings of film theorists like Christian Metz. [3]

Such developments look exciting, but readers of Anglo-American literary criticism might be surprised by my account of their prevalence. Barthes' call for a reorientation of critical attention, for an invigorating post-structuralist reformulation of the antique notion of 'authorship', has not yet been answered (or even clearly heard) within eighteenth-century literary studies. Within that fastidious world of 'literary history teaching, and public opinion' the traditional 'biographical person' of Henry Fielding remains all too resolutely alive and kicking.

Of course, within such apparent continuity of concern with a particular author, there will have been highly significant changes of emphasis. In a reversal of one time-honoured perspective, the recent reputation of the witty and panoramic Henry Fielding has been partly eclipsed by the extraordinary return to critical favour of his more prosaic, sombre and intense contemporary Samuel Richardson, to the extent that the imposing bulk of Clarissa now occupies a position of centrality in most interpretations of the eighteenth-century English novel, a position occupied for so long by Tom Jones. And whereas Fielding's debunking of Richardson's seriousness of purpose in his lampoon Shamela (1741) once seemed to many commentators like a refreshing breath of unpretentious sanity after the claustrophobic and repressive atmosphere of the original Pamela (1740), Fielding's strenuous bid for cultural authority and his high-handed exercise in artistic brokerage are no longer so easy for most commentators to endorse uncritically.

After the growth of woman-centred studies, and the more scrupulous attention to questions of sexual ideology, Fielding's masculinist parody often looks improperly dismissive, now seeming to many readers to be as repressive and as unimaginative of alternative social possibilities as Richardson's pious novel once did to their predecessors. Furthermore, Fielding's novels are now regularly presented as formative, emergent and volatile, rather than unified and coherent, his extended narratives being seen as internally riven and disfigured by the stubborn complexities of ideology, class and gender which they seek to encompass and naturalise. But nonetheless, although the nature of Fielding's literary reputation may have shifted radically over the last twenty-five years, and although his works are now interrogated and analysed in ways that would have seemed very strange not too long ago, the man himself yet remains in the forefront of the most fastidious critical attention. Whether or not Fielding needs us may be unreasonably hard to determine, but Barthes is surely correct in thinking that we still need him.

Needless to say, there are solidly material reasons why Fielding studies should remain so vibrant in an intellectual climate otherwise hostile to biographical study, and so internally contested. The necessary 'support system' for such traditional scholarly and critical activity is now more secure than ever before. At last, thanks to the work of the indefatigable Battestins, there is a broadly dependable and detailed (if by no means wholly uncontentious) biography, providing a much-needed replacement for the outdated and antiquarian 1918 version by Wilbur L. Cross, which was so eager to sanitise and defend Fielding from the received tradition of moral detraction, turning at least one blind eye to its subject's indiscretions. At the same time, more and more definitive editions of our man's prolific and various writings are being made available to scholars in the scrupulous 'Wesleyan' texts, bringing back into prominence whole areas of Fielding's literary output which had until now all but sunk beneath the critical horizon, and providing bibliographically reliable texts for most of his fiction. Previously murky and irrecoverable parts of Fielding's career – his early work in the theatre, his extensive periodical writing, his political position, his dealings with his wives, his magistracy – are at present being explored and illuminated by the diligence and intelligence of the most intrepid scholarship. Wider cultural and contextual issues – the development and status of the novel, the politics of the theatre, the conditions of periodical writing, the contemporary controversies over gender roles – are also under revitalising investigation, with Fielding's involvement in all of them becoming gradually clearer.

To take only one illustrative example, the more recent critical accounts of early eighteenth-century fiction, deliberate and self-conscious in their use of modern literary theory and sensitive to broader issues of cultural context, by Michael McKeon and J. Paul Hunter among others, pay no less attention to this author than did the more traditional versions offered by Ian Watt and Alan D. McKillop. In these newer accounts, Fielding may appear afresh, but as we shall see he still appears plentifully. So, flying in the face of Barthes' reservations about the security of authorship, for academics and scholars professing an interest in Henry Fielding, these are surprisingly fruitful and propitious times to be at work.

On closer examination, we discover (perhaps to no one's real surprise) that the accumulated efforts of the most rigorous scholarship have not managed to uncover a single, intact and coherent vision of the author 'Henry Fielding', unanimously recognised to be accurate and appropriate. Rather, as we might expect, different scholars have offered portraits of their subject which have discernible family resemblances and areas of overlap, but which differ markedly and significantly in their interpretive stance, creating specific points of contention, and even from time to time threatening the breakdown of the fragile critical consensus. Emphasising what these accounts have in common may be a way of perpetuating a broad paradigm of scholarly consensus, but drawing attention to their differences may put that paradigm in jeopardy.

A clear case in point would be the surprisingly hostile reception which met the first publication of the Battestin biography in 1989. No one could fault the authors for their diligence or their scholarly approach. However, their overall interpretation of Fielding's career still seemed to many to be too clear cut. The biography divides its subject's life up into four main episodes – 'A West Country boyhood and Eton (1707–26)', 'Playwright and libertine (1727–39)', 'Politics, novels, and the law (1739–49)', 'Magistrate and reformer (1749–54)' – giving an astonishingly schematic narrative shape to what is on examination a very volatile and shifting career. And for some scholars, perhaps over-habituated to the one-sided version of Fielding offered by Cross, Battestin's suggestions about the possibility of incestuous tangles in Fielding's adolescence were calumnious, and they reacted with surprisingly vehement outrage and infuriation. The biographer's role as recorder of events has in this case been overtaken by the contending pressures to provide a coherent narrative, and come up with something new.

These basic biographical uncertainties are clearly disconcerting, but they are not the sole area for critical contention. Great differences of emphasis can also be found in different scholars' assessments of Fielding's political alignments, or in their presentation of his conscious and unconscious views on the complex questions of gender. These differences are apparent enough in the work of critics who approach the subject in broadly similar ways, but divisions are obviously more pronounced in critics who arrive at their arguments from self-consciously different ideological positions. Battestin's Fielding not only differs from Cross's, but also from Michael McKeon's, and none of these is entirely similar to my own. Even if we do not wish to go as far along the road to critical relativism as Barthes occasionally seems to, and even without resorting to a wholly non-historicist or semiotic account of these narratives, we may yet have to acknowledge that our posited author ('he') is a highly volatile construction, inconsistent, evasive, and persistently awkward to define.

Perhaps it might be argued that such epistemic uncertainty is inevitable and eventually untroubling. It could be seen as simply a healthy part of the fabric of any pluralist critical discourse, only to be expected with a subject at once as public and as inscrutable as this one – 'Fielding' in all his varieties could serve as a kind of cautionary token of the reluctance to think of all questions as answerable, all problems soluble. The controversies identified so far are after all no more than the conventionally understood difficulties of historical biography, and they must beset the study of Defoe, Swift and Pope, indeed of any historical figure, no less than they disconcert the study of Fielding. If they are especially intensified in this particular case, it is perhaps not because of specific procedural uncertainties, but an inevitable consequence of the scarcity of recoverable private writing. Despite recent discoveries of private correspondence, and the various periodical essays now claimed as Fielding's by Battestin and others, the canon of his writing is still uncertain, sadly lacking in some of the most important biographical clues. Even after decades of the most intensely inquisitive and scrupulous scholarship, there are still very few existing letters from Fielding, and no private diary or journal has yet been discovered. As a result, his inner feelings and what we might call his 'interiority' remain hidden from critical scrutiny.

But it would still be wrong to see this as a problem peculiar to Fielding. With the hegemonic power of irony in the literary world of the time, British eighteenth-century authors never offered wholly transparent or unmediated accounts of themselves and their attitudes on the page. In consequence, attempting to reconstruct the actual living personalities of authors from their own writing has always involved circuitous manoeuvres, intelligent guesswork and a talent for obliqueness. With this author, just as with Swift, Pope and so many others, identification, attribution and interpretation are complicated by the many different self-projections found in the various literary *personae* Fielding adopted. Fielding's very first published work, *The Masquerade, a Poem* (1728), is attributed on the title-page to none other than 'Lemuel Gulliver, Poet Laureat to the King of Lilliput', and the playful construction of alternative authorial identities did not stop there. From 'Harry Luckless' the impecunious master-puppeteer in *The Author's Farce* (1730) and 'H. Scriblerus Secundus' the alleged author of *The Tragedy of Tragedies* (1731) and other Haymarket plays, from the comically belligerent 'Captain Hercules Vinegar' of the periodical *The Champion* (1739–42) and the assured 'Sir Alexander Drawcansir' of *The Covent-Garden Journal* (1752), to those magisterial figures, at once benign and irascible, who narrate and preside over the comic novels, Fielding appears throughout his career in a host of disguises and transformations. Articulating the relationship between these self-projections and the concealed creator himself is going to be no easy business, and, as we shall see, various critics have given very different accounts of the matter over the years.

So while I am describing certain recently formulated problems involved in identifying the role of authorship, it must be seen that the specific enigma of 'Henry Fielding' is not exclusively the result of a post-structuralist conspiracy. Contemporary eighteenth-century commentators, too, were interestingly uncertain about Fielding's private character, even when they were in a position to be much more confident of his public identity, of what Barthes calls his 'civil status'. Although he attracted both vociferous supporters and powerful detractors in his own day, and although the Richardson/Fielding controversy was intensely argued from various positions throughout the 1740s and beyond, there were clear and recurrent points of contention in the contemporary estimate of the author's real personality and character, of what Pope would have called his 'ruling Passion'.

The points of uncertainty were many, but the most insistently argued one involved Fielding's class affiliations and allegiances. Significantly, many contemporary observers remarked on what they saw as a perplexing disparity between the man and his work, as though Fielding's allegedly dissolute or 'low' writing had to be seen as an indecorous or inappropriate articulation of his privileged social position and class status. The tone of contemporary discussion as a result is often one of extreme puzzlement and suspicion, across the shifting and disputed class divide – why, many eighteenth-century commentators asked, is one of *us* apparently writing like one of *them*?

A few examples may help confirm the point. In an all-star gathering of Augustan literary eminences, James Boswell recalled how Dr Johnson sometimes approvingly quoted Samuel Richardson's remark that 'had he not known who Fielding was, he should have believed he was an ostler'.[4] Richardson's actual bafflement and exasperation at the behaviour of his literary rival was in fact even more elaborate than Boswell's (or Johnson's) recollection of it, with the fullest version reading 'it is beyond my conception, that a man of family, and who had some learning, and who is really a writer, should descend so excessively low, in all his pieces'.[5] The litany of 'family' and 'learning' is a familiar one, and the accusation that Fielding's writing was 'low' quickly became commonplace. When George Cheyne, corpulent physician to the gentry, denounced Fielding's work as suited to 'entertain none but porters and watchmen', he was making clear the sense of class-based hostility to Fielding's dalliance below stairs felt by many.[6]

The Eton- and Leyden-educated patrician figure of Henry Fielding seemed to some of his contemporaries to be violating the unwritten laws of social and literary decorum by writing such undignified books, such 'low' works, and in consequence eighteenth-century commentators seem to have found it particularly difficult to get his character and his career into any coherent perspective. And Fielding himself did not refrain from joining in this debate. In the extensive preliminary chapters in both *Joseph Andrews* and *Tom Jones*, the author (or, I should more cautiously say, a self-conscious and ironised version of the author) aggressively engages in dialogue with his critics and interrogates these very concerns with 'lowness' and literary prestige.

Such persistent uncertainties of focus, and the recurrent sense that the author may have something to answer for, beset the history of Fielding's reputation. Alongside other self-consciously controversialist eighteenth-century authors and public figures, Fielding was subject to persistent caricatures and lampoons in the contemporary press, his identity smeared and obscured by the accusations and deliberate misinterpretations of others to the point where it now becomes almost indeterminate and irrecoverable. Many Augustan writers were clearly aware of this problem, and they responded to it in a number of ways. The fragmentation of personal identity which Alexander Pope so feverishly announces in his *Epistle to Dr Arbuthnot* (1735) and which reappears so emphatically throughout his *Imitations of Horace* (1733–8) is only one among many contending accounts of the enigma of the public literary personality in the eighteenth-century world of letters. As Pope sees it, by entering the realm of print, the fortunate writer may gain fame and a public, but only at the cost of losing control of his own personality and becoming prey to misrepresentation and the onslaughts of the deranged, the spiteful and the envious – in other words, the reading public. Indeed, by means of his own character sketches in the *Epistles to Several Persons* and the *Dunciad*, Pope sought to retaliate by creating his own privileged gallery of misrepresentations, images of his famous and infamous contemporaries which subsequent commentators have too frequently mistaken as accurate.

Jonathan Swift, too, discovered ironic solace in recognising his powerlessness to prevent the creation of misconceptions surrounding his private character, and in his mock-elegiac poem 'Verses on the Death of Dr Swift' (1731?), he affects to enjoy the spectacle of the controversy continuing even after his death:

> Now Grub Street wits are all employed;
> With elegies the town is cloyed:
> Some paragraph in every paper,
> To curse the Dean, or bless the Drapier.[7]

For Pope and for Swift, such public misrepresentation left a great deal of room for the writer to deny responsibility for the reception of his work, and to play elaborate games of misdirection, but it also encouraged intense exasperation at the difficulties of conveying clear meanings to a resistant, obtuse and ill-informed audience. The ludic element to be found in misattribution was exploited famously by Swift in his *Bickerstaff Papers* (1708), where, writing as 'Isaac Bickerstaff', an astrologer, he played an elaborate practical joke on a genuinely popular astrologer, John Partridge, announcing the certainty of that man's imminent death. That 'Bickerstaff' was taken seriously, to the extent that Partridge's name was removed from the rolls of active writers held by the Stationers' Company, shows the public's willingness to be imposed upon, and the problems of sifting the genuine from the fake. In this case, the death of the author John Partridge was contrived by an elaborate hoax. Later in the century, and on a more philosophical level, the complex entanglement and disentanglement of the figures of Laurence Sterne, Parson Yorick, and Tristram Shandy laid out the ontological problem of the identity of the author well in advance of post-structuralist speculation.

Fielding, too, was immersed in this world of misidentifications and misunderstandings, and moved through it as both a victim and a perpetrator. As a well-known controversial satiric dramatist, he was subjected to persistent caricature and misrepresentation, even though these were not as insistently vituperative or scandalous as the ones heaped on the Scriblerians. However, many of the most pervasive contemporary assessments of Fielding's character were highly pejorative, driven by ideological and personal hostility. The sharpest and most consistent point of attack, as already indicated, lay in what was seen as his unbecoming or indecorous conduct, with the more hostile commentators taking great pleasure in censuring Fielding's well-known fondness for drinking and for rather *louche* female company, and many took umbrage at his seemingly flagrant attempts at social climbing, at 'place-seeking'. For a number of the more censorious contemporary critics, Fielding's later fictional work only achieved its accuracy through its excessive 'lowness', its concentration upon farcical mishaps and sexual misadventures. To explain his fondness for such subjects, many writers resorted to rather casual biographical speculation, and it became virtually a commonplace to contrast Fielding's turbulent and complex personality with Samuel Richardson's alleged purity of heart.

In the first extended biographical sketch of Henry Fielding, Arthur Murphy's *Essay on the Life and Genius of Henry Fielding, Esq.* (1762), the character of the subject is seen as undergoing a perpetual and enfeebling conflict between its high-minded aspirations to a Socratic ideal of virtue, and the contrary pressures of vividly felt and powerful carnal appetites. In seeking after what he took to be the 'natural', Murphy suggests, Fielding bravely and dangerously consorted with the 'low', at no little cost to his personal reputation and, in the end, to his physical constitution. Such a convenient and simplistic caricature, with its undercurrent of a recognisable 'fatal flaw' in Fielding's make up, held sway for a surprisingly long time, reappearing virtually intact in Sir Walter Scott's influential essay on the author published in 1820, and still visible in outline throughout Cross's 1918 biography. The fact that the final section of the 1989 Battestin biography is called 'Consequences' indicates the surprising tenacity of this convenient narrative. However, even if some of the more high-minded modern critics have found it difficult to eradicate this judgemental perspective entirely, we must yet seek to be more circumspect and sceptical of such a convenient and orderly version of events.

That character-sketch and caricature were militant articulations of eighteenth-century social and political ideology is surely incontestable. As a result, we must see most of the contemporary descriptions of Fielding as more or less deliberate attempts to darken or lighten his character, rather than to represent it with anything corresponding to our anachronistic notions of scholarly accuracy. The problem for more recent commentators is that without such a pronounced judgemental reading, or without a simplifying diagrammatic or sentimental account like Murphy's, the authorial presence of 'Henry Fielding' becomes horribly blurred around the edges and begins to elude definition.

As a convenient illustration of the way Fielding's contemporary reputation was constructed and contested through the press, setting cumbersome terms of reference for subsequent writers, it is worth glancing briefly at that most bizarre book, An Apology for the Life of Mr. Colley Cibber, Comedian (1740), in which the egregious actor and poet laureate Cibber gives a very damning and dismissive early sketch of Fielding, 'whom I do not choose to name, unless it could be to his advantage, or that it were of importance'.[8]

For Colley Cibber, himself the subsequent target of sustained vituperative reprisal in Fielding's Joseph Andrews, as well as in the later versions of Pope's Dunciad, Fielding the playwright was no more than 'intrepidly abusive', 'in haste to get money'. In short, he was certainly not a figure to be taken seriously, best thought of as a minor irritant in the distinguished laureate's own triumphant career, but to be thought of as a personality above all. At this stage, there were many who would have agreed with Cibber on this issue, if on almost no other. A little later, after the great popular success of Fielding's fiction, such complaints about his personal avarice and rapacity may have dwindled somewhat, but they were quickly replaced by equally stentorian outbursts in many quarters about his low morals and weak character.

By the time of his premature death near Lisbon in 1754, aged only forty-seven, Fielding remained well known in his native land as a prominent and controversial public figure. In the contrasting contexts of his well-publicised early life in the theatre and his later more sober but equally visible career in the law, Fielding was, to put it crudely, known to be the extremely unpopular author of two extremely popular comic novels, and of one less popular serious novel. For some, Fielding's transformation from playwright to magistrate was a brazen and remarkably public version of the metamorphosis of poacher into game-keeper. Furthermore, Fielding was regularly represented by his contemporaries as a flagrant example of someone whose iconoclastic and irreverent earlier work was later hypocritically repudiated by an author obviously rewriting the narrative of his own life in search of personal advancement.

The spectacle of the scurrilous playwright turning into the grave and censorious magistrate was one which many found hard to take. In the absence of any more convincing or intimate personal testimony, this reputation for duplicity and hypocrisy long outlived him. During the later eighteenth century, at least as much print was expended on anatomising Fielding's complex character and personality as on articulating his work. Some of this discussion was sympathetic – most notably the fulsome praise offered by Edward Gibbon – but considerably more of it was hostile. As the editors of the appropriate *Critical Heritage* volume put it, 'this would have been a very bulky book indeed if it had included criticism of Fielding the man'.[9]

Such hostility and censoriousness reverberate long beyond the confines of the eighteenth century, setting a restrictive and awkward agenda for subsequent writers. Even when commentators found something in Fielding to praise – as when Coleridge so stoutly defended the skill and artifice of the plot of *Tom Jones* – the inherited version of the author's character still provoked hesitancy and reservation. Throughout the nineteenth century, the legacy of this judgemental version of Fielding was all-pervasive, and even writers as sympathetic as William Hazlitt had to take it as their point of departure. Consequently, when William Makepeace Thackeray began his recuperative panegyrical account of Fielding's life in 1853, he had to struggle to free himself from the moralistic straitjacket in which he felt his Augustan predecessors had placed him. The key passage of Thackeray's essay is worth quoting in full, as an example of the way Fielding's character is seen as something to be fought over, to be made and remade within the requirements of different intellectual contexts. In modern terms, Thackeray is 'laundering' his subject, turning the licentious Augustan man about town into a more suitable figure who would not embarrass or discomfort the more prudish sensibilities of the English Victorian reading public:

> I cannot offer or hope to make a hero out of Harry Fielding. Why hide his faults? Why conceal his weaknesses in a cloud of periphrases? Why not show him, like him as he is, not robed in a marble toga, and draped and polished in a heroic attitude, but with inked ruffles, and claret stains on his tarnished lace coat, and on his manly face the marks of good fellowship, of illness, of kindness, of care, and wine. Stained as you see him, and worn by care and dissipation, that man retains some of the most precious and splendid human qualities and endowments. He has an admirable natural love of truth, the keenest antipathy to hypocrisy, the happiest satirical gift of laughing it to scorn. His wit is wonderfully wise and detective; it flashes upon a rogue and lightens up a rascal like a policeman's lantern. He is one of the manliest and kindliest of human beings: in the midst of all his perfections, he respects female innocence and infantine tenderness, as you would suppose such a great-hearted, courageous soul would respect and care for them. He could not be so brave, generous, truth-telling as he is, were he not infinitely merciful, pitiful, and tender. He will give any man his purse – he can't help kindness and profusion. He may have low tastes, but not a mean mind; he admires with all his heart good and virtuous men, stoops to no flattery, bears no rancour, disdains all disloyal arts, does his public duty uprightly, is fondly loved by his family, and dies at his work.[10]

In a remarkable piece of sleight of hand, Thackeray's protestation of inadequacy at the beginning of this passage seems wholly gestural and insubstantial once his mighty threnody begins to swell. When compared to Thackeray's well-known revulsion at some of Swift's work, this passage looks very deliberate and organised in its attempt to purify the image of Fielding, to turn him into a venerable precedent for Thackeray's own work.

The insistent denial of heroism notwithstanding, only an exceptionally churlish person would find the subsequent string of compliments unsatisfying. As a character reference, Thackeray's portrait is so glowing that it could virtually be read in the dark. After all, the powerful and detailed catalogue on the positive side is scarcely balanced by a list of concomitant weaknesses. The fact that this care-worn and humane Fielding occasionally dribbled claret down his shirt-front (I shall be frank with you – I have done that myself) becomes endearingly trivial when put alongside his prodigious generosity of spirit and purse, his open-heartedness, his bravery, his honesty, his closeness to his family, his lack of guile, and all the rest of his redeeming qualities. Of course, it may be that Thackeray's own more positive terms of reference are now just as disconcerting as those he is trying to dispel – it is not obviously encouraging that he ends up by praising 'the manly, the English Harry Fielding' – but the point still remains that Thackeray's biographical strategy is more creative than descriptive, seeking to rebuild his author in the style which both he and his audience would prefer him to be.

Thackeray's revisionist account of Fielding is a very dramatic indication of the mutability or plasticity of authorship, which is to remain a focal point of the present study. As we shall see in the ensuing pages, there may be a body of factual information at the heart of the enquiry, but nonetheless the superstructure of interpretation built upon it will take many different shapes. Every 'Fielding' is somebody's Fielding – including my own. His alleged authorship has to be marked by whatever are taken to be the most salient features of the texts discussed, or of eighteenth-century fiction in general, or by a declared or concealed or simply internalised judgemental version of Fielding's character. Interpretations are built upon other interpretations, and any 'facts' available are buried beneath a great weight of conjecture. Thackeray's version may now seem outrageously partial, sexist and nationalist, but at least he makes his evaluative perspective clear. Not all writers do this with anything like Thackeray's lack of embarrassment, and many keep their values as secretively as possible.

However, protestations of disinterest in this field are always suspect, and the recoverable versions of 'Henry Fielding' described and exploited by critics and commentators can never be wholly innocent of covert or explicit ideological manipulation. Fielding's identity, and his presence in his fiction, remains something to be fought over, not something to be assumed. Thus, when one recent scholar claims to have found an identifiable Fielding lying at rest beyond these vicissitudes, I cannot but be sceptical:

> It is not my purpose to parade modish critical approaches, so readers anxious to discover the feminist's Fielding, or the deconstructionist's Fielding, or the neo-Marxist's Fielding, will catch at best only accidental glimpses of him here. This book is meant to introduce Fielding's major fiction.[11]

Would that this point of unproblematic objectivity, certainty and freedom from bias were really possible! Just as much as that writer, I too would be unhappy about offering anything like a 'parade' of 'modish critical approaches', or a wholly pluralist compendium of perspectives on Fielding. But, alas, the evaluative certainty about what really constitutes 'Fielding', and what might properly be considered to be his 'major works', needs a lot more investigation than the quoted critic has enthusiasm for. The point of consensus or neutrality he yearns for simply no longer exists. Instead, the theoretical and institutional framework of literary enquiry is always in place, supporting some individual statements and assessments, discouraging others, whether critics are prepared to recognise it or not, and the historical and philosophical uncertainties of interpreting text and context cannot be made to disappear simply by telling them to go elsewhere.

Conscious of the complex epistemological and critical problems surrounding the notion of authorship, and aware of the peculiar difficulties raised by the case of this author, I am very hesitant about finding any uncontentious, verifiable transcendental signifier called 'Fielding' to shore up the remarks I might make about the novels. In fact, despite the fervent protestations of disinterest, even the account of 'Fielding' offered by the critic quoted above (Simon Varey) turns out to be a judiciously presented, well-informed and extremely interesting version of the prevailing orthodoxy. But the fact that one version has become orthodox does not make it any less of a selective and interpretive account; it remains as much of a textual construction as any of the novels under discussion.

As this brief extract from Varey's book shows, the introduction of Fielding's 'major works' can still be presented as non-controversial, observing the elaborate formalities and conventions of traditional critical exegesis. However, while such a presentation may indeed not be feminist or deconstructionist or neo-Marxist or any such thing, it remains defiantly traditionalist and historicist.

To put the point in as unadorned a way as possible: no matter how hard you may try to cleanse your writing of theoretical or ideological affiliations, or hypothesis and conjecture, they stubbornly linger, at best going underground. And denying that you have a clear-cut critical affiliation is no guarantee that you do not in fact have one, whether you choose to recognise it or not.

The problem for anyone writing about this subject today is thus not that there is too little information about the author to allow for reliable representation, but rather that there is such a polyphony (or cacophony) of accounts that the literary world seems over-congested with 'Fieldings' all vying for attention. Each of these figures is able to claim some authority, but none of them can get wholly free of contention. So, if all commentary is selective and interpretive, can anyone at all be trusted? And what are then the criteria for accuracy or acceptability?

From such an unequivocally bald statement, it looks as though I am drifting helplessly towards a wholly relativist account of 'Fielding', abandoning positivist enquiry as too grossly contaminated by the prior ideological commitments and affiliations of the enquirers. However, that would clearly be too large and decisive a move to make on the basis of the sketchy evidence so far presented, and it would also be pragmatically unattractive and intellectually disadvantageous. My version of Fielding looks increasingly like what Richard Rorty calls 'the culminating reinterpretation of our predecessors' reinterpretation of their predecessors' reinterpretation . . .'. Although I see the process of reinterpretation as discontinuous and volatile rather than stealthily progressive, I believe Rorty's account sounds the most appropriate so far. My Fielding is not a clearly sculpted monument to be revered, but a much less stable edifice, constantly under maintenance and reconstruction. To quote Rorty again, the subject of this book is one of those 'artefacts whose fundamental design we often have to alter'.[12]

Without fully endorsing Rorty's philosophical pragmatism, I feel there is much in what he says. Tempting though it would be to start from scratch, to assume that all the inherited earlier versions of 'Fielding' did not prejudice contemporary enquiry and that they could simply be dispelled, their presence and persistence has to be acknowledged and somehow accommodated. In one debilitating sense, this turns literary criticism into nothing more (or nothing less?) than a commentary upon commentaries. Yet I see no immediate alternative, if something called 'Henry Fielding' is to remain installed as the prime focus of concern, and if his interactions with his social and historical contexts are to be given due prominence. For just as 'Fielding' is a collaborative and partly speculative construction, so too are his historical contexts. After all, the received versions of authors and their contexts are often created to suit requirements other than those of literary critics, and their functions can be more diverse than mere scholars can identify – anyone who has ever been to a Burns Supper can perhaps begin to see the magnitude of the problem. However, as the waters of Fielding's personality and context grow muddier, and as we recognise in them only more and more clearly our own reflections, there yet remains the possibility of pausing and seeking to start somewhere else. So: if we cannot firmly grasp the author, can we still engage with his works?

Serious and ironic men

In *Beylism*, in the *Stendhal-Club*, and in other manifestations – especially marked in the case of Stendhal – of the fetishism of the author, there is at least one good thing; they save us, or divert us, from another sort of idolatry, which is no less serious, and today more dangerous, namely, the fetishism of the work – conceived as a closed, complete, absolute subject.[13]

The question being addressed so far is: Do we still need Henry Fielding? In fact, do sophisticated literary critics still need to worry about authors at all? Faced with all the problems of accuracy and disinterest which beset positivist scholarship and biography, might it be best to abandon the project entirely, and cheerfully invent the Fielding which best suits our purposes? After all, many of the commentators described so far seem to have exercised a great deal of creative license in their accounts of 'Fielding', refashioning him to fit the spirit of the age or the particular requirements of the occasion. So should we just ignore the epistemological problems and make a celebratory fetish of Henry Fielding, whoever he might really have been, perhaps creating an idolatrous Fielding Club and holding regular Fielding Suppers (potentially rather boisterous evenings!) to commemorate his birthday, the day before Shakespeare's? Like a number of other British authors (Dickens, Shakespeare, Florence Nightingale), Fielding could then begin to appear on our stamps and tea-towels and bank-notes, becoming part of the signifying system of authentic Britishness.

Clearly, any such procedure can all too easily be made to look absurd – although it seems to work with Shakespeare. Instead of inventing a fantasy figure, an imaginary friend for lonely literary critics, we might prefer to seek some other more reliable source of meaning. Perhaps it will be possible to find a hermeneutic perspective which will allow us to read these challenging and vital texts either entirely on their own, or within their various literary and social and historical contexts, without becoming enmeshed in the tangles of authorial presence or intention. In short, can we get rid of the disconcerting and evasive presence of 'Henry Fielding' and still have something interesting and informative to talk about?

If the controlling author-figure really is to be banished, the most obvious and immediately available replacement for him or her is the literary work itself, the 'text'. In this case, instead of trying to look at Henry Fielding's *Tom Jones*, we might seek to solve or diminish the interpretive problems by concentrating on a complex verbal and linguistic construction called *Tom Jones* in splendid isolation. We might thus extract the book from its local contexts, and examine its formal principles of construction – in essence, we might attempt to read it simply as a lot of words on a lot of pages. Of course, this idea is by no means new. The notion of the relative autonomy of the literary text – what Gerard Genette in the opening quotation denounces as 'the fetishism of the work' – has indeed been seen as a very attractive option for certain literary critics at various points in the past, and has left a legacy of reading practices and terminology which need to be assessed.

The earlier structuralist work of Roland Barthes mentioned in the previous section is clearly affiliated to the autonomy of the literary artefact, culminating in his transitional 1971 essay 'From Work to Text'. However, Barthes is a special case, and less idiosyncratic alignments relevant to the present study can be found in the otherwise disparate projects of the Russian Formalists of the 1920s and the Anglo-American 'New Critics' of the 1940s and 1950s. Each of these loose critical groupings had its own distinct reasons for minimising the role of the author. For the Formalists active in the early days of the Soviet Union, the post-revolutionary desire for an objective science of the literary text, and the linguistically derived study of the formal devices of language meant that the biographical element in literature was given a very low critical priority. Authors themselves might, after all, be tainted by their disreputable bourgeois origins or their reactionary political affiliations, and yet critics might still wish to be able to read their books more or less independently.

In dealing with narrative, the central Formalist enterprise involved discovering the many different ways an original 'story' (*fabula*) might be turned into the visible 'plot' (*sjuzhet*), without the commentator having to express great concern or curiosity about the social status, ideological affiliations or historical personage of the plotter. For such a critic, it would be the narrative formulation of *Tom Jones* which was the proper subject of attention, not the book's connections with or allusions to the events or contexts of its author's life. In fact, apart from Viktor Shklovsky's flamboyant essay on *Tristram Shandy* and some remarks by Boris Tomashevsky on the technique of 'defamiliarisation' in *Gulliver's Travels*, there is very little Formalist commentary on eighteenth-century fiction, but the possibilities remain.[14]

For the more disparate grouping of Anglo-American 'New Critics', the concentration upon 'the words on the page' arose more from a desire to cleanse reading of its residue of affective sentimentality than from any overt desire to desensitise its political contexts. Nonetheless, the aim of the critic as thus understood was to assemble an 'objective' reading of a literary text, unblemished by any considerations of authorial intention. Unlike Formalists, however, the New Critics retained confidence in the ability of fine writing to offer a critique of life, and as a result they were less interested in cataloguing the various literary devices which constituted a text and more interested in examining the enriching meanings which might be drawn from a work of literature, employing procedures of 'close reading' not easily adapted to the sprawling energies of eighteenth-century fiction. As with the Formalists, few New Critics turned their attention to this field, although William Empson's essay on *Tom Jones* is a notable exception.

To call such commentators 'fetishists of the text' might seem crude and unfair, and it would certainly be wrong to present either group as monolithic or unanimous in its allegiances. Indeed, the original Formalist account of narrative has been greatly refined and developed in subsequent years, and given greater analytic subtlety by many later writers including Barthes, Emile Benveniste, Mieke Bal and Seymour Chatman, of whom more later. However, no matter what differences of emphasis or orientation may be discerned, the point remains that for critics of Formalist or New Critical persuasion and their successors the question of the immediate biographical or social context of any piece of writing could not be centrally or perhaps even remotely relevant to the authorised critical procedures to be used in articulating it.

I offer these brief sketches to introduce some of the most important positions within the debate about Fielding's fiction. Each affiliation has in its own way occasionally permeated the present field of study, but, as I have suggested already, critical work on eighteenth-century English writing is conventionally much less self-consciously theorised and positioned than, say, the equivalent work on Romanticism or Modernism. For whatever reason, critics working in this area rarely make firm declarations of ideological or theoretical alignment, and the broad humanist consensus remains intact.

Nonetheless, there have been a few significant exceptions, the most notable being R. S. Crane's outstanding text-centred demonstration of the intricate symmetrical construction of Fielding's most widely read novel in his 1952 essay 'The Concept of Plot and the Plot of Tom Jones'.[15] As will be seen in a later chapter on that novel, Crane's essay is one of the most stimulating accounts of the workings of narrative to have been offered in eighteenth-century studies, and it cannot be overlooked in any subsequent discussion of Tom Jones. However, brilliant as his systematic unravelling of the novel is, Crane offers no expressed theoretical commitment (he has often be labelled as a 'Chicago Aristotelian', but the name really means very little) and his analysis flatters to deceive if mistaken as a rigorous exercise in either Russian-style Formalism or its Anglo-American equivalent. Instead of developing the technical vocabulary of *fabula* and *sjuzhet* (or their many equivalents, like Chatman's 'story' and 'discourse'), Crane inherits a more traditional organicist and Aristotelian notion of plotting. Following Coleridge, Crane accepts the idea that the organisation of a literary work through a plot is a quest for formal unity or coherence, and maintains that the successful literary text represents a triumph of order over contingency and shapelessness.

As he willingly volunteers, Crane remains within the more traditional practices of humane literary study, however detailed and 'textual' his work might seem. Indeed, at one point he takes issue with the dismissive remarks about Fielding's importance in F.R. Leavis' *The Great Tradition* (1948), where Leavis quickly identifies 'the limits of the essential interests' offered by *Tom Jones*. Despite the appearance of dissent, Crane does not investigate the premises of Leavis's case about the relative merits of different authors, but instead seeks to discover other features of this particular book which even the most committed Leavisite might admire. So although it expresses an unusually rigorous interest in those features of prose upon which Formalists habitually concentrated, Crane's analysis is a broadly Aristotelian account of narrative, refining and developing the original Coleridgean terms of reference, still integrated within the humanist critical context which claims that the construction of plot is one of the greatest vehicles for a novelist's art and craft.

Crane's essay, then, offers a reverent defence of his author's artistry rather than a specific example of a theoretical project designed to facilitate a more general account of the technical or formal features of narrative. And while the essay is descriptive in its orientation, the aim of the project is at heart evaluative – to install Fielding in his rightful place at the beginning of 'The Great Tradition'. Crane's procedure, however, relies not on the tracing of lineage or lines of development, but on the elaborate description of an autonomous artistic object:

> . . . the method is one which depends on the analytical isolation of works of art, as finished products, from the circumstances and processes of their origin.   (Crane, p. 646)

Whether it is as easy as Crane thinks to conceive of novels as 'finished' remains to be seen, and maybe the material processes of origin impose more pressures than he is able to consider. Even so, Crane still stands apart from more conventional Fielding scholars by his unusual willingness to provide detailed local analysis of text, a truly rare thing in such an author-centred critical field.

Crane's compromises between formalism and evaluative humanism are well known to specialists in the field, and they represent the most successful infiltration of close analysis into eighteenth-century studies. Self-evidently, neither New Critics nor Formalists were able to articulate the clutter and business of the eighteenth-century English novel, its dialectic between developed form and discursiveness, its oscillation between the mimetic and the self-reflexive, its comprehensiveness, its multiple voices and modes of address, or its complex layers of irony. Indeed, where the New Critics concentrated on individual poems, Formalist analysis at its most stimulating seems more at home with a corpus of relatively short texts than with a single long work. The example of Vladimir Propp's *Morphology of the Folk Tale* (1928), where the author systematises an assembly of affinities and identifies the recurrent 'functions' in folk narratives is a clear case. And while much of the more generally applicable semiotic discussion of narrative structures, offered by such commentators as Genette, Greimas and Eco, has bearing on the dominant and emergent forms of eighteenth-century English fiction, they are usually reluctant to deal in specific cases, preferring to discuss a more abstract and depersonalised system of narrativity.

However, without for the moment donning the necessary protective clothing and entering the germ-free environment of semiotic studies, there is clearly still room for a text-centred and non-authorial analysis of the eighteenth-century English novel. Until very recently, it has been in the loosely defined field of 'rhetoric' that this project has been carried on, with a few selected 'canonical' novels (often including *Joseph Andrews* and *Tom Jones*) being articulated as deliberately assembled and structured exercises in communication. In such analysis, the historical personage of the author is given little prominence, if he or she is incorporated at all, and the main thrust of the discussion lies in uncovering the linguistic codes and conventions of communicative procedure. It is possible to see Barthes himself (especially in *S/Z*) as a practising rhetorician, and to see rhetoric as the study of the internal, formal ways in which texts achieve recognisable significance. However, the term 'rhetoric' itself is slippery, open to many different interpretations, and it is worth seeing the form it has most regularly taken on its journeys through eighteenth-century studies.

Although the word 'rhetoric' as used in this context derives initially from classical studies of language – from the work of Aristotle, Cicero and Quintillian on the techniques of persuasion in public discourse – it has subsequently taken on much wider significance. At one extreme, 'rhetoric' is broadly synonymous with 'grammar', and the rhetoric of a work or text is simply the most comprehensive catalogue of formal and linguistic devices exploited within it. More selectively, 'rhetoric' can involve study only of the especially stylised or deliberate features of language and form, as in

Samuel Johnson's 1755 *Dictionary* definition of the term: 'the act of speaking not merely with propriety, but with art and elegance.' Both of these orthodox definitions can be cited as appropriate in the present discussion, but there remains another, of more immediate significance. At the farthest extreme, 'rhetoric' means much more than the systematised internal operations of any piece of language. Indeed, for some recent commentators, 'rhetoric' can be taken to refer to the power invested in language (and in language-users) to reshape the world, and so the capacity for 'rhetoric' can even be made to become one of the defining properties of the human condition.

In this last context, Stanley Fish, writing in 1990, offers a suggestive distinction between two opposed ways of thinking about human identity. There is, on the one hand, the figure of 'serious man' who expresses confidence in an irreducible singleness of identity, and in his secure place within a knowable existent material universe. On the other hand, there is his more volatile postmodernist counterpart 'rhetorical man' who 'manipulates reality, establishing through his words the imperatives and urgencies to which he and his fellows must respond . . . manipulates or fabricates himself, simultaneously conceiving of and occupying the roles that become first possible and then mandatory given the social structure his rhetoric has put in place.'[16] The ideological quarrel between the serious and the rhetorical is, according to Fish, at least as old as the hills. But at the moment, in our fragmented and relativist post-modern culture 'the fortunes of rhetorical man are on the upswing'.

Following in the footsteps of the historian of science Thomas Kuhn (behind whom lies the powerful figure of Nietzsche), Fish uses this distinction to argue that all claims to objectivity and knowledge made within the humane disciplines are, literally, rhetorical. As his argument goes on, he follows through the implications of this idea until he has developed a sweeping demystification of the cognitive pretentions of most conventional assumptions. Like Richard Rorty, mentioned in the previous section, Fish refuses to see commentary as an unproblematic means of access to knowledge, and in its combination of scepticism and creativity, his version of the rhetorical may yet offer us a way out of the impasse of authorship.

Fish's argument has attracted a great deal of attention and commentary, and I introduce it here as a benchmark of possibilities. But although it will be exploited later, Fish's argument is not one most readers would immediately associate with Anglo-American eighteenth-century studies. Rhetorical study of eighteenth-century fiction conventionally proceeds with the scrupulous forensic caution and seriousness of R. S. Crane, a truly serious man, as far removed from Fish's exuberant and relativist assumptions as can be conceived. Like the equally controversial scepticism about the bases of critical authority, described polemically in his book *Is There a Text in This Class?* (1980), Fish's account of rhetoric cheerfully embraces the possibilities of indeterminacy and phenomenological imprecision. More conservative versions of the subject shy away from such iconoclastic verve, and prefer to cling to the more reassuring classical notion that rhetoric is a knowable and describable repository of technical and linguistic devices, literary techniques which can be identified and itemised in fixed and determinate texts.

These two writers, Crane and Fish, can serve as representatives of the two most extreme and opposed positions in non-authorial critical thinking. For Crane, in the *Tom Jones* essay at least, literary works are determinate, spatial and open to skilled analysis. For Fish, the same texts are constantly volatile, temporal and available for recreation within critical discourse. In the years between 1952 and 1990, as we might expect, a range of positions has been adopted, but it would be wrong to construct some kind of progress from Crane's old-fashioned serious determinacy to Fish's new-fangled rhetorical volatility. Rather, the debate about Fielding's work has eddied between these two poles of influence, and neither has achieved clear supremacy at any point.

So, what are these interim positions, and what do they do with Fielding? In the most widely read English study of rhetoric published this century, Wayne C. Booth's *The Rhetoric of Fiction* (1961), individual novels (including two by Fielding) are articulated in terms of the formal narrative techniques adopted within them to ensure artful communication. Consciously adopting a synchronic perspective, Booth (like Crane) tries to avoid concern with broader contextual issues, or with the personalities of individual writers, or with lines of literary influence. For him, it remains a matter of little relevance that the novels under consideration may purport to describe a material world, or may seem to express the psychology of their authors. Booth's primary concerns remain the technical procedures of the fictional narratives under examination, and their use of the resources of rhetoric to render experience communicable.

The Rhetoric of Fiction starts off as an exercise in literary taxonomy, itemising the main varieties of narrative technique and Jamesian

'points of view' without ostensibly taking sides between them.
However, as his discussion of Fielding in particular shows, Booth's
commentary, like Crane's, is still at its heart recognisably evaluative.
Conscious of his inheritance of the deeply serious mantle of Henry
James, Booth even expresses concern that his analytic procedures may
be thought too reductive – 'in treating technique as rhetoric, I may
seem to have reduced the free and inexplicable processes of the
creative imagination to the crafty calculations of commercial
entertainers'.[17] Booth's reverence for these 'inexplicable processes'
puts him much nearer to Crane than to Fish, making him confront his
discomfort at the egalitarian element in rhetorical study. Clearly
disturbed by the notion that he may be helping these rogues in their
'crafty calculations', Booth retreats behind an evaluative veil, and
strictly limits his attention to canonical texts, in which he finds a
workable but crude and over-schematic distinction between 'reliable'
and 'unreliable' narrators.

Although this distinction is difficult to sustain, it offers Booth a
diagrammatic way of representing and articulating a number of
eighteenth-century novels, notably *Tom Jones* and *Tristram Shandy*.
When dealing with Fielding's novel, Booth concentrates less on the
'spatial' features of the text, and more on the developed relationship
between the narrator and the reader. From his account of the
interaction between narrator and 'narratee', Booth goes on to discuss
the overlapping but not identical relationship within the text between
the implied author and the implied reader, and to speculate about the
supervising relationship beyond the text between the real author and
the real reader.[18] In going beyond formal analysis of plotting to look
at procedures of address and communication, Booth is able to
confront the constantly interrupting, cajoling and coercive figure of
the narrator in Fielding's novel – a device which had previously
created great difficulties for those critics who sought to encompass
eighteenth-century fiction in the embrace of verisimilitude.

Indeed, for a great many commentators, the intrusive narrator is
something of an embarrassment. As Ian Watt put it in *The Rise of the
Novel*, 'few readers would like to be without the prefatory chapters, or
Fielding's diverting asides, but they undoubtedly derogate from the
reality of the narrative'.[19] Despite the way he affects to distance
himself, Watt seems to be one of these 'few readers', since this most
prominent feature of both *Joseph Andrews* and *Tom Jones* is
incompatible with his paradigm of 'formal realism', as displayed by

Bunyan, Defoe and Richardson. Like so many commentators under the spell of Henry James, Watt betrays a disposition to prefer novelists who 'show' their readers what is happening to those who insist on butting in and 'telling' them. As a consequence, he can never be completely comfortable with the interventionist figure of Fielding, eventually more or less dismissing *Tom Jones* as 'only part novel'. Although he is ostensibly describing eighteenth-century fiction as it was, Watt is eager to tidy it up, to chart a consistent teleology – a 'rise of the novel' – in which practices of oral and early printed story-telling like intrusive narrators and digressions are gradually shed in favour of pseudo-sophisticated nineteenth-century models of 'realism'. By refusing to conform to this pattern, Fielding finds himself excluded from the pageant.

For a great many critics, then, the superiority of mimetic ('showing') procedures of narrative over diegetic ('telling') alternatives goes virtually without saying. R.S. Crane, for instance, finds it hard to read Fielding without acknowledging just such a prejudice:

> It could be shown, I think, that as compared with most of his predecessors, the author of *Tom Jones* had moved a long way in the direction of the imitative and dramatic. Yet it cannot be denied that in many chapters he merely states and that in even the most successful of the scenes in which action and dialogue predominate he leaves far less to inference than we are disposed to like.   (Crane, p. 639)

However, where Watt sees the intrusive narrator as a kind of amiable anachronism, over-garrulous and incorrigible in offering his 'diverting asides', and where Crane simply finds him more prominent 'than we are disposed to like', Booth tries to offer a more positive account. Although encumbered by more than enough prejudices of his own (against the ambiguities and ironies of twentieth-century fiction, for example), and although as infatuated as Crane with the 'finished' and 'controlled' nature of novels, Booth tries to keep an open mind on the question of the intrusive narrator. As far as he is concerned, the house of fiction is capacious, and there is nothing indecorous or dishonourable in an author ransacking all the possibilities of narrative communication, be they direct or indirect.

Being less committed to the notion of verisimilitude, Booth can attempt to understand the role of the narrator in *Tom Jones* in broadly functional terms. In fact, his argumentative strategy of legitimation is increasingly paradoxical. Where we might expect a full-bloodied defence of the diegetic principle ('telling'), Booth actually strives to incorporate the narrator into the main fabric of the narrative, turning him from being the vehicle of quasi-authorial 'telling' into yet another character in a more complex, more deftly orchestrated piece of 'showing'. Alongside the main plot of Tom's mishaps and adventures, Booth detects an important 'sub-plot' in which the narratee and the narrator start out as antagonists, then grow fonder of each other, before finally parting as friends. The narrator is thus not an irritating or needlessly diverting intrusion into the plot, but an essential component in a plot even richer and more variegated than that discovered by Crane.

But the question remains: Who is this narrator? Can it conceivably be Fielding? When he comes to sum up his case, Booth seems clear that the narrator in Tom Jones is not to be read as simply an oblique representation of the author himself:

> Was Fielding literally infirm when he wrote that sentence? It matters not in the least. It is not Fielding we care about but the narrator he created to speak in his name.   (Booth, p. 218)

The line of separation is clearly drawn – the narrator is a detailed and fully realised character, with whom the reader (or at least the narratee) develops a complex relationship, who represents a greater moral norm than any of the other characters to be encountered in the tale, but who yet remains separable from the inscrutable and perhaps finally invisible controlling author. The narrator is thus not Fielding himself, but Fielding's proxy. To put the distinction in the more technical terms of Gerard Genette, the narrator is no longer an 'extra-diegetic' agency of narration, but an incorporated character in a more complex novelistic structure, a character who belongs in the gallery of models alongside Tom, Blifil, Allworthy, Sophia and all the others.

Within Booth's account of Fielding's work, however, there is a great deal of uncertainty about the focus of attention, which becomes apparent in the lexical confusion which quickly entangles him. Within only four pages (Booth, pp. 215–19) a whole range of diverse terms is assembled to describe the subject, indicating the covert essentialism of the analysis. The recognisable narrating voice in the text is variously referred to as 'the implied author', 'the dramatized

Fielding', 'the narrator', 'Fielding-as-narrator', 'Fielding's dramatic version of himself', 'the author' and 'this self'. Such a battery of expressions, a thesaurus of its own, indicates Booth's lack of adequate descriptive terminology to effect the vital distinction between the real and the implied authors. Booth is obviously trying to transform the obtrusive 'telling' voice of the text into something fully dramatised, something 'shown', for reasons which have more to do with his own overall approach to writing and the hegemony of the mimetic paradigm than with the quiddity of Fielding's novel. Instead of being the tiresome interloper barely tolerated by Watt, the narrator becomes a presence, a standard of judgement within the novel, and a repository of values, consistent and fully realised. To put it in suitably allusive terms: the narrator's role in *Tom Jones*, as Booth sees it, is to act as Virgil to the reader's Dante.

Booth arrives at this position through his search for unity and stability in the book. Indeed, he claims that his account of the narrator is necessary 'if we wish to claim that *Tom Jones* is a unified work of art and not half-novel, half-essay' (Booth, p. 216). Perhaps this sounds reasonable enough, but only if the arguments against its being 'half-novel, half-essay' are obvious and overwhelming. However, these reasons remain hidden as unexamined assumptions about the rightful nature of fiction, rather than as carefully delineated and defended positions.

After all, what is so wrong with the idea that *Tom Jones* is a mixed and inconsistent text? The fundamental grounds for Booth's resistance to the hybrid form, or for Watt's, are never clearly spelt out, but they seem to arise from other commitments, allegiances and affiliations which have to be seen as ideological rather than as purely literary. As Frederic Jameson claims, Booth's critical procedures are determined by a prior commitment to stable cultural values and to moral wholeness:

> Booth's book is a defence of the omniscient narrator, the implied author or reliable commentator, who unobtrusively but strategically makes his presence between reader and characters felt in such a way that the former is provided with the standards by which to judge the latter properly. The implied author is of course not the real author either, but rather the absolute embodiment of positive cultural values.[20]

'Fielding-as-narrator' thus comes to represent 'the absolute embodiment of positive cultural values'. The narrator dramatically ceases to be a tedious lapel-grabber, egregiously breaking the frame of verisimilitude, and turns instead into a kind of SuperFielding, the author's very best version of himself, a dramatic reappearance of Thackeray's manly hero, now cleansed even of those stubborn claret stains.

In a bizarre twist to Booth's account, the intrusive narrator of *Tom Jones* comes to represent the same standards of value espoused by the much more withdrawn narrator of *Emma*, the obvious differences between these figures submerged by one overwhelmingly important similarity: ' "Jane Austen", like "Henry Fielding", is a paragon of wit, wisdom, and virtue' (Booth, p. 264).

It surely becomes troubling when what is ostensibly a formalist analysis of a text turns into another kind of author-worship with a few more inverted commas thrown in. Booth's resistance to narrative polyphony, and his desire for consistency and wholeness (not to mention wholesomeness) seem in the end to disfigure his presentation. Eventually he finds in the narrative, not an unmediated version of the author himself, but a dramatised account of that author's finest moments. But yet when he says that 'he' finds such a figure, to whom is he referring?

> . . . the same distinction must be made between myself as reader and the often very different self who goes about paying bills, repairing leaky faucets, and failing in generosity and wisdom. It is only as I read that I become the self whose beliefs must coincide with the author's . . . The author creates, in short, an image of himself and another image of his reader; he makes his reader, as he makes his second self, and the most successful reading is the one in which the created selves, author and reader, can find complete agreement.   (Booth, pp. 137–8)

So the already complex case is further complicated by the appearance of the reader. Fielding creates 'Fielding' and then he goes further and creates 'Booth' to read him, no doubt admiringly. 'Fielding-as-narrator' constructs an appropriate counterpart in 'Booth-as-narratee', imposing constraints and limitations on their relationship and requiring due deference. Presumably, just as the author's second self is a heightened and selective version of his personality, the created reader will be an equally purified figure – the high-minded 'Booth' who plumbs the text is not the same prompt-paying Booth who plumbs the kitchen.

While it is inevitable and desirable that rhetorical analysis pay due attention to the results of the oratorical processes within the text, Booth's account of the role of the reader seems extremely narrow and over-determined. In the less collaborationist terms of Louis Althusser, style or rhetoric 'interpellates' the reader, hailing him or her in a specific way, setting the terms of address and establishing the conventions of the relationship between the reader and the particular text. All manner of relationships might hereby be constructed, and yet for Booth, the practice of reading is always a process of heightening, with the willing and deferential reader being raised to the level of sophistication of the implied author.

For all its influence, Booth's account of Fielding's fiction eventually seems too rigidly moralist, too sermonising and in the end self-congratulatory to cope with the book's vituperative energy, its internal dialectic and its serpentine convolutions of plot. For the narratives (as I read them anyway – this is 'Bell-as-narratee' speaking) simply do not offer consistently friendly or flattering interpellations, hailing me as subtle and perceptive. Quite the reverse, for they deliberately patronise me, confronting me with my own errors, describing me as a 'little reptile of a critic' every so often and forcing me off balance whenever they choose to.

My major objection to Booth's account of rhetoric is that it is too single-minded, too solemn and reified in its treatment of the text – in short it is unquestionably the reading of a 'serious man'. By removing the narratives from their social and political context, Booth has gained space to incorporate his own reading, but he has universalised it to the point where it becomes the only legitimate reading. Even more than Crane, he requires Fielding to lift himself and his reader out of the mire of narrative confusion, by means of the largely benign and humane supervisory figure of the narrator. The elements of mischievous play, of deliberate confusion and misdirection, prominent in my own recreation of all of Fielding's work seem to be wholly obliterated in Booth's account, just as they are in the standard biographical accounts, from Murphy's to Battestin's.

Booth's influential study is not the only rhetorical account of Fielding. In John Preston's *The Created Self: The Reader's Role in Eighteenth-Century Fiction* (1970), Fielding's novels are articulated through their capacity to persuade, their attempt to construct an appropriate reader for themselves through positioning and emphasis. Preston's study goes much closer to an Althusserian idea of interpellation, without actually mentioning it, and seems to allow the reader more creative freedom, however much reading may eventually be supervised by the narrator's or the author's control:

There are, then, areas of meaning which the narrator does not even mention. But his reticence does not prevent us becoming conscious of them. Thus the book begins to escape from the narrow designs imposed on it, from the conscious intention of the narrator . . . the author leaves the book to itself, or rather, to the reader. In other words, Fielding has been able, by means of the plot, to create a reader wise enough to create the book he reads. [21]

Combining and extending the work of Crane on the complexities of the plot and Booth on Fielding-as-narrator, Preston moves away from the rhetorical towards what he calls an 'epistemological' reading of *Tom Jones*. Preston believes that the book offers a rhetorical training in discernment, setting various traps for the reader, with a view to educating him (and it is always 'him', alas) in the ways of the world.

Although it may be stretching the term 'rhetoric' to include a reading such as this, Preston's account of the interaction of the narrator and Fielding, and his emphasis on the suasive features of the text place him as a negotiating figure between the poles of Crane and Fish. Although he introduces more volatility by concentrating upon the reader, Preston yet shares Booth's view of the book as elevating, of the narrator/author as a discernible centre of wisdom who orchestrates the characters in terms of their relative credulity and sagacity, seeking to create a knowing, generous and perceptive (yet not wholly cynical) reader.

Despite the terms of reference established early in his argument, Preston has surprisingly little to say about any reader's *actual* response, preferring to demonstrate instead what he presents as the reader's *required* response. Unlike the more provocative and unstable versions of reading offered in Barthes' later writing and in Stanley Fish's 'affective stylistics', this particular argument is based on a very determinate and static account of the book, with little real evocation of the relativity or the positioning of specific readers. For Preston, there may be, and may have been, many different readers of *Tom Jones*, but there can in the end only be one successful reading of the book. That competent reading is to be created by the intelligent interaction of Fielding, his narrator, and the right kind of deferential, remarkably passive reader, who brings to the book only the human capacity for regular error and a humble willingness to accept eventual correction at the hands of the supervisory author.

The account of reading Fielding offered by Preston starts off provocatively, but ends up rather tamely, with the incontestable text still seen as the sole repository of authority, supervising and governing its readings. Indeed, Preston incorporates reservations about the more conservative tendency in his argument when he invites further discussion – 'I should be glad to feel that such an approach might prompt other more radical enquiries into the nature of the reader's role in fiction' (Preston, p. 3). Preston himself has little to offer in this more radical direction, but that is not the end of the matter, and the line of Fielding criticism running through Crane, Booth and Preston next takes in the reader-centred theory of Wolfgang Iser.

In his books *The Implied Reader* (1974) and *The Act of Reading* (1978), Iser regularly cites the work of Fielding as a paradigm case of the text partly constructed by the intelligent reader. Like the implied reader invented by Booth, Iser's 'reader' still lacks flesh, blood, prejudices and the elementary skills of household maintenance, remaining a rather abstract personage, neither historicised nor gendered, and Iser seems extremely unwilling to let go of his desire for a neutral, 'unbiased' and orderly reading. However, even with these liberal compromises, which go strongly against the spirit of more radical historicised reception theory, Iser accepts a less concrete and stable notion of the literary text than any we have encountered up to this point. He moves towards the indeterminacy of Barthes and Fish, yet refuses to turn the text into an unsupervised play area where free-associating readers may make merry. In fact, Iser's particular version of reception theory is a careful mixture of the traditional scholarly interpretive concerns and some broader sense of how individual readers might bring something to their reading. The reader then becomes more of a participant in the making of the text, and less of a spectator, albeit a participant held under strict authorial supervision:

> The participation of the reader could not be stimulated if everything were laid out in front of him. This means that the formulated text must shade off, through allusions and suggestions, into a text that is unformulated though nonetheless intended. Only in this way can the reader's imagination be given the scope it needs; the written text furnishes it with indications which enable it to conjure up what the text does not reveal.[22]

In Iser's formulation, then, there are always gaps in the text, gaps which permit the reader of a novel a certain restricted freedom of interpretive movement. However, this 'unformulated' text remains 'nonetheless intended', and so eventually by sleight of hand the authorial power of supervision and the supremacy of the author's intention is retained.

What exactly is involved in keeping the reader on probation, or even under house arrest like this? As Iser puts it, he (always 'he' again, at least in the English translations) is granted a degree of interpretive freedom, but only within a framework where the big decisions are all made for him by the author, and there is never any doubt that these big decisions remain unquestionable. When Iser deals with the challenges to the reader in the prefatory chapters of *Joseph Andrews* and *Tom Jones*, he describes the textual strategies very well, but he rarely lives up to the radical potential of the theory of reading outlined in his later book. As one commentator puts it:

> . . . more troublesome for Iser's enterprise is the fact that here and elsewhere freedom is granted to the reader only when it doesn't really count much at all. If Tom Jones is a pound or two lighter, an inch or two taller, or if his eyes are a darker shade of blue are matters left to the reader. In these areas we are permitted to exercise a certain liberty in filling in blanks. But when it comes to the meaning of sections of the novel or the work in its entirety, Iser leaves no room for deviating from 'the message'. The indeterminate often seems to involve only the trivial and non-essential details; where meaning is produced, however, the reader either travels the predetermined path or misunderstands the text. [23]

These are damaging criticisms of Iser's position, and they seem wholly justified, illustrating a wider problem in contemporary Fielding studies. The critics dealt with in this section, from Crane to Iser, have, for their various reasons, been eager to remove the author from the texts, but, like an uninvited party-goer, he has always managed to sneak back in. Even here, in the most radical account of his work so far, it is Fielding who remains energetically at work behind the scenes, creating the illusion of reader freedom. And for Iser that freedom is at heart only an illusion, for the author or narrator still exercises real control, even over suggestions and implications. Seeing the spectre of indeterminacy and anarchy looming before him, Iser is only too happy to welcome Fielding back, on whatever terms he chooses.

Having brandished the fetish of the author in the opening section, and replaced him with the fetish of the work in this section, I have only succeeded in identifying problems. Crane, Booth, Preston and

Iser have not obviously overcome the difficulties of reading Fielding's novels without Fielding's help, and the developmental model of Ian Watt, mentioned briefly, seemed equally uncomfortable with these texts. So what is to be done? Is there a way of making sense of authorial presence without being in awe of it? Is there a way of reconciling the apparently conflicting demands of textual authority and interpretive freedom? You will not be surprised, by hefting this volume in your hands, to discover that I do not think the debate should be wound up at this point. But yet the problems remain large and imposing, and another prefatory section is required to bring them into line.

The return of the author?

It may be observed by the reader, that in pursuing the foregoing train of reflections, sight has been lost of HENRY FIELDING: but it never was intended, in this little tract, to observe the rules of strict biography.[24]

Regarding our troublesome subject, the author Henry Fielding, the position now seems to be that while commentators may not be able to live with him, they cannot live without him. In the abstract, the author himself or herself (or even itself) has been revealed to be a highly volatile and changeable construction, created and defined through the perspectives of various sets of critical and biographical practices, surrounded by methodological and practical uncertainties. In this particular case, it is obvious that from the early eighteenth century onwards Fielding's image and his reputation have fluctuated greatly in response to the persuasions and commitments of those discussing him.

Nonetheless, it has proved to be no easy matter to dispel this controversy simply by discarding him. Although there are several critical positions which are not firmly wedded to the biographical presence of an expressive author, they too have been seen to present their own attendant problems. The contending claims of formalism or rhetoric or reception theory to dispense with the author or to introduce a more attainable replacement, whether it be the narrator or an interpellating authorial 'second self' or a 'narratee' (a curious creature often mistaken by sailors for a mermaid) or the 'implied reader' or even the actual flesh and blood page-turning reader, have all had something to offer but have all foundered on the rocks eventually.

Of course, my examination of alternatives to 'the author' has scarcely been exhaustive. It may yet be discovered that there is more to narrative poetics than Wayne C. Booth offers, and more in reception theory than in the work of Wolfgang Iser. However, since these commentators represent the best-known versions of their respective approaches within the field of eighteenth-century studies, and since each has particular relevance for the case of Henry Fielding, they may stand as paradigm cases. So, for the moment at least, it looks disquietingly as though the denotative term 'Henry Fielding', with or without those tiresomely restraining handcuffs of inverted commas, remains no more than a necessary fiction of some kind, needing scrupulous attention and interrogation whenever sighted.

Does this mean that 'he' lives only as a personal pronoun, an elusive 'shifter' in more senses than one? Perhaps 'he' not only accumulates all the conventional philosophical difficulties which attach to the use of proper names, but also disintegrates on closer contact, to the extent that the 'Fielding' on display in subsequent pages can be no more than a phantasm of my own making, a personalised projection of my reading of eighteenth-century English novels, a convenient device for the ostentatious display of my critical and rhetorical faculties, and, who knows, perhaps even a stimulus to my professional advancement.

Fortunately, this depressing possibility is not the end of the matter, and there is still some point in my own 'narratee' continuing to read on. Everything said so far about the problems involved in the more conventional biographical versions of literary and historical study of the eighteenth-century English novel has rehearsed reasonably familiar reservations about positivist scholarship, reservations sharpened in the turmoil of post-structuralist controversy and by no means restricted to the study of Fielding. Problems in the formulation of 'the author' have been among the most intense areas of debate within post-structuralist thinking, and for the most part the debate has been troubled and inconclusive, more sweepingly destructive of received ideas and 'common-sense' assumptions than constructive of comprehensible and coherent replacements for them. But not all of the discussion of authorship has been quite so negative. There have been still further attempts to reassess the problem of the author which will repay attention, and which may yet provide a provocative context

and critical vocabulary for the treatment of what I still cannot refrain
from calling Fielding's fiction.

Despite all the problems identified, the discredited author has
stubbornly refused to leave the critical arena. In recent years, indeed,
there has been something of a more positive return to the questions of
authorship and authority in literary and adjacent areas of study, albeit
one couched in terminology far removed from the more traditional
vocabulary of biographical scholarship. Let us take the best known of
these developments first. In film studies since the later 1950s there
have been relevant debates surrounding the notion of the 'auteur',
concerned with identifying the personal stamp of a particular
film-maker, say John Ford or Alfred Hitchcock, on an essentially
collaborative work like a film emerging from the Hollywood studio
system.[25] Given that the director (or whoever is seen as the 'auteur')
has little initial control over the choice of material, he or she may
resort to flamboyant stylistic techniques to personalise the work, or
may offer priority to particular features which lie relatively dormant in
the original source. The 'auteur' is thus not the sole generator of
meaning in the text, but a more limited figure, who may both
facilitate and impede the text's ability to convey clear messages.

A convenient illustration to help begin to see the relevance of this
issue would be to look at the way the 1958 hard-boiled crime novel
The Executioners by the prolific 'pulp' writer John D. MacDonald was
treated by different film-makers. The original novel is a stylised
account of the violent reprisal carried out by a criminal on the family
of the man who originally helped to convict him. Following
recognisable patterns of crime-writing, it is an accessible 'readerly' text
in which generic conventions are obeyed, and the narrative draws on
the tacit expectations of its competent readers. It was first made into
the film *Cape Fear*, directed for Universal Studios by the versatile J.
Lee Thompson in 1961. In this version, the inherited material is more
or less directly fashioned into cinematic terms by a competent
technician, and the film's distinguishing features lie in its skilled use
of narrative tension and its charismatic central performance by Robert
Mitchum rather than in any 'authorial' presence. As a narrative, it
follows the contours of the original text closely, and seems to give
priority to those episodes which are made prominent by MacDonald.
Thirty years later, however, it was remade by the self-conscious
'auteur' Martin Scorsese, and given a wholly different interpretation.
In the later film, Scorsese reads his original texts against the grain,

exploring the gaps and silences in the earlier works. New tensions and complications are introduced, and the remake becomes a deliberate, stylised reading (almost a misreading) of the precedent texts, playing with the assumptions and conventions of the popular form it emerges from. The menaced family are no longer representatives of integrity or innocence, and the menacing figure has much greater diabolic energy. The new film makes a number of quite deliberate references to the old one, by casting original actors in different parts, and setting up similar scenes used to different narrative ends. All of this is interesting in its own terms, and supplies film bores with the kind of material that leaves them with such large gaps in their social calendars. However, it is not all just a matter of game-playing. There are clear points of tension between the later director's vision and the horizons of expectation of the material, and these moments of stress allow the work to be explored within the protocols of Scorsese's output, emphasising the themes of guilt, reprisal and expiation which are prominent elsewhere, in earlier films like *Mean Streets* and *Taxi Driver*.

As this example suggests, the named 'auteur' (by no means an uncontroversial or uncontested term in itself) then serves as a way of ascribing complex meaning and significance to essentially popular texts, and as a means of making explicit connections between the internal drama of a film and a wider network of ideological affiliations. In this particular case, Scorsese's film acts as a reappraisal of the original 1950s' texts as much as a rendition of them, entering into dialogue with them and their assumptions. Furthermore, the 'auteur', problematically or otherwise, offers a way of bringing together otherwise disparate films, or of identifying individualised commitments as recognisable points of continuity across different texts, and at the very least it provides a useful focal point for the articulation of cinematic productions, without seeing the named figure as the only point of origin of the final work. Reading the text as a Robert De Niro film, for example, draws attention to different meanings than reading it as Scorsese's work. As the Scorsese example indicates, 'auteur' theory allows for the relation between author and text to be adversarial and combative, rather than simply expressive.

In dealing with a medium which was reluctant to display or venerate individuated authors for its works until comparatively recently, and which has always situated itself in the popular terrain, film studies start out less encumbered by the received and possibly oppressive critical tradition. As a consequence, they may make more visible some of the procedural problems which are also to be faced in literary study, without the usual disabling prejudices. In the debate surrounding the 'auteur' we get a salutary defamiliarisation of a recognisable issue, couched in what may seem to be unusual terms, but which nonetheless offer provocative avenues for exploration. These may need to be investigated before the relevance of such terminology to Fielding's fiction becomes apparent.

In its earliest forms, as expressed in a polemical article by François Truffaut in the French critical journal *Cahiers du Cinema* in 1954, the theory of the 'auteur' was offered principally as a way of developing intellectually serious study of film by reclaiming the hitherto neglected importance of the individual creative personality in a collaborative medium, a medium previously discussed almost exclusively in terms of technical innovation or genre or entertainment value. Clearly, extensive critical consideration had already been lavished on certain powerful and charismatic individual figures in the cinema, like D.W. Griffith or René Clair or Orson Welles, but no real rationale or coherent methodology had been evolved, limiting the focus of attention to a few obviously 'maverick' and unrepresentative artists like these. In the first formulation of 'auteur' theory, the figure of the director was selected as the dominant guiding intelligence behind individual film texts, orchestrating and personalising even those films which had been mediated through the studio system or those which fell into convenient generic categories like the 'western,' the 'women's picture' or the *'film noir'*.

Following Truffaut's 1954 account with more or less fidelity, self-conscious 'auteur' studies have taken film beyond the otherwise dominant notion of genre, and have subsequently brought into prominence the work of author/directors as diverse (and, some would say, similar) as Howard Hawks and Akira Kurosawa, Woody Allen and Fritz Lang, Jean-Luc Godard and Jerry Lewis. Interestingly, the critical vocabulary used to articulate cinema in this way has passed over into the area of production and enhanced the status of the director in practice, to the extent that many working directors now claim patrimony for their films by a signature at the opening, just as the authors of novels were beginning to do in the early eighteenth century.

Although directors still retain their centrality in this discipline, just as authors do in literary criticism, the idea of the 'auteur' in film has gradually developed greater sophistication, offering up other influential participants in film-making as candidates, like screen-writers or editors or 'stars' or cinematographers or lighting technicians, or other more idiosyncratic controlling figures like Walt Disney or Samuel Goldwyn. The list continues to grow, but there are clear limits to candidacy, and, as far as I know, no one has yet proposed a distributor or projectionist as 'auteur', however much the competence or affiliations of such a figure might affect the public perception of individual films.

The relevance of this project to more conventional literary study will become clearer in time, but on first inspection it may seem paradoxical that just as the new-style 'auteur' was being drawn through Paris on an elaborate band-wagon, the old-style 'author' was being unceremoniously bundled out of the other side of town. However, the two events are not as flagrantly contradictory as they might at first appear, and the new term 'auteur' is an altogether more flexible and tentative critical formulation, which could be used as a replacement for the increasingly discredited and disreputable term 'author'.

The two kinds of study may seem to overlap, and may occasionally merge. The earlier authorial studies of Griffith or Welles, for example, are largely indistinguishable from old-fashioned 'life and works' criticism so familiar in the representation of canonical figures like Fielding. Nonetheless, the points of divergence between the two ways of thinking are more striking than the occasional moments of convergence. To put the matter as simply as possible, acknowledging the risk of over-simplification, the most significant difference between 'auteur' and conventional author-centred study is that the former is *a posteriori* in orientation, while the latter is firmly *a priori*. Where film studies try to build a coherent figure from a body of work, recognising points of continuity and recurrent emphasis no matter what the interference from other important contributing features, author study as conventionally understood tries to read the works in question through the prior figure of their only begetter. And whereas literary study sees almost all texts as 'authored', film study in this formulation recognises that those films which may be attributed to an 'auteur' are unusual and deviant. Arising from overpoweringly material circumstances of production, and designed for commercial con-sumption, most film texts are generic and do not invite the individualist or expressive perspectives which silently dominate literary study.

Film theorist Jim Kitses puts the issues surrounding 'auteur' theory as follows:

> The term describes a basic principle and a method, no more and no less: the idea of personal authorship in the cinema and – of key importance – the concomitant responsibility to honour all of a director's works by a systematic examination in order to trace characteristic themes, structures, and formal qualities. In this light the idea of the 'auteur' does not seem to me to solve all our problems as much as to crystallise them.[26]

Kitses seeks in 'auteurism' a loose alliance, a question of emphasis rather than a detailed programme of study. The notion of the 'auteur' does not even answer all the difficulties of film criticism, never mind the particular set of problems raised by the specific nature of eighteenth-century literary production. Yet it offers a less tendentious way of focusing on the personal touch or voicing which can sometimes be found in films, uncovered through scrupulous and informed comparative retrospectives, visible despite all the other interferences and obstructions. In the Hollywood cinema in particular the director rarely (if ever) enjoyed complete creative control over all aspects of film-making, yet some aspects of his (or very occasionally *her*) filmic personality could still be discerned. These elements of personality or individual ideological commitment were not directly expressed within in a film, but were instead mediated by the form, impeded or facilitated by the material and the moment of production.

Despite the obvious peculiarities of the medium of film, and the obvious differences between the cinema and the literary world, there are things in 'auteurism' which cross over surprisingly well from one to the other. In particular, it is this notion of the creative figure struggling with inherited material, not always of his or her own choosing, and deliberately or inadvertently personalising it which I believe offers exciting possibilities for the discussion of Fielding. And, of course, 'auteur' criticism takes for granted the polyphony of any text – the way it represents a compendium of expressive voices, some of which may be in contention – to an extent which is directly opposed to the prevailing monist assumptions of most literary critics.

Although occasionally overstated by its advocates, 'auteur' theory does not seek to be all-encompassing. It has to be emphasised that by no means all films have a recognisable 'auteur', just as not all literary texts are authored, and some may be seen as the work of several

competing or collaborating creative figures. The discovery of the
'auteur' is not automatic, but 'involves an operation of decipherment'
in which either a core of meanings or motifs or a repertoire of stylistic
devices could be recognised and attributed.[27] The 'auteur', then,
certainly need not be thought of as identical with the historical
personage whose name appears somewhere in the titles of any film – a
point of emphasis which this way of thinking shares with the
narrative poetics of the last section – yet nor is the 'auteur' always a
deliberately deployed 'second self'.

The case of Alfred Hitchcock is perhaps the most complex and
instructive example, as well as the most widely debated. According to
many 'auteur' theorists, including Truffaut himself, there are
recognisable and recurrent Hitchcockian themes and motifs, clearly
visible in his films – mistaken identity, the arbitrariness of guilt,
people falling from tall buildings, and attractive but glacial blonde
women having a bad time. It is tempting to look for personal
explanations for the prominence of these motifs – in Hitchcock's
Jesuit background or in the darker depths of his psychology – as
several of the writers in *Cahiers du Cinema* sought to do in the 1960s,
but it is at least as important to recognise the way these motifs are
articulated through the development of a new and idiosyncratic
cinematic language. However, once these technical and thematic
features have been isolated and identified, they are freed from
authorial protection. Some Hitchcock films convey most, if not all of
these recurrent tropes (*Vertigo, Rear Window, Psycho*), and some only
a few (*Lifeboat, Rope, Topaz*). More confusingly, once the repertoire of
motifs and devices had been recognised, some very Hitchcockian films
did not personally involve him in any way (Stanley Donen's *Charade*,
Brian de Palma's *Body Double*). And just to make the picture even
harder to decipher, Hitchcock himself enjoyed the celebrity of the
director to an unusual degree, and quite deliberately made a fetish
of himself by his teasing cameo appearances in his own films, and
by his mordant self-publicising, a rare and splendidly disruptive
example of the ways in which a critical theory can impinge on
creative practice.

The marks of 'auteurship' may thus be recondite internal patterns
or recurring ideological positions, or a set of stylistic mannerisms,
which need not necessarily be located within the personality of an
actual living being, or thought of as the results of expressed or implied
authorial intentions. 'Auteur' theory humanises and personalises the

objects of study, while retaining the material centrality of the text, and it does not have to concern itself greatly with matters of biography as traditionally understood. Unlike the version of authorial study prominent in traditional literary scholarship, 'auteurism' does not impose supererogatory biographical assumptions upon the texts being articulated, and it is unusually responsive to the ways in which the medium employed both encourages and inhibits personal expression.

Some of this work on 'auteurism' has by now found its way into more mainstream literary study, but it has had little extensive influence so far on historical perspectives, offering itself instead mainly as a cult of personalities. The polemical urgency of Truffaut is now long passed, and 'auteur' theory has developed through a convergence with generic criticism (in the work of Jim Kitses), structuralist readings of film (Peter Wollen) and the big bow-wow strain of semiotics (*Screen*). Yet its hesitancy and its attempt to negotiate all the complexities of attribution and authorship make 'auteurism' in my view a particularly fertile and unjustly neglected avenue for historical and materialist literary criticism. Its particular configuration of individual creativity, the material circumstances of production, and the mediation of personal expression through awkward and resistant forms makes it especially relevant, I believe, to Fielding, writing as he was at the moment of the rapid and unprecedented technological development of the early novel.

At first sight, to talk of Fielding as 'auteur' might seem modish and anachronistic, but I shall argue more expansively later that in the way he inherits a body of uncongenial and awkward material, then revises it in the light of his own ideological and personal commitments, devising his stylistic palette as he goes along, creating points of tension and conflict between form and content, Fielding operates in a way more comparable with the film director than with the solitary writer familiar from traditional critical accounts. Across the range of his novels, we may be able to discern his recurrent preoccupations, his concerns with cultural authority, with sexual conduct and the proper definition of masculinity, and with the threat of social disorder, often reappearing *in spite of* the material he is working with, voiced in a particular way.

But, you may be asking, who says these are his preoccupations? Who says these are his recurrent concerns? Well, I do, and I think the books do, but that is for later. There is clearly still a great deal to be argued out, not least to find a way to incorporate a historical perspective alongside the formalist bias of this method, but for the moment, please accept what I hope is a tantalising foretaste of Fielding the 'auteur'.

Film theory has developed relatively rapidly, and its terms of reference often seem to be deliberately defined in opposition to those prevailing in literary study. However, even within the realm of traditional textual scholarship there has of late been a reinvigorated concern with the vexed questions of authorship and authority, inspired mainly by the rediscovered work of Mikhail Bakhtin and his associates, and subsequently infiltrating the emergent school of thinking loosely called 'cultural materialism' or, rather more grandly, 'New Historicism'. Indeed, such has been the renewal of concern with these questions that, according to some, 'authorship has proved a magnetic topic for literary studies and is now identified as an index of the current state of literary history and theory'.[28]

Put bluntly, the 'current state of literary history and theory' goes something like this: the theoretical and practical arguments against traditional authorial study coming from semiotics and post-structuralism might be compelling and persuasive, making it difficult hereafter to treat 'Fielding' or whoever either as a recoverable historical person or as a figure held in the isolation block of literary tradition. But all the same, the ensuing impulse to dispense with the author altogether, replacing that figure at best with the experiential *frisson* offered by Barthes, causes at least as much unease from a different direction. In this particular case, Fielding's known public life is hard to shrug off. Those vivid and interventionist connections with society and culture which permeate Fielding's work, those moments of public commentary in his pamphlets and his plays, the ways in which his experience was decisively shaped by his social and political circumstances and his installation in a literary culture, all of these exert a pressure on my reading of his novels which no amount of logical stringency or philosophical niceness could persuade me to disregard. To treat, say, *Amelia* without looking at the way it mediates contemporary thinking about the status of women or about masculinity smacks of bad faith and evasiveness. To pretend that the placing of the narrative of *Tom Jones* in the dramatic and significant year of 1745 is not germane to its structure or meaning seems equally contrary. And although the case of Fielding is heightened and dramatised by his highly visible and controversial public life in the theatre and later in the magistracy, these reservations must surely apply to other eighteenth-century authors just as much.

Also, the complex processes of reading and writing always seem more humanised and historicised than any strictly semiotic version of them has room for, perhaps less formalist than 'auteur' theory really has space for. Reading seems to demand an attempt at historical location, at recognising a mediated version of a particular culture, held in the historical construction of writing. But even so, if Fielding's novels are not just canvasses on which his private preoccupations can be discerned, but also acts of historical revisionism, how are the connections and interactions between text and context to be made? And what form does this revisionist, interpretive 'author' now take?

In Michel Foucault's 1969 essay 'What is an Author?', an attempt at synthesis is offered. In explicit refutation of Barthes' early essays on the one hand and of Jacques Derrida's work on *écriture* on the other, Foucault acknowledges the disappearance of the author as a historical event, while seeking a partial reinstatement of authorial presence, although in an overtly historicised and materialist way. Barthes allowed the author back in either as a 'guest', a 'figure in the carpet', or as a collaborator in a hectic moment of *jouissance*.[29] Foucault's alternative and contending notion of what he comes to call the 'author-function' is undoubtedly put forward with more rigour, and even if his argument is less joyfully impressionistic than Barthes, Foucault makes more of the necessary concessions to the pressure of history.

He starts by looking at the history of the term 'author', part of the historical process of individualised and personalised explanation, now seemingly redundant. For Foucault, the main enterprise when dealing with the machinery of authorship is not to pay homage to the few great minds of European culture and respectfully trace their influence, but to 'reexamine the empty space left by the author's disappearance; we should attentively observe, along its gaps and fault lines, its new demarcations, and the reapportionment of this void; we should await the fluid functions released by this disappearance'.[30] By reappraising an inadequate notion of authorship he himself had used in the context of Marx, Ricardo, Buffon, Linnaeus, Darwin and other prominent 'authors' in his earlier works *The Order of Things* (1966) and *The Archaeology of Knowledge* (1969), Foucault looks for such new demarcations, 'fluid functions', identifying central activities of the idea of the author in literary criticism.

As well as offering a convenient means of classification for diverse texts, the named 'author' has a wider talismanic value:

> The author explains the presence of certain events within a text, as well as their transformations, distortions, and their various modifications (and this through an author's biography or by reference to his particular point of view, in the analysis of his social preferences and his position within a class or by delineating his fundamental objectives). The author also constitutes a principle of unity in writing where any unevenness of production is ascribed to changes caused by evolution, maturation, or outside influence. In addition, the author serves to neutralize the contradictions that are found in a series of texts. Governing this function is the belief that there must be – at a particular level of an author's thought, of his conscious or unconscious desire – a point where contradictions are resolved, where the incompatible elements can be shown to relate to one another or to cohere around a fundamental and originating contradiction. Finally, the author is a particular source of expression who, in more or less finished terms, is manifested equally well, and with similar validity, in a text, in letters, fragments, drafts, and so forth.   (Foucault, pp. 128–9)

For Foucault, this conception of 'author' is no more than a modern reformulation of Saint Jerome's principles of authenticity, and no matter how elaborately it may be expressed, its assumptions remain naive and insupportable. Although useful and suggestive in many cases, maybe even unavoidable, 'author' is a term exploited by its users to create the illusion of a fundamental unity, and to 'rarefy' the text.

In an acknowledged variant of Booth's 'second self', Foucault distinguishes between the author 'in the sense of the individual who delivered the speech or wrote the text in question' and the author as 'the unifying principle in a particular group of writings or statements, lying at the origins of their significance, as the seat of their coherence'.[31] It is the latter he seeks to define, to describe rather than to replace, and he has little to say about the former and its relation to particular texts. As opposed to the texts which he claims do not require the signature of an author (orders, contracts, casual remarks) there are the texts of literature, philosophy and occasionally science, which reach towards an author either as an index of truthfulness or as a guarantee of individuality.

So the role of the author's name, of 'Henry Fielding', is not wholly descriptive nor indicative of origin, but rarefactory: 'discourse that possesses an author's name is not to be immediately consumed and forgotten . . . its status and its manner of reception are regulated by the culture in which it circulates' (Foucault, p.123). This is consistent with the way the named 'auteur' enhanced the value of film, but the most important point here is Foucault's account of the factors which bring the author into being. In orthodox historicist accounts, including Ian Watt's 'rise of the novel', it is the pressing force of history, the intersections of moment and possibility, the powerful coalescence of emergent material features of literary production and the intellectual and social spirit of the times, which bring authors like Defoe, Richardson and Fielding into existence. For Foucault, on the other hand, authors are not functions of history, but functions of discourse: 'the author's name is not a function of a man's civil status, nor is it fictional; it is situated in the breach, among the discontinuities, which gives rise to new groups of discourse and their singular mode of existence' (Foucault, p. 123).

The key term in this formulation is 'discourse', and it resists easy definition, given the way Foucault uses it to cover a multitude of signs. In the context of this particular argument, 'discourse' refers to an apparently autonomous system of language, internally coherent and consistent, based around one central term. Political discourse is the body of language that surrounds and constitutes the notion of government; legal discourse is the body of language surrounding and constituting the law. In this case, then, the aggrandised figures of authors are seen as functions of literary discourse, where their function is to preserve the illusion of coherence in debate, at the cost of perpetuating fantasy and replicating illusions. But although the 'author' is a function of literary discourse, the term arises from the point of contact (and friction) between that discourse and legal discourse. In historical terms, the author was willed into existence partly through the requirements of the penal code, from the need to identify and control transgressive writing, requirements which led to the individualised system of authorial copyright and ownership.

So in Foucault's argument, the 'author-function' is a kind of legal fiction, restricted in its applications and behaviour. In modern times, we project our ways of handling texts around these created figures, and we recognise different templates of construction: 'a "philosopher" and a "poet" are not constructed in the same manner, and the author of an eighteenth-century novel was formed differently from the modern novelist' (Foucault, p. 127). Here we see the ways in which

Foucault's argument begins to connect with the notion of the 'auteur' and with the study of Fielding's fiction. Although he is more concerned with the term 'author' as it refers to initiators of discursive practices (Freud and Marx are the examples chosen), he takes an eighteenth-century example when illustrating the 'author' as that person to whom the production of a particular text is conventionally imputed:

> . . . one could say that Ann Radcliffe did not simply write *The Mysteries of Udolpho* and a few other novels, but also made possible the appearance of Gothic Romances at the beginning of the nineteenth century . . . The novels of Ann Radcliffe put into circulation a certain number of resemblances and analogies patterned on her work – various characteristic signs, figures, relationships, and structures that could be integrated into other books. In short, to say that Ann Radcliffe created the Gothic Romance means that there are certain elements common to her works and to the nineteenth-century Gothic romance: the heroine ruined by her own innocence, the secret fortress that functions as a counter-city, the outlaw-hero who swears revenge on the world that has cursed him . . .   (Foucault, p. 132)

Although Foucault's presentation of the history of the Gothic novel in Britain is rather odd, we may see the overall pattern of his argument, which moves in a direction directly opposite to the present one. Foucault is eager to discover a way of using 'author' which will apply to Freud and Marx, rather than exclusively to the producers of eighteenth-century fiction. The author-function referred to as 'Ann Radcliffe' is created by our desire for a point of origin. The discourse of literary criticism, governed by the restrictive protocols of origin and influence, installs 'Radcliffe' securely in this formal genealogy. Like an 'auteur', the author is here recognised retrospectively, by formal analysis within a historical and developmental perspective.

So whereas Foucault's essay starts by offering a clear analysis of the problems involved in the formulation of the 'author', he ends up lacking a suitable replacement, preferring instead to uncover the ideological machinery by means of which the problem has emerged. The terms he evolves may be appropriate for 'initiators of discursive practices', the grand narrators of our culture, but as his brief account of Ann Radcliffe shows, he has little that is helpful to offer on the topic of Fielding. As he says himself, 'there is a decided absence of positive propositions in this essay' (Foucault, p. 136). However, his terms of reference may yet be capable of greater development than he offers here. In fact, elsewhere he offers more complex analyses of the historical and social pressures on discourse, looking at the reasons why literary critics have been drawn to offer individuated accounts of literary history. As he put it in 1972, 'in every society the production of discourse is at once controlled, selected, organised and redistributed according to a certain number of procedures, whose role is to avert its powers and its dangers, to cope with chance events, to evade its ponderous, awesome materiality'.[32]

The figure of the author, as conventionally constructed by literary critics, has been one such procedure, and it is my aim to confront the 'ponderous, awesome materiality' of eighteenth-century fiction. In traditional accounts, criticism seeks to subdue the internal contradictions and volatility of its texts by emphasising the dominant and supervisory wisdom of the personal point of origin of literary production. The function of the time-honoured 'author' has been to bring internal tensions under control, to make texts under review capable of coherence, to deflect attention from the fissures to the prevailing wholeness of mind postulated behind them, and eventually to enable literary history to recount its own teleological narrative. By bringing together *Shamela*, *Joseph Andrews*, *Jonathan Wild*, *Tom Jones*, *Amelia* and the other texts as Henry Fielding's books, as his sole intellectual property, we envisage a rich and detailed source of explanation for them, even if it is a source which we have seen to be elusive and indistinct. We also construct a convenient icon called 'Henry Fielding' as inventor of a discursive practice whom we can then install in the processional development of the English novel, comfortably filling the space between the traditional book-ends called 'Daniel Defoe' and 'Samuel Richardson' on the one side, and 'Tobias Smollett' and 'Charlotte Lennox' on the other.

By looking at the notion of the 'auteur', we see the possibilities of a much looser configuration of authorship, and a much less proprietorial one. By extracting parts of Foucault's argument, we get to see the ideological functions of the traditional notion of authorship, and we may then feel even more impelled to find an alternative formulation. In order to release texts from the custodial sentence of authorial control, we must remember that they intersect not only with a particular life, but also with a culture, a body of existing literary material, a technology, and a mode of distribution, and that they engage in dialogue with a host of other texts.

To do justice to that complex lattice, we must discuss another strain of radical thinking, that surrounding Mikhail Bakhtin:

> Literature enters the surrounding ideological reality as an independent part of it, occupying a special place within it in the form of specifically organized verbal works with a specific structure proper to them alone. This structure, like any ideological structure, refracts socio-economic being in its coming-to-be, and refracts it in its own way. But at the same time literature in its 'content' reflects and refracts the reflections and refractions of other literary spheres (ethics, cognition, political doctrines, religion, etc.), i.e. literature reflects in its 'content' that ideological purview as a whole, of which it itself is a part.[33]

Although these are possibly not the words of Bakhtin himself – there is a teasing material uncertainty about his own authorial presence which I shall for obvious reasons presently ignore – they can serve as a brief manifesto for everything that he and his associates tried to achieve. For Bakhtin, the formal analysis of literary works is essential, but not in the bloodless style of earlier efforts. Instead, literature must be seen both in itself and in its social context. Critics are required to articulate literary works in the 'specific structure proper to them alone', but must also find a way of expressing how that specific structure 'reflects and refracts the reflections and refractions of other ideological spheres'.

Even more comprehensively than Foucault, Bakhtin concentrates on the literary text as a mechanism within language, but he sees it in a much wider context than that of authorial control, largely because of his account of language as an interactive social construction. In his long and detailed study *Problems in Dostoyevsky's Poetics* (1927/1963), for instance, he rarely mentions the personality or character of the author under consideration, but looks instead at the principles of construction of some remarkable novels. As he puts it, Dostoyevsky's work has been misunderstood because critics have at best an inadequate vocabulary to describe the internal complexities of narrative, and have consistently sought for an authoritative and veridical voice in texts which do not seem to offer one. This is not to be explained solely by 'the methodological helplessness of critical thought', but by the essentially elusive nature of the authorial presence: 'the plurality of independent and unmerged voices and consciousnesses and the genuine polyphony of full-valued voices are in fact characteristics of Dostoyevsky's novels'.[34] Because of the multivocal rendering of these narratives, they simply do not yield a totalising authorial reading, and the specific psychological, moral or ideological character of their creator thus need not figure prominently in commentary upon them.

Despite this decentralised and impersonalised conception of the novels, Bakhtin was remarkably unembarrassed about using the name 'Dostoyevsky' in his discussion. Nonetheless, he was extremely eager to clarify its referent, to distinguish between the author as private individual and the author as literary creator. As one explanatory commentary puts it, 'the author is not a single, fixed entity so much as a capacity, an energy . . . What has importance is not who an author is, but how, when, and where she is.'[35] In distinguishing so clearly between the 'author-person' (who remains outside the text) and the 'author-creator' (who is produced within it) Bakhtin was exploiting a route already familiar within Russian Formalism. However, by strenuously historicising the text, rather than its author, he offers a way of concentrating upon the 'how, when, and where' of any literary product, rather than exclusively cataloguing its internal repertoire of stylistic mechanisms and devices.

Bakhtin seems to have started out thinking that the multivocality he described was a highly distinctive and innovative feature of Dostoyevsky's work, but later he came to see it as characteristic of narrative fiction as a whole. Although the representation of multiple voices in these books by the Russian novelist might be more obvious and more easily visible than elsewhere, it is really no more than an intensification of what Bakhtin identifies as the 'dialogic' tendencies of all extended prose.

The word 'dialogic' is a key term, and it needs some explanation before it can be appropriated here. For Bakhtin, language is never a vehicle for the unmediated representation of the material world. Any utterance may purport to convey information about the world, but it simultaneously reproduces or parodies or incorporates other previous utterances about its ostensible subject – language is, to use an alternative formulation, essentially intertextual. The producer of a literary text thus never sits in front of a wholly blank piece of paper, awaiting the flash of unprecedented inspiration and consummate originality, since the subjects are already half-formed, the descriptive phrases half-spoken, the whole system awaiting further intervention. In the heightened and self-conscious language of the literary text, this dialogue with existing texts, this multivocality was foregrounded, but not, as the Russian Formalists thought, simply to exploit and display the linguistic resources and conventions of language. Rather, the dialogic work flaunted its awareness of language as the site of ideological conflict: 'the dialogic work accepted that its production was a historical act: not the signification of a static reality by a lonely subject but an active discursive intervention conditioned by precise social and historical circumstances'.[36]

The notion of the author as a 'lonely subject' is thus to be abandoned. In its place, there is the generative and subversive power of language itself, multivocal and festive:

> Thus at any given moment of its historical existence, language is heteroglot from top to bottom: it represents the co-existence of socio-ideological contradictions between the present and the past, between differing epochs of the past, between different socio-ideological groups in the present, between tendencies, schools, circles and so forth, all given a bodily form. These 'languages' of heteroglossia intersect with each other in a variety of ways, forming new socially typifying 'languages'. [37]

As well as offering this perception about the 'double-voiced' nature of language, Bakhtin replenishes study of the eighteenth-century novel by his version of the history of novelistic discourse. He sees it as a constant process of internal subversion, of rift and schism, rather than as a stately procession of great minds, and his combative account of writing seems peculiarly appropriate to Fielding's work. The impulse towards the parodic, the comic and the subversive in Fielding's writing, and its repeated concern about who governs discourse, are key problems and issues in reading Fielding which Bakhtin's ideas can help articulate. By using these terms, and the flexible idea of the 'auteur', the notion of Fielding as a 'lonely subject', the individual who remains the focus of biographical attention, will be dispersed in favour of Fielding as the site of heteroglot confrontation, as the location of contesting pressures, as a voice amid voicings, struggling to be heard amid the cacophony.

But is it really legitimate to put Fielding's fiction alongside Dostoyevsky's as dialogic or heteroglot? It might seem odd to use these less determinate terms in the context of writing so strictly commandeered and apparently held under narratorial control as Fielding's. Nonetheless, the ensuing chapters will demonstrate that in Bakhtin's suggestive phrasing we may find a way of recognising the deepest and most persistent concerns of these books without undue anxiety about the character of their 'author-personality'.

At this point, you may well still be asking who I mean by Henry Fielding. And answer comes there none. In the face of all the difficulties and complexities already identified, I want to set up a confrontation or dialogue between two figures. There is first of all the Foucauldian 'author-function' of Henry Fielding, existing within the discourse of literary criticism, whom we encountered in the opening section, a constant site of ideological dispute. Then there is the Bakhtinian 'author-creator' Fielding, who is produced within the texts themselves, narrating and seeking to preside over them, provoking and sustaining his own ideological skirmishes. Neither of these figures is precisely coincident with any known historical personage, and the nearest we may get to a sustainable compromise between the two is some 'auteur' going by the remarkably familiar name of 'Henry Fielding'.

So as the Fieldings begin to multiply before my eyes, it may be time to get on with the main part of the argument. Accordingly, the next chapter will concentrate on Fielding's emergence into the adversarial world of prose fiction with the parodic *Shamela*, published in 1741, and will concentrate on the combative and dialogic relation that work has with the earlier work of Samuel Richardson. As a final twist to the uncertainties about authorship discussed in this chapter, it is worth pointing out that Fielding never owned up to having written this book; that his name does not appear on its original title-page, where it is attributed to a 'Mr Conny Keyber'; and that at the time it was published only a very small group of intimates would have been able to identify the author of *Pamela*.[38] So not only is our concern with authors fraught with epistemological and methodological difficulties, it is also anachronistic. In short, after all this fuss about authorship, the following chapter will discuss a book Fielding did not admit to writing, about another book of whose author he was ignorant.

Notes and references

1.   Henry Fielding, 'A Modern Glossary', *The Covent-Garden Journal* (14.1.1752), ed. Bertrand A. Goldgar (Oxford, 1988), p. 35.

2. Roland Barthes, *The Pleasure of the Text* (1973), translated by Richard Millar (New York, 1975), p. 27.

3. See the discussion of recent thinking on this topic in John Caughie (ed.), *Theories of Authorship: A Reader* (London, 1981), pp. 199–207. See also the note on 'author' in Leon S. Roudiez's introduction to Julia Kristeva, *Desire in Language*, trans. Thomas Gora, Alice Jardine and Leon S. Roudiez (Oxford, 1980), p. 13.

4. *Boswell's Life of Johnson*, ed. G.B. Hill and L.F. Powell (6 vols, Oxford, 1934–50), ii, 174.

5. Samuel Richardson, letter to Lady Bradshaigh, 23 February 1752, in John Carroll (ed.), *Selected Letters of Samuel Richardson* (London, 1964), pp. 198–9.

6. George Cheyne, letter to Samuel Richardson, 9 March 1742, quoted in Claude Rawson (ed.), *Penguin Critical Guides: Henry Fielding* (Harmondsworth, 1973), p. 59.

7. Jonathan Swift, 'Verses on the Death of Dr Swift', in Pat Rogers (ed.), *Jonathan Swift: The Complete Poems* (Harmondsworth, 1983), p. 489.

8. Colley Cibber, *An Apology for the Life of Mr Colley Cibber, Comedian* (1740), Everyman edn (London, 1976), p. 147.

9. Ronald Paulson and Thomas Lockwood (eds), *Henry Fielding: The Critical Heritage* (London and New York, 1969), p. xxi.

10. William Makepeace Thackeray, 'Hogarth, Smollett and Fielding', in *The English Humourists of the Eighteenth Century* (London, 1858), pp. 270–1.

11. Simon Varey, *Henry Fielding* (Cambridge, 1986), p. vii.

12. Richard Rorty, 'Philosophy as a Kind of Writing', on *Consequences of Pragmatism* (Minnesota, 1982), p. 92.

13. Gerard Genette, *Figures of Literary Discourse*, trans. Alan Sheridan (Oxford, 1982), p. 147.

14. See Victor Shklovsky, 'Sterne's *Tristram Shandy*: Stylistic Commentary', in *Russian Formalism: Four Essays*, ed. Lee T. Lemon and Marion J. Reis (Lincoln, Nebraska, 1965), pp. 25–57. I have tried to exploit Russian Formalist terminology in the reading of Defoe in my essay 'Narrators and Narrative in Defoe', *Novel: A Forum on Fiction* 18 (1985), 154–72.

15. See R.S. Crane, 'The Concept of Plot and the Plot of *Tom Jones*', in *Critics and Criticism*, ed. R.S. Crane (Chicago and London, 1952), pp. 616–47. The choice of the year 1952 as the starting point for modern Fielding studies may look arbitrary, but it is the year of the present writer's birth, and so marks the beginning of the contemporary period as far as he is concerned.

16. Stanley Fish, 'Rhetoric', in *Critical Terms of Literary Study*, ed. Frank Lentricchia and Thomas McLaughlin (Chicago and London, 1990), p. 208. In making this distinction, Fish acknowledges a debt to Richard Lanham, *The Motives of Eloquence* (New Haven, 1976).

17. Wayne C. Booth, *The Rhetoric of Fiction* (Chicago and London, 1961), Preface. Further page references will be incorporated in the text.

18. Seymour Chatman, *Story and Discourse: Narrative Structure in Fiction and Film* (Ithaca, NY, 1978), pp. 147–51.

19. Ian Watt, *The Rise of the Novel* (London, 1957), p. 298.

20. Frederic Jameson, *Marxism and Form* (Princeton, NJ, 1971), pp. 355–9.

21. John Preston, *The Created Self: The Reader's Role in Eighteenth-Century Fiction* (London, 1970), pp. 112–13. Further page references will be incorporated in the text.

22. Wolfgang Iser, *The Implied Reader* (Baltimore and London, 1974), p. 31.

23. Robert C. Holub, *Reception Theory: A Critical Introduction* (London, 1984), pp. 105–6.

24. Arthur Murphy, 'An Essay on the Life and Genius of Henry Fielding, Esq.' (1762), in *Henry Fielding: The Critical Heritage*, ed. Ronald Paulson and Thomas Lockwood (London and New York, 1969), p. 411.

25. See 'Auteurism', in John Caughie (ed.), *Theories of Authorship* (London, 1981), pp. 7–121.

26. Jim Kitses, *Horizons West* (Blommington and London, 1969), p. 7.

27. Peter Wollen, *Signs and Meanings in the Cinema* (3rd edn, London, 1972), p. 77.

28. David Saunders and Ian Hunter, 'Lessons From the "Literary": How to Historicize Authorship', *Critical Inquiry* 17 (1991), 479.

29. Roland Barthes, 'From Work to Text' (1971), in *Image-Music-Text: Selected Essays*, trans. Stephen Heath (Glasgow, 1977), p. 161.

30. Michel Foucault, 'What is an Author?' (1969), in *Language, Counter-Memory, Practice*, ed. Donald F. Bouchard, trans. Donald F. Bouchard and Sherry Siomon (Oxford, 1977), p. 121. Further page references, incorporated in the text, will refer to this edition.

31. Michel Foucault, 'The Discourse on Language', in *The Archaeology of Knowledge*, trans. A.M. Sheridan Smith and Rupert Swyer (New York, 1972), p. 221.

32. Foucault, 'The Discourse on Language', p. 216.

33. P.N. Medvedev, *The Immediate Tasks Facing Literary-Historical Science* (1928), trans. C.R. Pike, in *Russian Poetics in Translation, Vol. 10: Bakhtin School Papers* (Oxford, 1983), p. 75.

34. M.M. Bakhtin, *Problems in Dostoyevsky's Poetics* (2nd edn, 1963), trans. R.W. Rotsel (no place of publication indicated, 1973), p. 4.

35. Katerina Clark and Michael Holquist, *Mikhail Bakhtin* (Cambridge, Mass., and London, 1984), p. 88.

36. Ken Hirschop, 'Bakhtin, Discourse and Democracy', *New Left Review* 160 (1986), 93.

37. Mikhail Bakhtin, 'Discourse in the Novel', in *The Dialogic Imagination:*

Four Essays, ed. Michael Holquist, trans. Caryl Emerson and Michael Holquist (Austin, Texas, 1981), p. 291

38. See C.B. Woods, 'Fielding and the Authorship of *Shamela*', *Philological Quarterly* 25 (1946), 248–72.

CHAPTER 2
Cultural contests

Pamela into *Shamela*

An Apology for the Life of Mrs. Shamela Andrews, In which, the many notorious Falsehoods and Misrepresentations of a Book called *Pamela*, are exposed and refuted; and all the matchless Arts of that young Politician, set in a true and just Light. Together with a full Account of all that passed between her and Parson *Arthur Williams*; whose character is represented in a manner something different from what he bears in *Pamela*. The whole being exact Copies of authentick Papers delivered to the Editor. Necessary to be had in all Families. By Mr. *Conny Keyber*.

Original title page of *Shamela* (1741)

The anonymous publication of the novel entitled *Pamela; or, Virtue Rewarded* in two volumes on 6 November 1740 was one of the great focal points of eighteenth-century British literary culture. For many reasons, after the appearance of *Pamela*, literature in English, especially prose fiction, was never to be quite the same again. This particular novel not only enjoyed enormous and controversial popular success at once, it also set the terms of reference and engagement for a great deal of subsequent English and European fiction, including Henry Fielding's first published venture into extended prose narrative. To make sense of Fielding's appropriation of the form of the novel, and to assess the reasons behind his attempt at cultural intervention, it is essential to see how his work interacts with and transforms the material at its disposal, especially with the complex and inconsistent material provided by *Pamela*.

The earlier novel offers an account, told through relatively unstylised and plainly told letters and journal entries, of how the eponymous heroine Pamela Andrews, a simple young serving girl in employment a long way from home, aged only fifteen at the beginning of her account, holds out against the improper and increasingly coercive sexual advances of her master, a prosperous country squire identified in the text only as Mr B—. Although he treats her very badly, and exerts great pressure upon her, Pamela's resistance is prolonged and articulate. Since Mr B— is both her employer and the local Justice of the Peace, the law incarnate, she has no obvious avenue to safety, and her letters become increasingly desperate. Eventually, the perceived threat to her chastity builds up to the extent that she tries to run away, only to be intercepted and restrained by her master and his wicked accomplices, Mrs Jewkes and Mr Colbrand.

However, as her anxiety increases, so too does her desire to reform the predatory squire, and, remarkably, she even begins to fall in love with him despite the circumstances. As this happens, her tormentor gets hold of her journal and some of her letters, and the spirit they display affects him so much that he begins to relent and starts to treat her with genuine courtesy and respect, seeing her for the first time as a fellow human being rather than as an object for his own desires. Towards the end of the tale, Mr B— reforms. Pamela then leaves behind her humble status and becomes the squire's wife, an elevated station in life to which she rapidly and unproblematically accustoms herself.

On each subsequent publication during its author's lifetime, the text of *Pamela* was revised and extended. However, the central fable of virtue rewarded remained constant, and the techniques of representation and narration did not fundamentally change. Alongside the detailed account of what happened on virtually a moment-by-moment basis, presented largely through the heroine's epistolary perspective, readers of all the editions were offered prolonged reflections on the morality of events, and advice about proper behaviour, voiced by the various participants. In its unadorned way, *Pamela* is a tale both frightening in its revelation of the power and depravity of Mr B—, and yet eventually reassuring in its representation of the remarkable triumph of the pure chaste Pamela. Its extraordinary appeal may be derived from this combination of apprehension and reassurance, by the way it both endangers and empowers its heroine, before finally relocating her and accommodating her within 'exalted' society. For all its apparent artlessness, *Pamela* now seems like an extraordinarily powerful attempt both to discover and to smooth over the contradictions in the dominant ideologies of the day, both social and sexual. For all its accessible simplicity, it looks like a book trying to negotiate between an attractive illusion of social mobility based on virtue or personal merit and a rigid framework of hierarchy, seeking to give a powerful voice to its lower-class heroine without radically undermining a fundamentally conservative vision of society.

The popular success of *Pamela* was immediate and unprecedented, with five subsequent editions appearing within twelve months, alongside numerous piracies, continuations, adaptations and sundry merchandising sidelines, from pictures on fans and teacups to displays of life-size waxworks of the main characters. As well as the various unauthorised continuations, a rather less successful authorised sequel, *Pamela in her Exalted Condition*, haphazardly recounting her adventures as a wife and her often self-congratulatory reflections on her new condition, appeared in December 1741.

The reasons for the sudden and extraordinary popularity of the novel, for the 'frenzy' it created, may now be hard to reconstruct, but there can be no doubting either its instant commercial success, or the intense public controversy it provoked at the time and which it even continues to provoke in eighteenth-century studies today. Perhaps the most salient and disorienting literary feature of the book is the way it combines immediacy and rumination, without relying on the directive extra-diegetic intrusion of a narrator, the whole tale offering a lengthy mixture of drama and sermonising which might be experienced with different priority by different readers. The very compendiousness of the book, its internal tensions, and its highly discursive narration, have led inevitably to the production of radically different and contending readings being offered within different interpretive communities. As we shall see, Henry Fielding's cynical 'reading' of *Pamela* was only one of many eighteenth-century readings, but it was one which sought to achieve hegemonic power by both redefining the original text and reappraising its meanings.

While it may still appear to us, as to many contemporary readers, that *Pamela* was an entirely new kind of text – 'novel' in all senses of that word – it can also be seen emerging from precedent literary and para-literary forms, engaging in dialogue with them, and creating a potent new mixture from diverse existent materials. Although obviously uninformed by the various classical and European models of prose fiction so prominent in Fielding's later work and in the developed novel of the mid-century as produced by Tobias Smollett and Charlotte Lennox, the seemingly artless narrative of the original

Pamela nonetheless reappraises several native British traditions, drawing on the competing frameworks of the religious and practical guide on the one hand and the tempestuous female romance on the other. In many ways, the contradictory impulses brought in from the various precedent texts force *Pamela* to become a book caught up in conflict with itself. Not only does it starkly juxtapose its drama and its moralising, it is also a text in which contending egalitarian and hierarchical elements fight it out, in which passion and restraint are set at odds, and in which readers are interpellated or hailed as alternatively prurient and solemn as the pages turn.

Looking at *Pamela* from a traditional authorial perspective, we discover that its begetter (conventionally posing anonymously as only its editor in a preface) was one Samuel Richardson, a stout fifty-year-old tradesman, who was at this time successfully running a substantial printing and publishing business in London. Unschooled in the classics or in what was conventionally understood at the time to be 'polite' literature, and very comfortably accommodated within his mercantile community, Richardson seems an unlikely figure to provoke any kind of frenzy. Indeed, once his identity as an author was made known, many contemporary commentators took him to be a curious phenomenon of nature rather than the studied product of art. And such an assessment was by no means always positive in its emphasis. As Sir John Hawkins, the early biographer of Samuel Johnson, put it in 1787:

> I might here speak of Richardson as a writer of fictitious history, but that he wrote for amusement, and that the profits of his writings, though very great, were accidental. He was a man of no learning nor reading, but had a vivid imagination, which he let loose in reflections on human life and manners, till it became so distended with sentiments, that for his own ease, he was necessitated to vent them on paper.[1]

The image of the 'distended' Richardson evoked here is not meant to be an especially flattering or ennobling one – perhaps it is yet another sly reference to that figure's famed corpulence – and the representation of his writing as a kind of involuntary easing of internal blockages is, to say the least, disconcerting.

But it is the accidental and involuntary nature of the popular success of *Pamela* that arrests this unsympathetic critic's attention, just as it had earlier arrested Fielding's. Hawkins, by describing the book as an unpremeditated explosion of sentiments, allows for its power, and creates a frame of reference in which its inconsistencies might be explained away as artlessness. Given Richardson's lack of appropriate literary qualifications or expertise, *Pamela* becomes a book without a proper author, a book which is better read as a spontaneous or accidental outburst than as a carefully controlled production. By describing Richardson as he does, Hawkins makes the authorial presence in the book almost negligible, and the writer turns from being the organiser, director or proprietor of the text into a kind of impersonal *conduit* through which the eventual narrative emerges. Richardson, that is to say, may well have actually written or compiled the book, but he could not be held *responsible* for the finished product.

Ironically, the well-known history of the writing of *Pamela* seems to lend some authority to this curious version of it. There is an extensively documented account of how two prominent and commercially motivated London booksellers, John Osborn and Charles Rivington, invited Richardson in 1739 to compile a book of sample letters, to provide models of important correspondence which would be of use to the inexperienced or semi-literate in the daily conduct of their affairs. Richardson agreed, and his *Familiar Letters on Important Occasions*, although not eventually published until 1741, included specimens of correspondence between a serving girl and her distant family. Clearly, this preparatory work in 1739 offered a model for some of the basic drama as well as many of the formal devices for the more fully developed novel later to emerge as *Pamela*.[2] Whatever the mercenary motives of Osborn and Rivington, Richardson's project in compiling the letter-writer was not exclusively commercial; it was at the same time to be educative and didactic in a very broad sense. Not only was he offering accessible and imitable models for lower-class correspondence, he was also following in the tradition of his own earlier *Apprentice's Vade Mecum* (1733) and precedent texts such as Defoe's *The Family Instructor* (1715), providing a vernacular conduct-book, designed to offer guidance on appropriate behaviour and advice about how to negotiate problems of status in a rapidly changing world to uncertain and under-confident readers.

That a highly dramatic novel grew from this prosaic stimulus is surprising enough, but when combined with Richardson's subsequent remarks (made in a letter in 1753) about how the germ of the narrative was an anecdote dimly remembered from some twenty-five years earlier, the composition of *Pamela* seems less and less deliberate, and the text less controlled or programmatic, less 'finished'. The book begins to take on significance and status far beyond that which its author could have understood or recognised. It is not just that Richardson was from the outset disqualified from 'proper' authorship by his lack of learning, as Hawkins clearly suggested, but that the text he somehow inadvertently produced took on significances and complexities of much greater resonance from the cultural fabric of his writing and from the moment of its intervention. And, of course, it remains highly probable that different readers may have found in the book much more (or even much less) than Richardson knew that he had put there.

In fact, as Margaret Anne Doody has convincingly shown, *Pamela* can be seen as a complex synthesis of a whole range of existent popular writings, as an adroit, if wholly unconscious exercise in intertextuality.[3] The novel draws not only on the recent conduct book, but also on the native traditions of fable and romance, especially the often despised and 'low' forms of women's writing. Learning from the established popular works of Penelope Aubin, Jane Barker, Elizabeth Rowe, Mary Davys and Eliza Haywood, among others, familiar to him through his activities as a printer, Richardson the novelist brought together the existing impassioned seduction narrative and the more formal tale of elaborate courtship. From Aubin's popular novels of the 1720s in particular, Richardson had at his disposal the ideas of female virtue in distress and the struggle for the survival of chastity (or at least virginity), which he could rewrite through his own mercantile perspective. And from other female writers, Richardson and his readers were given templates of narrative in which women were put under pressure, in which virtue and integrity eventually secured remarkable triumphs over passion and jeopardy.[4]

So although, for the present purposes, it is attractive to see *Pamela* as opening a dialogue with *Shamela* and *Joseph Andrews* in turn, it would really be fairer to see it as also continuing one with these earlier texts. This novel is not an autonomous object, nor is it an unambiguous or deliberate statement of its author's ideological position. Rather, it is best seen as a complex and polyphonic text in which radically different and at times incompatible ideological positions are voiced – and perhaps voiced differently in the various revisions and adaptations. The simple hierarchical model of the conduct book becomes inappropriate and abrasive in the presence of the more volatile sexual ideology at work elsewhere. Richardson's control over the processional narrative, the actual blow-by-blow sequence of events, may be tight, but his control over its resonant meanings is relatively slack. As a result, his novel is full of ideological interference, with pious moralising and almost revolutionary outbursts sitting uncomfortably side by side, at once restraining and empowering readers. Residual traces of the impassioned female romance are juxtaposed with emergent filaments of social mobility, and the text eventually becomes a compendium of diverse ideological possibilities rather than a carefully orchestrated or directed whole. The 'author' fails to intervene decisively in this cacophony, or to arbitrate between the contending positions, and readers are left to impose coherence on the text by selecting from it the particular emphasis that suits their reading appetite best. The text on the page thus remains incomplete, awaiting the interpretive guidance of particular readers in specific reading contexts.

With the benefits of distance and hindsight, the confusions of meaning and purpose in *Pamela*, which may have partly provoked Fielding's hostile response, are now relatively easy to identify, often being located in the question of the heroine's status and the significance of her chastity/virginity. Clearly, the orthodox reading of the book, as preached from many eighteenth-century pulpits, was that temptation was to be resisted, no matter how strong it might be, and that virtue might be its own reward. Thus, some of Pamela's more outspoken remarks can be naturalised within an overall moral or religious ideology. At one point, she makes what look like uncompromisingly egalitarian statements:

> Were my *life* in question, instead of my *virtue*, I would not wish to involve any body in the least difficulty for so worthless a poor creature. But, O sir! my *soul* is of equal importance with the soul of a princess, though in quality I am but upon a foot with the meanest slave.[5]

Pamela's sense of personal integrity here – her belief that her soul is absolutely valuable – jostles against her acknowledgement that her rank, or, as she puts it, her 'quality', is humble and relatively worthless. Even in this brief passage, the text seems to introduce contending meanings and to slip out of firm authorial control. Is Pamela's statement to be read as an endorsement of the prevailing social hierarchy, recognising its paradoxes, or as an enlightened refusal to submit to its demands? Or is it simply an unexamined contra-diction, clumsily interrupting the narrative and needlessly deflecting attention from the sequence of events?

There are many such moments of ideological stress uncomfortably contained within the narrative structure of the novel. At one point, Pamela insists on her personal integrity in terms which are very dismissive of the vanity of the rich:

> One may see by it how poor people are despised by the rich and the great! And yet we were all on a foot originally. Surely these proud people never think what a short stage life is; and that, with all their vanity, a time is coming, when they shall be on a level with us . . . O keep me, Heaven! from their *high* condition, if my mind shall ever be tainted with *their* vice!   (*Pamela*, p. 294)

Pamela cries out for understanding, and offers a class-based (or 'quality'-based) hostility to the vices of the wealthy, modulated through a more egalitarian religious ideology. But of course she herself has been transformed into one of these wealthy people by the end of the novel, achieving the '*high* position' about which she here expresses uncertainties, and the reward she receives for retaining her 'virtue' is significantly more material than it is spiritual.

Such confusion over the value of hierarchy is discoverable throughout the book, and the issue of Pamela's true status never seems to be fully under authorial control. Similarly, it is perplexing that after her spirited and intense resistance to her master's encroachments, and her insistence on her equal spiritual worth, when she comes to be socially relocated towards the end she promises the most abject obedience in her wedding vows:

> 'Know *you* any impediment?' I blushed, and said softly, 'None, sir, but my great unworthiness.' Then followed the sweet words, '*Wilt thou have this woman to thy wedded wife*', &c. and I began to take courage a little, when my dearest master answered audibly to this question, '*I will*'. But I could only make a curt'sy, when they asked *me*; though, I am sure, my *heart* was readier than my *speech*, and answered to every article of *obey, serve, love, honour*.   (*Pamela*, p. 374)

After the abduction and the privations Pamela has suffered, not to mention Mr B—'s acknowledged treatment of a previous mistress,

Sally Godfrey, whom he has virtually exiled in Jamaica, the heroine's willingness to accept her new husband and master without reservation or hesitation seems quite remarkable. Is this voluntary self-abasement a contradiction of her earlier independence, or can it be read as a continuation of her selfhood by different means? As she herself says immediately afterwards, describing her own career in the third-person to her parents, the transformation in Mr B— has been spectacularly sudden – '. . . thus the dear, once naughty assailer of her innocence, by a blessed turn of Providence, is become the kind, the generous protector and rewarder of it!' (p. 375). To describe the predatory seducer (and kidnapper) Mr B— as 'once naughty' seems remarkably restrained, trivialising and tolerating his behaviour, and it does a radical disservice to the heightened drama and intensity of the earlier narrative.

The point of contact between proper self-assertion and 'knowing your place' is a major point of friction in this text, and the book's subtitle, *Virtue Rewarded*, could be inflected in different ways. In the most conventional reading, these points of stress are invisible, and the text naturalises an ideology which may have been internally fraught but which held important meanings for its lower-class subjects. By acting upon principle, upon an intuitively understood code of conduct, the humble could yet instruct (and reform) the proud. Just as the humble heroine becomes exalted, lower-class readers could feel themselves aggrandised by the experience of the text, rewarded for their integrity and their fidelity.

That might account for the popularity of Richardson's work with one audience, but for readers as unsympathetic as the more patrician and literate Fielding, the book was a ridiculous farrago. Under the disguise of piety, it did not seek to consolidate the value of Pamela's chastity so much as raise the price of her virginity. Fielding took the success of *Pamela*, a text he clearly saw as incoherent, unintelligent, ungrammatical and morally fraudulent, to be an index of the woeful credulity of the times. More than just a facile piece of writing, it reflected the effects of the failure of those in positions of prominence to behave with due dignity or proper authority. In an age in which Colley Cibber could be made poet laureate, and Sir Robert Walpole could be the First Minister of State, the success of the low-brow novel epitomised by *Pamela* simply reinforced the sense of imminent cultural collapse and declining standards in contemporary life which Fielding's fiction returns to again and again.

Fielding's *Apology for the Life of Mrs Shamela Andrews*, then, published as a pamphlet on 4 April 1741, after three editions of *Pamela* had appeared, is not just a topical parodic rewriting of Richardson's novel designed to make fun of its specific literary shortcomings. It is also a much wider assault on the inadequacy of the moral and intellectual life of the times conducted through the perspective of the precedent novel, engaging in dialogue with its declared ideology and its more covert assumptions, and thereby with the much wider issue of identifying who may and who may not legitimately lay claim to cultural authority.

Returning to the terms of reference laid out in the previous chapter, it is clear that the kind of parody found in *Shamela* is always a dialogic exercise. As Mikhail Bakhtin puts it, the parodic text speaks with two tongues:

> . . . an author can also make use of another person's word for his own purposes by inserting a new semantic orientation into a word which already has – and retains – its own orientation. In that case, such a word, by virtue of its task, must be perceived as belonging to another person. Then two semantic orientations, two voices are present in a single word. The parodistic word is of this type . . .[6]

In *Shamela*, Fielding pursues his own aims by imposing just this kind of new intention on his predecessor. The authorial strategy in his book is to commandeer the ambiguities and uncertainties of the original narrative, and to make them cohere around a single, ridiculously travestied reading of that text by an act of jeering mimicry. The technique of caricaturing existing texts to make them seem ridiculous was already thoroughly familiar in the adversarial literary world of eighteenth-century England. In Fielding's earlier theatrical career, he had produced various plays which relied on the bathetic effect of just this kind of travesty, notably *The Tragedy of Tragedies* (1731) and *The Covent-Garden Tragedy* (1732), and throughout the pages of his periodical *The Champion* (1739–41) he had exploited the 'double-voicing' devices of selective exaggeration and parody to denounce what he saw as the imbecility and pomposity of his literary (and commercial) rivals.

That Fielding's appropriation of the original text was persuasive to many cannot be doubted. He may have disfigured Richardson's work irretrievably, but he did so in a way that affirmed his own cultural authority over the low-brow interloper and rival, which seems to have persuaded at least some others to revise their opinions likewise. As an anonymous poem in the *London Magazine* in June 1741 put it:

Admired *Pamela*, till *Shamela* shown,
Appear'd in every colour – but her own:
Uncensur'd she remained in borrow'd light,
No nun more chaste, few angels shone so bright.
But now the idol we no more adore,
Jervis a bawd, and our chaste nymph a w——.[7]

It may be that this revision appealed more to the sophisticated coffee-house *literati* than to the common reader, newly enfranchised into literature, but nonetheless *Shamela* seems to have made a great impact of its own. So how did Fielding manage this extraordinary redirection of emphasis? How did he frame the original text in such a way as to make it seem so ridiculous and inept to certain kinds of reader? And what were the prime targets of his satiric attack?

The attempt to rewrite Richardson's text as a catch-penny burlesque begins on the title page, where this new slim volume is described as being 'Necessary to be had in all FAMILIES'. The hit at the commercial success of *Pamela* is only the first part of Fielding's basic reorientation of the book, moving it entirely away from questions of morality and insistently towards questions of money. Put very simply, Fielding turns the central figure of the narrative from being a frightened and naive female victim clinging on to her integrity in the face of Mr B—'s attacks into an accomplished mercenary prostitute who deftly cons the gullible 'Mr Booby' into marriage with the assistance of her worldly accomplices Mrs Jervis and Parson Williams – the isolated, vulnerable figure on whom others gang up is thus not the helpless lower-class female, but the witless upper-class male.

'Shamela' is a prostitute's daughter, and her correspondence with her mother steadily and brazenly reveals the plot to soak Mr Booby of his money by arousing (but, of course, not satisfying) his sexual interest in attractive young serving girls. So Fielding's version of the story immediately reverses the terms of reference of the original: where Pamela is victim, Shamela is predator; where Mr B— is rakish, Booby is oafish; where Pamela acts from integrity, Shamela feigns and pretends; and where Pamela strives alone for honesty, Shamela

contrives trickery with her accomplices. The whole coinage of
Richardson's text is devalued by Fielding's transformation of the
heroine's secret aims, as she famously puts it:

> I thought once of making a little Fortune by my Person. I now intend
> to make a great one by my Vartue.[8]

So it seems that Shamela (and, of course, by implication Pamela as
well) is more artful than a mere prostitute, having hit upon an
altogether more remunerative and painless way of making a living –
'Vartue'. For these characters, as Fielding (mis)represents them, it is
even easier to fake integrity than to fake orgasm, and the rewards to
be gained from such skilled deception are concomitantly greater.

This is clearly an unfair and partial misreading of *Pamela*,
deliberately blind to its more liberating or egalitarian possibilities, and
to its pathos. But the point of Fielding's exercise is that it is not to be
seen as constructing a new meaning which might gratuitously be
imposed on the original, but rather that it claims to offer a revelation
of the *real* meaning hidden away and obscured within the original, the
real voice hidden under the cultivated accent of protestation.
According to Fielding, Pamela's 'virtue', about which she makes so
much fuss, is after all really only 'vartue', a secret desire for social
climbing and a talent for cunning personal advancement, and it is
thus clearly not worth all the protestation she makes. Fielding's book
swiftly and flagrantly rewrites the sexual politics of the basic plot,
removing the notion that men are predators and women victims, and
replacing it with the contending notion that the crafty are predatory
and the gullible are their prey, irrespective of gender.

In this way, *Shamela* avoids a sexual politics which is gendered, and
gives us instead one which is 'intelligenced', if I may put it that way.
We return here to the traditional Jonsonian or Restoration comic
world of fools and knaves, where women hold secret power, a move
which provides a way of defusing the topical energies of Richardson's
text, which are taken out of the immediate social context, and
relocated in this familiar literary world of farce and duplicity. By
offering such a familiar and exclusively literary set of references,
Shamela covertly decontextualises and redirects the sexual ideology of
its source. From Fielding's perspective, the 'newness' of *Pamela* is seen
only to be a hypocritical veneer, and to be a rather unconvincing one
at that.

There is little to be gained by citing extensive parallel passages from the two books, since Fielding's point is made much more rapidly than Richardson's, and since he is trying to draw a single consistent meaning from (and into) an ambiguous and compendious text. Yet it is worth looking at Shamela's preparations for her wedding night in comparison with Pamela's. Whereas the social concerns of Richardson's novel meant that Pamela had to persuade Mr B— 's family of her worthiness, while striving to convince her own family that she had not lost her right to their respect, Fielding's Shamela has an altogether simpler task to perform before the great event:

> In my last I left off at our sitting down to Supper on our Wedding Night, where I behaved with as much Bashfulness as the purest Virgin in the World could have done. The most difficult Task was for me to blush; however, by holding my Breath, and squeezing my Cheeks with my Handkerchief, I did pretty well. . . . at last I went to Bed, and my Husband soon leapt in after me; where I shall only assure you, I acted my Part in such a manner, that no Bridegroom was ever better satisfied with his Bride's Virginity. And to confess the Truth, I might have been well satisfied too, if I had never been acquainted with Parson *Williams*.
>
> (*Shamela*, p. 347)

The creation of 'Vartue' here is certainly comic, and the farce is deftly handled. But as a reading of the precedent text it is clearly reductive in the extreme, as well as profoundly coercive, failing to engage with the complexities of rank or 'quality' which are so prominent in the original.

And it is not only the meanings of the original book that are ridiculed in the parody. Elsewhere, Fielding makes clear his view of the manifest absurdity of Richardson's blow-by-blow narrative technique. In a very funny, but uneasily tempered passage, he offers a ridiculous travesty of the breathless epistolary style:

> *Thursday Night, Twelve o'Clock*
> Mrs. *Jervis* and I are just in Bed, and the Door unlocked; if my Master should come – Odsbods! I hear him just coming in at the Door. You see I write in the present Tense, as Parson *Williams* says. Well, he is in Bed between us, we both shamming a Sleep, he steals his Hand into my Bosom, which I, as if in my Sleep, press close to me with mine, and then pretend to awake. – I no sooner see him, but I scream out to Mrs. *Jervis*, she feigns likewise but just to come to herself; we both begin, she

to becall, and I to bescratch very liberally. After having made a pretty free Use of my Fingers, without any great Regard to the Parts I attack'd, I counterfeit a swoon. Mrs. *Jervis* then cries out, O, Sir, what have you done, you have murthered poor *Pamela*: she is gone, she is gone. –

O *what a Difficulty it is to keep one's Countenance, when a violent Laugh desires to burst forth*.   (*Shamela*, p. 330)

The full vocabulary of fraudulence is encapsulated here – 'shamming', 'pretend', 'feigns', 'counterfeit' – and our privileged access to the event allows us to recognise its truly farcical nature. Yet Fielding's point in parodying the immediacy of the present tense epistolary style is to show us how Richardson himself is complicit in the act of counterfeiting. By giving up control of the narrative to the characters, he is merely pretending not to be an author, failing to acknowledge publicly his directive responsibilities in shaping his narrative. And if we follow Fielding's argument, we are forced to see that by pretending not to be an author, by failing to live up to his organisational responsibilities, Richardson is disqualified from the genuine writer's position of real cultural authority.

Fielding's intervention is thus a comic travesty of both the sexual drama of the original and its manner of literary representation. However, it moves beyond any single point of reference, and goes well beyond the confines of the spoof, taking the occasion to develop greater dialogue with the manifold weaknesses of contemporary culture. The meaning and success of *Pamela* becomes a focal point for the analysis of cultural decline. It is significant that the title-page describes the heroine as a 'young Politician', for Fielding here begins his fictional reinterpretation of contemporary political life, an authorial concern which is continuously prominent throughout *Joseph Andrews*, *Jonathan Wild*, *Tom Jones* and *Amelia*.

Around this apparently casual exercise in parody, Fielding assembles a group of representative figures who stand for the contemporary abuses of taste and failures of cultural responsibility which he is eager to castigate. On the title-page, the author is represented as a 'Mr. Conny Keyber', a clear caricature of the egregious Colley Cibber, man of the theatre, poet laureate, and recent author of the similarly titled *An Apology for the Life of Mr. Colley Cibber, Comedian*, (1740).

As mentioned already, Fielding and Cibber were bitter and persistent antagonists – Cibber had passed disparaging remarks about

Fielding in his *Apology*, and Fielding had immediately retaliated through the pages of *The Champion* in April and May 1740. But the feud between the two figures, only one of many feuds in Fielding's combative career, went back to the earlier period when Cibber had been largely in control of the Drury Lane theatre. In Fielding's play *The Author's Farce*, published and performed in 1730, the year Cibber received the accolade of the laureateship, the actor-manager had been caricatured as the theatrical tyrant 'Marplay', as the ridiculous thespian 'Sir Farcical Comic', and had even slightingly been referred to in person as the suspiciously German-sounding 'Keyber'. The renewed assault on Cibber in *Shamela* not only shows Fielding's remarkable ability to harbour grudges and sustain resentment over a long period, it offers up 'Keyber' as a representative of the wider cultural failings of Hanoverian England. The first name 'Conny' is not only a dismissive slang term evocative of fools, rabbits and the female pudenda, it also aligns Cibber with another prominent literary figure, Conyers Middleton, the apparently pompous and self-important author of *The History of the Life of Marcus Tullius Cicero* (1741), a respectable enough scholarly work which seems to have irritated Fielding intensely, largely on account of its obseqious and fulsome dedication to the appalling Lord Hervey.[9]

For Fielding, the success of these works, as of the anonymous *Pamela* itself, was indicative of serious and disquieting errors of discernment in contemporary culture, which his parody is more than willing to address. As well as transforming the internal drama of the narrative into an all-too-familiar Restoration romp, Fielding contextualises its popular success by slyly setting it alongside other examples of the contemporary failure of taste, compiling corroborative illustrations of equally incompetent texts and fraudulent characters from the surrounding world. The point is made clearer in the dedicatory epistle to *Shamela*, which not only parodies Richardson's shameless incorporation of 'puffs' for his book, which had started modestly enough and then expanded greatly with the second edition of February 1741, but makes the link between literary production and political corruption much clearer. The letter from Keyber 'To Miss Fanny' brings into the text the notorious figure of Lord Hervey, already travestied by Pope as 'Lord Fanny' in his *First Satire of the Second Book of Horace Imitated* (1733) and as 'Sporus', the butterfly broken upon the wheel in his *Epistle to Dr Arbuthnot* (1735). Hervey's close association with the court and with Walpole's regime surreptitiously implicates major political figures in this satiric attack, and at the same time it begins Fielding's fictional examination of the ideology of masculinity.

The letter to Miss Fanny pretends to follow the fulsome style of Conyers Middleton's own dedication to Hervey, excessively panegyrical and unstinting in its encomium, but it simultaneously makes oblique references to Hervey's reputation for 'hermaphroditic' sexual practices, eventually producing a ridiculous mixture of vanity and inept self-revelation:

> *First*, then, Madam, I must tell the World, that you have tickled up and brightned many Strokes in this Work by your Pencil.
>
> *Secondly*, you have intimately conversed with me, one of the greatest Wits and scholars of my Age.
>
> *Thirdly*, You keep very good Hours, and frequently spend an useful Day before others begin to enjoy it. This will I take my Oath on; for I am admitted to your Presence in a Morning before other People's Servants are up; when I constantly found you reading in good Books; and if ever I have drawn you upon me, I have always felt you very heavy.   (*Shamela*, p. 317)

It is clear that there is no direct satire on Samuel Richardson here. Indeed it has now been established by scholars that Fielding was actually unaware of Richardson's identity as the author of *Pamela* at this point, and that he bore him no personal animus. Richardson was acquainted with Fielding's sister, Sarah, with whose own novels he was involved, and the actual author is never directly or personally targeted in *Shamela*. Instead, the satire is directed at the ridiculous and blinkered vanity of over- ambitious contemporary authors in general – seen also in the commendatory letter from 'the Editor to Himself' – and at a number of other more familiar targets. However the Cibber/Middleton figure, unwittingly revealing himself to be Hervey's catamite, also stands for the widespread corruption of taste and morality which Fielding saw as a particularly disturbing feature of upper-class life at the time, a motif which appears constantly throughout his fiction. By relocating the book in this way, Fielding is not disparaging Richardson's personal qualifications, but taking an opportunity to attack other pretenders to the dignity and gravity of authorship.

The Cibber/Middleton figure, and Lord Hervey, represent Fielding's contemptuous view of many of his fellow-authors, and other features of the text are introduced in order to ridicule the equally bogus qualifications of the contemporary reading public. In the preliminary exchange between two members of the clergy, the views put forward by 'Parson Oliver' seem to be close to Fielding's own understanding of *Pamela*:

> The instruction which it conveys to Servant-Maids, is, I think, very plainly this, To look out for their Masters as sharp as they can. The Consequences of which will be, besides Neglect of their Business, and the using all Manner of Means to come at Ornaments of their Persons, that if the Master is not a Fool, they will be debauched by him; and if he is a Fool, they will marry him.   (*Shamela*, p. 324)

Oliver represents the worldly, sensible reader of *Pamela*, as constructed and recommended by Fielding, explicitly contrasted by the credulous, unwitting 'Parson Tickletext', who expresses his steamy infatuation with the book. Tickletext has been so taken up with the book, that he has joined his fellow clergymen in extolling its merits from the pulpit – 'for we have made it our common Business here, not only to cry it up, but to preach it up likewise' (*Shamela*, p. 321). Tickletext is here reiterating the praise heaped on the book by the wonderfully named Reverend Benjamin Slocock of St Saviour's Southwark earlier in the year. He may be voicing a common view, but it is soon apparent that, underneath the piety, the *real* pleasure to be had from the text is more ticklish than he seems to realise:

> This Book is the 'SOUL of *Religion*, Good-Breeding, Discretion, Good-Nature, Wit, Fancy, Fine Thought, and Morality. There is an Ease, a natural Air, a dignified Simplicity, and MEASURED FULLNESS in it, that RESEMBLING LIFE, OUT-GLOWS IT. The Author hath reconciled the *pleasing* to the *proper*; the Thought is every where exactly cloathed by the Expression; and becomes its Dress as *roundly* and as close as *Pamela* her Country Habit; or *as she doth her no Habit*, when modest Beauty seeks to hide itself, by casting off the Pride of Ornament, and displays itself without any Covering;' which it frequently doth in this admirable Work, and presents Images to the Reader, which the coldest Zealot cannot read without Emotion.   (*Shamela*, p. 321)

Parson Tickletext here unwittingly gives an exhilarating anticipation of Roland Barthes in combining intertextuality – the quoted passage comes from the prefatory material to the second edition of *Pamela* –

and perhaps the earliest recorded account of reading as an exercise in *jouissance*. The pleasure of this text for this reader is clearly sexual, seen in the way Tickletext mentally undresses the heroine – 'Oh! I feel an Emotion even while I am relating this: Methinks I see *Pamela* at this Instant, with all the Pride of Ornament cast off' (*Shamela*, p. 322) – and his ridiculously lurid fantasies alert the reader to the prurient and semi-pornographic nature of the tale of female suffering.

The incorporation of Tickletext has slightly more to do with the satire on Richardson's novel than the introduction of Conny Keyber and Miss Fanny, since there are scenes in the original text which do seem to be 'warm' in a way Tickletext would recognise and enjoy. However, its real role is to begin the discussion of issues which become increasingly prominent in *Joseph Andrews*: the role of the clergy in contemporary culture and the dubious nature of religious 'enthusiasm'. Just as Shamela's virtue is inauthentic, so too is the piety of Tickletext and, even more obviously, that of Williams. The clergy play only a small role in *Pamela* and Fielding introduces this idea into his spoof to attack a related issue of the day more than to parody the precedent novel. He adumbrates this idea much more elaborately later on, but in *Shamela* itself, Methodism and the doctrine associated with the controversial figures of George Whitefield and John Wesley enter as new topics in the continuing dialogue, consequences of his engagement with the public 'frenzy' surrounding the earlier book rather than precise renderings of its internal workings.

The main idea running through Fielding's parody is that his heroine protests virtue without possessing it, and a number of devices are introduced to show that this was not an isolated phenomenon peculiar to the participants in Richardson's novel. In the world of contemporary religion, the Methodist movement seemed to Fielding to be giving scandalous legitimacy to such forms of outward show by concentrating on 'faith' rather than 'works' as the criteria for true piety. Parson Tickletext himself seems to be an example of the unconscious hypocrite the book is designed to expose, and within the narrative there are other indications of a growing concern with the proper and improper forms of religious observation.

At the beginning, Shamela receives from her mother a copy of 'one of Mr. *Whitefield's* Sermons, and also the Dealings with him' (*Shamela*, p. 328), from which she is encouraged to learn how best to ensnare her 'rich Fool', Mr Booby. Later, when she hears Parson Williams preach, the Methodist message is even more flagrantly caricatured:

Well, on *Sunday* Parson *Williams* came, according to his Promise, and an excellent Sermon he preached; his Text was, *Be not Righteous over-much*; and indeed he handled it in a very fine way; he shewed us that the Bible doth not require too much Goodness of us, and that People very often call things Goodness that are not so. That to go to Church, and to pray, and to sing Psalms, and to honour the Clergy, and to repent, is true Religion; and 'tis not doing good to one another, for that is one of the greatest Sins we can commit, when we don't do it for the sake of Religion. That those People who talk of Vartue and Morality, are the wickedest of all Persons. That 'tis not what we do, but what we believe, that must save us, and a great many other good Things; I wish I could remember them all. (*Shamela*, p. 336)

The ideas outlined here are, of course, a grotesque travesty of Whitefield's actual views, but within the text they smear the enthusiasts by a process of guilt through association. Yet although it provides greater resonance for the events portrayed, the subject of devotional enthusiasm is not central to the enquiry in this particular narrative. Rather, it is a recurrent concern of Fielding the *auteur*, visible in earlier periodical writing and elsewhere, which gets written on top of the farcical adventures, adding to them without really developing them along any consistent thematic line. As far as Fielding is concerned, his new text is capacious enough to incorporate a whole range of slanders and caricatures, and he is not to be exclusively restricted to a simple reworking of *Pamela* if other opportunities present themselves.

Parson Williams, as we know, is the father of Shamela's illegitimate child (who is referred to, but does not appear in the narrative), and in the text Fielding is having fun with the character for the sake of it, as well as using him to blacken Methodist ideas. Williams is knowing and mercenary, whereas the hapless Tickletext is simply naive. Yet by the end of the book, a traditional comic reversal has taken place: Tickletext is sadder but wiser, and Williams is publicly exposed as a fraud:

P. S. Since I writ, I have a certain Account, that Mr. *Booby* hath caught his Wife in bed with *Williams*; hath turned her off, and is prosecuting him in the spiritual Court. (*Shamela*, p. 357)

The traditional literary taxonomy of knaves and fools is reinstated, and the pamphlet concludes. By now it is clear that as well as rewriting the original *Pamela*, to expose its technical crudities and its mercenary attitudes, Fielding is seizing on the whole *Pamela* phenomenon as an opportunity to castigate the contemporary state of his culture. Under the government of Walpole, referred to as '*his Honour*' by 'John Puff' in the prefatory letters, Fielding sees a society driven by money and outward show, hopelessly gullible and lacking in substance. By engaging in dialogue with that culture's most celebrated literary document, Samuel Richardson's *Pamela*, Fielding is able to begin to build a platform from which he may announce his own oppositional concerns and attitudes.

However, the attempt to rewrite *Pamela* through his own perspective is not wholly consistent. In this text, as in earlier eighteenth-century exercises in such dialogue as *The Beggar's Opera* or *Gulliver's Travels* or *The Rape of the Lock* and so many others, there are elements of struggle between the material on hand and the emergent ideas. The simple parody of Richardson becomes a pretext for a wider cultural analysis, but the basic caricature leaves Fielding insufficient room to develop the further themes he introduces. Seeing him as *auteur*, we might suggest that in this particular work his later themes are nascent, but not fully formed or contained within the text, which has its own momentum. Not that this is necessarily a bad thing. *Shamela* is a volatile text, struggling to contain a broad agenda of cultural criticism within the framework of the anti-*Pamela*. It shows Fielding's desire to sit in place as arbiter of the good taste of his age, but it could not really be called an example of that cherished 'good taste'. The exercise in arbitration or cultural brokerage it conducts is undisciplined, splenetic and at times unfocused, repeating in a slightly different and more self-aware form the lack of cohesion which Fielding identified in the original novel. In order to put to rights both the literary ineptitude of *Pamela* and the weaknesses endemic in the culture which produced and celebrated it, Fielding had to appropriate the popular form of the novel and much more systematically redefine its function. In *Joseph Andrews*, which we shall now examine, he sought to carry on the cultural and commercial combat by other means.

Notes and references

1. Sir John Hawkins, *The Life of Samuel Johnson Ll.D.* (1787), ed. Bertram H. Davis (London, 1962), p. 96.

2. See T.C. Duncan Eaves and Ben D. Kimpel, *Samuel Richardson: A Biography* (Oxford, 1971), pp. 86–99.

3. Margaret Anne Doody, *A Natural Passion: A Study of the Novels of Samuel Richardson* (Oxford, 1974), pp. 14–35.

4. See Jane Spencer, *The Rise of the Woman Novelist: From Aphra Behn to Jane Austen* (Oxford, 1986), pp. 75–90.

5. Samuel Richardson, *Pamela, or Virtue Rewarded* (1970), ed. Peter Sabor, with an introduction by Margaret Doody (Harmondsworth, 1980), p. 197. Further references will be to this edition, and will be incorporated in the text.

6. Mikhail Bakhtin, *Problems in Dostoyevsky's Poetics* (2nd edn, 1963), trans. R.W. Rotsel (no place of publication indicated, 1973), pp. 156–7.

7. Quoted in *Henry Fielding: The Critical Heritage*, ed. Ronald Paulson and Thomas Lockwood (London and New York, 1969), p. 116.

8. Henry Fielding, *An Apology for the Life of Mrs Shamela Andrews* (1741), ed. Douglas Brooks-Davies (Oxford, 1970), p. 342. Further references will be incorporated in the text.

9. See Glenn W. Hatfield, *Henry Fielding and the Language of Irony* (Chicago and London, 1968), p. 149.

CHAPTER 3
Making the novel

The science of authoring

As it is possible the mere *English* Reader may have a different Idea of
Romance with the Author of these little Volumes; and may
consequently expect a kind of Entertainment, not to be found, nor
which was even intended, in the following Pages; it may not be
improper to premise a few Words concerning this kind of Writing,
which I do not remember to have seen hitherto attempted in our
Language. [1]

There are, besides these more obvious Benefits, several others which
our Readers enjoy from this Art of dividing; tho' perhaps most of them
too mysterious to be presently understood, by any who are not initiated
into the Science of *Authoring*.   (JA, p. 79)

The 'little Volumes' modestly referred to here are better known to us
as the novel *Joseph Andrews*, originally published in two small
duodecimo books, unattributed to any named author, on 22 February
1742. As expressed on the original frontispiece, the full title of the
work is *The History of the Adventures of Joseph Andrews, and of his
Friend Mr. Abraham Adams. Written in Imitation of the Manner of
Cervantes, Author of Don Quixote.* Interestingly, although there is
nothing here to alert prospective readers to the directive authorial
presence of Henry Fielding, another author of sorts is immediately
credited with the preliminary shaping of the work. So perhaps I
should revise my opening statement and indicate the prominence of
the name of the Spanish author Miguel de Cervantes within the title
itself, identifying a venerable writer, fully accomplished in 'the
Science of *Authoring*', whose work the new text is said deliberately to
imitate.

In fact, although this new book is conventionally reticent on the
subject of its own authorship, its opening pages bristle with

comparative references to other texts and writers – Homer, Aristotle, Fenelon, Shaftesbury, William Hogarth, 'the Abbé Bellegarde', Ben Jonson and William Congreve are all cited within the prefatory remarks, constructing a familiar classically oriented literary context in which the 'little Volumes' demand to be placed. In order to clarify what the preface calls 'this kind of Writing', there is copious citation of other authors and texts throughout the ensuing narrative. As in the parodic presentation of *Shamela*, readers are being invited to see this new production as a book among other books, both similar to and different from previous productions, as a highly self-conscious exercise in the mysterious business of 'Authoring'. In the introductory chapter proper, this intertextual space is made local and immediate. The dialogue with popular writing as personified by the successes of Samuel Richardson and Colley Cibber, so prominent in *Shamela*, is resumed, and the as-yet-unidentified writer of *Joseph Andrews* tries to establish suitably dignified and legitimate literary precedents for his own 'authoring' activities, provocatively placed alongside the rather less dignified and illegitimate ones provided for theirs.

From the first passage quoted above, it is clear that the anonymous author is trying to draw important distinctions between the native English traditions of popular fiction and the more elevated classical and European forms of narrative. And in this initial exchange, the question of who actually constitutes the modern readership is seen as of the utmost importance. The 'mere *English* Reader' dismissively hailed at the outset, full of inappropriate expectations and sadly lacking in literary expertise and competence, is to be distinguished from his (or, just as likely, her) more intelligent and literate counterparts 'the Classical Reader' and the 'sensible Reader':

> In the Diction I think, Burlesque itself may sometimes be admitted; of which many Instances will occur in this Work, as in the Descriptions of the Battles, and some other Places, not necessary to be pointed out to the Classical Reader; for whose Entertainment those Parodies or Burlesque Imitations are chiefly calculated. (JA, p. 4)

> . . . we should confine ourselves strictly to Nature from the just Imitation of which, will flow all the Pleasure we can this way convey to a sensible Reader. (*ibid.*)

Having set the prospective purchaser right in the unusually aggressive opening words, announcing that this book is not what its likely readers will have come to expect from fiction, the author expresses his yearning not only for a more congenial literary context, but also for a better class of customer, for a reader who is better prepared for the more up-market and demanding range of pleasures and challenges to be offered by the ensuing book.

As the argumentative preface continues, its author becomes more conscious that no such reader is likely to be forthcoming, and more aware that there is nothing to be done about such a sorry state of affairs. In the end, he compromises by hailing an audience which might not be particularly well informed or discriminating but which is at least relatively well disposed, reasonably affluent and decisively male:

> . . . I shall leave my good-natur'd Reader to apply my Piece to my Observations, and will detain him no longer than with a Word concerning the Characters in this Work . . .   (JA, p. 8)

The 'good-natur'd Reader' here addressed is welcomed into the dialogue and his discernment (if not his attention span) is rather unconvincingly flattered. However, the magic soon goes out of the relationship between writer and reader, and, as the book develops, the host's hospitality is intermittently rough and rather reluctantly offered.

The author's exasperation at the poor qualifications and incompetence of contemporary novel readers is quickly established. So, it must be asked, why does he then deign to write a novel at all? In the opening chapter, the narrator surrounds the notion of imaginative biography with subtle and disconcerting ironies, mainly designed to belittle the contemporary reading public and confront them with copious evidence of their poor taste and ignorance. Talking of exemplary biography, a broad category which accommodates his own volumes, he says:

> In this Light I have always regarded those Biographers who have recorded the Actions of great and worthy persons of both Sexes. Not to mention those antient Writers which of late days are little read, being written in obsolete, and, as they are generally thought, unintelligible Languages; such as *Plutarch*, *Nepos*, and others which I heard of in my Youth; our own Language affords many of excellent Use and Instruction, finely calculated to sow the Seeds of Virtue in Youth, and are easy to be comprehended by Persons of Moderate Capacity. Such

are the History of *John* the Great, who, by his brave and heroic Actions against Men of large and athletic Bodies, obtained the glorious Appellation of the Giant-killer; that of an Earl of *Warwick*, whose Christian Name was Guy; the Lives of *Argalus* and *Parthenia*, and above all, the History of those seven worthy Personages, the Champions of Christendom. In all of these, Delight is mixed with Instruction, and the Reader is almost as much improved as entertained.   (JA, pp. 15–16)

Of course, the imagined reader of these diverting chapbooks is really thought by Fielding to be wholly uninterested in such elevated Horatian categories, displaying no obvious desire for either 'Instruction' or 'Improvement', perhaps understandably preferring the more immediate pleasures of delight and entertainment. In response to this demand, the contemporary popular press, according to the author of *Joseph Andrews* at least, was offering only trivial diversion. As a result, the press as a whole could no longer make any legitimate claim to edification, or to the moral authority required for 'Instruction'.

With literature's entry into the recently developed market economy, the press inevitably set its sights too low for Fielding's taste, and pandered to the strongest wishes of its undiscerning sponsors, giving them what it thought they wanted, and what, in the absence of any alternative, they then came to think they wanted. And as the presiding voice of this novel goes on to argue, the two most flagrantly misleading patterns of behaviour for his contemporary readers thereby established were the lives of these two well-known reprobates, Mr Colley Cibber and Mrs Pamela Andrews.

In offering this brisk critique of the contemporary press at the beginning of *Joseph Andrews*, Fielding does not neglect the opportunity to return to the more single-mindedly satiric project of *Shamela* and ridicule both Richardson and Cibber yet again. However, the important difference is that the new text is significantly more expansive, no longer confined in the restrictive and chafing form of parody. In fact, this new book embraces the possibilities of a revitalised kind of novel-writing much more positively than its predecessor, for reasons which are both material and aesthetic, and instead of casting aspersions on the very form of the novel, *Joseph Andrews* tries to identify an acceptable way for its author to inhabit the newly developed form of fiction.

Having been made fully aware of the attractive (and immediate) commercial possibilities of the novel by his sale of *Joseph Andrews* to the bookseller Andrew Millar – to his apparent astonishment, the habitually impecunious Fielding was offered the seemingly huge sum of £200 for the book – he took the opportunity to develop his own terms of reference within the developing genre.[2] The financial side of his literary enterprises will be discussed in more detail later, in the context of the subscription publication of the *Miscellanies*, but for the moment it is important to dwell on the ways his engagement with the developing form of the novel gave him access to an unidentifiable but substantial public. In a text which is both a complex narrative of its own and a manifesto for a certain kind of fiction, Fielding negotiates with the demands and requirements of his new audience, consciously and ironically dropping his standards to what he sees as their level, while at the same time trying to remind them of just how much higher his own aesthetic and intellectual standards will always remain.

In the preface and the introductory chapters to three of the four books which comprise the narrative, as well as in passing remarks dispersed throughout the text, Fielding outlines his own authorised theory of fiction, expressed in a deliberate style at once more controlled than Richardson's immediate epistolary form, and more measured than Cibber's self-congratulatory excesses. Initially, he offers his readers a sly and self-consciously paradoxical account of the 'comic Epic-Poem in Prose', which takes as its subject 'the true Ridiculous' (JA, pp. 4, 6). The definition of legitimate writing and its content sketched at the beginning of the narrative is partly serious and partly ironic, acting as both a barrier to understanding the book and a means of access to it. The notion of the 'comic Epic-Poem in prose' is neither wholly facetious nor wholly playful, incorporating deliberate paradox and misdirection, while also seeking more forcefully to reclaim the possibilities of the revitalised comic novel as a legitimate means of expression for the properly qualified writer.

The offered definition deliberately flouts and disrupts the conventional aesthetic categories of the day. For more literate eighteenth-century readers, the 'comic' was thought of as the least elevated of the recognised literary forms, often associated with farce, to be distinguished from the defensible corrective or retributive force of satire on the one hand and the instructive gravity of tragedy on the other. Given the unavailability of Aristotle's treatise on comedy, and the apparent disappearance of Homer's alleged exercise in the 'low' style, the *Margites*, fondly mentioned in Parson Adams's disquisition on the classics in Book III, Chapter II, comic narrative lacked the distinguished classical support which many eighteenth-century commentators sought. However, the comic form was never without its supporters, and there had been a number of more recent indigenous attempts to legitimise comedy, which even Fielding's apparently ill-informed readers would have been likely to recognise.

In a number of ways, the Restoration theatre as practiced by George Etheredge, William Wycherley, Aphra Behn and William Congreve (to name only the better-known authors, or even *auteurs*) had blurred the distinction between satire and comedy, producing a hybrid dramatic form in which the attempt to expose and correct vice was encompassed by the more obvious desire to exploit and flaunt its comic possibilities. Fielding's own highly successful satirical drama of the 1730s had incorporated many of the racy features of his Restoration predecessors, as well as his own predilection for more topical parody and lampoon. However, after the introduction of the Licensing Act in 1737, heavily restricting access to the stage, these avenues were largely unavailable, and as his career progressed Fielding seems to have moved away from the boisterous energies of his plays, and moved towards a more compromised understanding of comedy, in which the satiric impulse is subdued and the ridicule is more restrained.

That is not to say that by embracing prose comedy Fielding was entirely turning his back on the corrective possibilities of writing. The native precedents available to him describing the role of comedy all included some sense that it had (or, at least, that it ought to have had) both censorious and celebratory powers, however variously they might be balanced. Such an argument can be found in the various hostile and supportive discussions of comedy by Jeremy Collier, William Temple, George Farquhar, Thomas Shadwell and many others in the late seventeenth and early eighteenth centuries, and was clearly part of the more widespread fabric of literary discussion.

In the preface to his 1671 play *An Evening's Love*, for example, John Dryden had sought to put the differing roles of comedy and farce into their proper perspective:

> Comedy consists, though of low persons, yet of natural actions and characters; I mean such humours, adventures, and designs as are to be found and met with in the world. Farce, on the other side, consists of forced humours and unnatural events. Comedy presents us with the

imperfections of human nature: farce entertains us with what is monstrous and chimerical. The one causes laughter in those who can judge of men and manners, by the lively representation of their folly and corruption; the other produces the same effect in those who can judge of neither, and that only by its extravagances. The first works on the judgement and fancy; the latter on fancy only: there is more of satisfaction in the former kind of laughter, and in the latter more of scorn.[3]

Without suggesting that this particular passage had any direct influence on the later novelist, I see Dryden's defensive and legitimising distinction between 'comedy' and 'farce' as consonant with Fielding's use of the term 'comic'. In practice, Fielding does not draw such a precise distinction between these two styles, but in his more schematic attempts at self-justification he is clearly in agreement with Dryden in trying to lift a defensible and respectable notion of comic writing out of the mire of derisive mockery and exaggeration, the new form being defined in opposition to what he saw as the fraudulent seriousness and solemnity of Richardson's novel and the pomposity of Cibber's autobiography.

In fact, the prefatory remarks to *Joseph Andrews* can be seen as continuing the discussion of the validity of comedy, appropriating the 'low' form to suit the purposes of the serious writer. At the risk of sounding anachronistic, I want to claim that throughout this discussion Fielding is enacting that distinction between the 'literary' and the 'popular' which Mikhail Bakhtin describes in *Rabelais and his World* (1965). In Bakhtin's argument, the 'comic' achieves such status and respectability as it has only when it changes from being predominantly carnal to being more cerebral, from being associated with riot and disorder to being a way of perceiving or imposing order. After a long period when the 'comic' could act as a powerful way of apprehending the grotesqueness of the world, of 'carnivalising' experience, collective and demotic in orientation, there is a point at which the 'comic' merely becomes the appropriate literary form for dealing with 'low' characters, just one part of the complete artist's palette, albeit now a more respectable and legitimate part. So the process of legitimation of comedy is one involving both gains and losses.[4]

Bakhtin's argument is generalised and European in orientation, looking most closely at Rabelais. In the more specific and restricted arena of British literary culture, it can be argued that the moment of transposition and incorporation of comedy arrives in 1742 with the publication of *Joseph Andrews*, which exploits and celebrates anarchic 'carnival' features, while at the same time seeking to keep them within carefully defined authorial control.

Conscious that the 'comic' is in need of redefinition if his dialogue with the existent literary traditions is to be fruitful, Fielding offers some lines of analysis of the term in his 'Author's Preface'. The first contrast offered is between comedy and 'the Burlesque':

> . . . no two Species of Writing can differ more widely than the Comic and the Burlesque: for as the latter is ever the Exhibition of what is monstrous and unnatural, and where our Delight, if we examine it, arises from the surprizing Absurdity, as in appropriating the Manners of the highest to the lowest, or *e converso*; so in the former, we should ever confine ourselves strictly to Nature from the just Imitation of which, will flow all the Pleasure we can this way convey to a sensible Reader. And perhaps, there is one Reason, why a Comic Writer should of all others be the least excused for deviating from Nature, since it may not be always so easy for a serious Poet to meet with the Great and the Admirable; but Life every where furnishes an accurate Observer with the Ridiculous.   (JA, p. 4)

Fielding dismisses the 'Burlesque' here as a vulgar and undignified genre, exhibiting only the monstrous and unnatural, an inappropriate medium for a sophisticated literary form – he sees it as Rabelaisian, in effect. It is interesting that he seeks to establish the legitimacy and authority of his argument by citing the views of the patrician philosopher Lord Shaftesbury, as expressed in his *Sensus Communis: An Essay on the Freedom of Wit and Humour* (1709), which are presented as being similar to his own. However, just as we begin to suspect the author of *Shamela* and such plays as *The Tragedy of Tragedies* of flagrant bad faith, he acknowledges a certain incongruity in his remarks by acknowledging his own earlier career as burlesque dramatist – 'I have had some little Success on the Stage this way' (JA, p. 5) – suggesting that Fielding's negotiation between derisive burlesque and instructive comedy is not yet over.

In the attempt to identify as clearly as possible the authority and legitimacy of the comic style of *Joseph Andrews*, Fielding next turns to contemporary painting for a serviceable distinction:

> Let us examine the Works of a Comic History-Painter, with those Performances which the *Italians* call *Caricatura*; where we shall find the true Excellence of the former, to consist in the exactest copying of Nature; insomuch, that a judicious Eye instantly rejects anything *outré*; any *Liberty which the Painter hath taken with the Features of that Alma Mater.* – Whereas in the *Caricatura* we allow all Licence. Its Aim is to exhibit Monsters, not Men; and all Distortions and Exaggerations whatever are within its proper Province.   (JA p. 5)

Once again, the distinction to be drawn is that between permissible exaggeration and improper distortion. The comic artist exaggerates (though only slightly) for the purposes of edification; the caricaturist or the writer of burlesque distorts and refracts as much as possible merely for the purposes of surprise and astonishment.

The specific example cited is that of Fielding's friend and contemporary, the graphic artist William Hogarth – 'He who would call the Ingenious *Hogarth* a Burlesque Painter, would, in my Opinion, do him very little Honour' (JA, p. 6). The comparison is at first surprising. Hogarth's vivid and stylised representations of faces and features seem to capitalise on the grotesque and to enjoy that very 'Licence' Fielding was apparently condemning. But it must be remembered that within his contemporary context, Hogarth was seeking to establish a style comparable to that for which Fielding argues here, negotiating between the existing patterns of heroic portraiture and more extravagantly grotesque caricature, giving the native 'comic' style greater currency and acceptability than it had previously enjoyed in British art.

Indeed, without labouring the point here it is arguable that the influence of Hogarth on Fielding is at least matched by the influence of Fielding on Hogarth, and that the two figures interacted creatively throughout their careers. Fielding refers to the artist in laudatory terms a number of times in his fiction, and the respect was clearly reciprocated. In April 1743, for instance, Hogarth produced an illustrative picture called *Characters and Caricaturas*, placing examples of his own style midway between comparable examples of idealisation and grotesque misrepresentation, beneath which is added: 'For a farther Explanation of the Difference betwixt *Character* and *Caricatura*, See the Preface to *Jo Andrews*.'[5]

The significance of this revisionist identification of the comic becomes clearer in the introductory chapter to Book III, where the author, amidst a series of dismissive and disparaging remarks about rival contemporary novel writers, tries to negotiate between the particular and the general in his own characterisation:

> I question not but several of my Readers will know the Lawyer in the Stage-Coach, the Moment they hear his Voice. It is likewise odds, but the Wit and the Prude meet with some of their Acquaintance, as well as all the rest of my Characters. To prevent therefore any such malicious Applications, I declare here once for all, I describe not Men, but Manners; not an Individual, but a Species. Perhaps it will be answered, Are not the Characters then taken from Life? To which I answer in the Affirmative; nay, I believe I might aver, that I have writ little more than I have seen. The Lawyer is not only alive, but hath been so these 4000 Years, and I hope G— will indulge his Life as many yet to come. (JA, p. 168)

Fielding here rehearses part of the conventional defence of satire as expressed by many of his contemporaries and immediate predecessors. Satire, according to Swift and Pope and many others, was defensible only when it dealt in particular cases of more general failings, avoiding the exclusively personal. Satirists, then, often attacked as vituperative or libellous, sought to defend themselves by their concerns for the common good, their alleged therapeutic or reformative powers, leaving aside the possible potency of satire as a form of personal reprisal. Of course, the legitimacy of this defence might be questioned, especially when put forward in the context of work like Pope's *Dunciad*, but plausible or not there can be no doubt that such defensive arguments were common currency in eighteenth-century English writing.

In keeping with this belief in generality, Fielding argues that the characters in this novel are not extraordinary fantasies of his own invention, but neither are they stylised portraits of specific, identifiable individuals drawn from life. They are instead representative of persistent and familiar human qualities, held up for useful ridicule by the high-minded and generous comic writer, not by the scurrilous and vindictive libeller. The effect of introducing satire into the novel according to this argument, is to enhance its reformative powers, by forcing people privately to confront their own weaknesses and failings:

> . . . his Appearance in the World is calculated for much more general and noble Purposes; not to expose one pitiful Wretch, to the small and

contemptible Circle of his Acquaintance; but to hold the Glass to thousands in their Closets, that they may contemplate their Deformity, and endeavour to reduce it, and thus by suffering private Mortification may avoid public Shame. This places the Boundary between, and distinguishes the Satirist from the Libeller; for the former privately corrects the Fault for the Benefit of the Person, like a Parent; the latter publickly exposes the Person himself, as an Example to others, like an Executioner.   (JA, pp. 168–9)

As well as surreptitiously and gleefully anticipating the commercial success of his book ('. . . thousands . . .'), Fielding here takes on the mantle of integrity conferred by the satirist. Steering a path between the derisive personalised lampoon of the caricaturist – an interesting example of which would be the representation of Fielding himself as 'Mr Spondy' in Tobias Smollett's *The Adventures of Peregrine Pickle* (1751) – and the hollow laughter of fools, Fielding strives towards a position of moral legitimacy and rightful authority. Eager to avoid confusion with those writers he saw as 'mere Jack-Puddings, whose Business is only to excite Laughter', Fielding seeks to convince his readers that he can temper his derisive mirth with some of the disinterested gravity of the satirist.[6]

Alongside the attempt to give dignity and status to the previously liminal comic form lies Fielding's attempt to reclaim the contested territory of the 'epic'. If comedy seemed irrecoverably tarnished by its association with 'low' subjects, the 'epic' for eighteenth-century readers was the most exalted, as well as the most elusive, of literary forms. Although Aristotle's *Poetics* had put tragedy at the top of the hierarchy of genres, most eighteenth-century commentators thought that the epic poem was the pinnacle of artistic achievement. As John Dryden put it in 1677:

Any man who will seriously consider the nature of an epic poem, how it agrees with that of poetry in general, which is to instruct and to delight, what actions it describes, and what persons they are chiefly whom it informs, will find it a work which is indeed full of difficulty in the attempt, but admirable when it is well performed.[7]

The epic may have seemed to many to be the highest goal any writer could seek, but it also seemed to an increasing number to be less and less possible actually to produce such a thing as time went by. Indeed, the whole notion of writing a genuine epic in the mundane world of early eighteenth-century England seemed to many commentators to have become self-evidently absurd, and the epic ideal had become heavily encrusted with ironies by the time of Fielding's intervention.

In 1727, Alexander Pope had pseudonymously published a parody of Longinus's treatise on the sublime, called *Peri Bathous, or The Art of Sinking in Poetry*. Writing as 'Martinus Scriblerus', indicating the hand of Swift and the other members of the Scriblerus Club in the project, Pope pours ironic scorn on such recent pretenders to poetic merit as Sir Richard Blackmore, author of what he presented as a feeble attempt at epic called *Prince Arthur* (1695), and Ambrose 'Namby-Pamby' Philips, author of *Pastorals* (1709). Part of this onslaught on the paucity of contemporary taste, also prominent in the various versions of Pope's own ironised epic the *Dunciad*, involved a recognition of how far current writing seemed to have sunk from its highest aspirations and its classical precedents, and in an appendix to the main text, Pope's readers are offered a 'Receipt to make an *Epic Poem*':

> An Epic Poem, as the Criticks agree, is the greatest Work Human Nature is capable of. They have already laid down many mechanical Rules for Compositions of this Sort, but at the same time they have cut off almost all Undertakers from the Possibility of ever performing them; for the first Qualification they unanimously require in a Poet, is a *Genius*. I shall here endeavour (for the Benefit of my Countrymen) to make it manifest, that Epick Poems may be made *without a Genius*, nay without Learning or much Reading. This must necessarily be of great Use to all those who confess they never *Read*, and of whom the world is convinc'd they never *Learn* . . .[8]

So, in the modern world, the elevated and exalted epic proper is no longer possible – neither writers nor readers are adequately equipped to cope with its grandeur of vision or with its comprehensiveness. In its place, Pope ironically recommends his own recipe for an instant substitute.

Fielding's account of the contemporary world of letters, as we have already seen from *Shamela* and as is obvious throughout the pages of *The Champion* and *The Covent-Garden Journal*, is no more flattering than Pope's. For both writers, the recent commercialisation of writing and the growth of a new reading public had brought about (or had been a symptom of) a rapid collapse of aesthetic and moral standards, and the epic hereafter could only prove elusive in any form other than the ironic or self-parodying, like *The Rape of the Lock* or the *Dunciad*.

If there is a difference in emphasis between Pope and Fielding it is that, writing fifteen or more years after *Peri Bathous*, Fielding has even less confidence in the expertise and expectations of his readership, and his relationship with them is even more fraught and adversarial. The note of reassuring Scriblerian complicity which is audible in Pope, where he is ironically addressing a small community of fellow wits, never makes itself heard above the cacophony of Fielding's one-sided dialogue with the imagined readers of his novels.

Later in *Peri Bathous*, Pope describes the ingredients of the 'Fable' as it appears in modern epic:

> Take out of any old Poem, History-book, Romance, or Legend (for Instance *Geffry of Monmouth* or *Don Belianis of Greece*) those Parts of Story which afford most Scope for *Long Descriptions*: Put these Pieces together, and throw all the Adventures you fancy into *one Tale*. Then, take a Hero, whom you may chuse for the Sound of his Name, and put him into the midst of these Adventures: There let him *work*, for twelve Books; at the end of which you may take him out, ready prepared to *conquer* or to *marry*; it being necessary that the Conclusion of an Epick Poem be *fortunate*.   (Pope, pp. 206–7)

As we shall see in the subsequent discussion of *Jonathan Wild* and *A Journey From This World to the Next*, Fielding was obviously in sympathy with the Scriblerian account of the controversy between the Ancients and the Moderns, of which *Peri Bathous* is only a small part, and Pope's account of how to produce a modern epic undoubtedly infiltrates the text of *Joseph Andrews*. Fielding was also clearly aware of the existence of Pope's parody, although perhaps not of its authorship, and wrote approvingly of it several times in *Tom Jones* and in *The Covent-Garden Journal*, which includes a continuation of his own called *Peri Tharsus, or The Art of Swaggering in Print* (1752). (*CGJ*, pp. 231–3).

So when Fielding offers the teasing definition of the 'comic Epic-Poem in prose' at the opening of his novel, he is reiterating contemporary ironic confusions about the function of the epic as well as seeking to reclaim and legitimise a new version of the comic. As he so deliberately phrases it, the 'Epic-Poem' in the 1740s is contained within, perhaps stifled by the 'comic . . . in prose'. Like a noble beast in a circus, the great machinery of the epic is being asked to perform its business within the undignified surroundings of the comic novel, and the discrepancies between human aspiration and human achievement – the great theme of all ironic writing – are thereby made glaringly obvious in the form of the book as well as in its content.

When Fielding introduces the conventional epic simile in *Joseph Andrews*, which he does regularly, its effect is simultaneously to expose the ordinariness of the world described within the text and dramatise the bathos of trying to ennoble that world through extravagant literary conventions:

> Now the Rake *Hesperus* had called for his Breeches, and having well rubbed his drowsy Eyes, prepared to dress himself for all Night; by whose Example his Brother Rakes on Earth likewise leave those Beds, in which they had slept away the Day. Now *Thetis* the good Housewife began to put on the Pot in order to regale the good Man *Phebus*, after his daily Labours were over. In vulgar Language, it was in the Evening when *Joseph* attended his Lady's Orders.   (JA, p. 33)

The bathetic ending here, and the hints of social satire throughout, recall the way elevated conventions and styles were appropriated and exploited in anti-pastoral poems like Jonathan Swift's 'Description of the Morning' (1709) or his 'Description of a City Shower' (1710). But Fielding's dialogue with the epic and with the expectations of his readers is more sustained, and more complex in its effects than these accessible anti-pastorals. He offers what Michael McKeon, writing in the context of Fielding's *Jonathan Wild*, calls 'a double critique', in this case interrogating the ordinariness of the world by the dignity of epic style, and interrogating the high-falutin' pretentions of epic by the obduracy of the day-to-day world, the whole enterprise being, as we saw, 'Written in Imitation of the Manner of Cervantes'.[9]

The dialogue with the epic, and with Cervantes, is not exclusively contained within the narrator's commentary. As well as dealing with a journey, albeit a rather inconsequential and haphazard one, and containing conventional epic episodes in ironised form, like mock battles, the book offers at least one character who maintains the heroic spirit and stature of classical precedent. The custodian of epic expectations within the tale itself, and the most obvious counterpart of the great chivalric knight Don Quixote, is Abraham Adams, the bookish and pedantic parson, whose elevated view of the world is in constant collision with the rough humbling experiences provided in a comic novel.

In a very precise sense, Parson Adams lives by the book: 'Adams return'd, "his Question would be properer, what kind of Beauty was the chief in Poetry, for that *Homer* was equally excellent in them all" ' (*JA*, p. 175). Living by Homer and by Aeschylus and by all the other writers he cites seems, on the face of it, to be intrinsically noble, but in the context of this narrative it continues to become farcical. When Adams quotes an appropriate passage of Horace (in the original Latin, of course) to Beau Didapper, the Beau replies that 'he did not understand *Welch*' (*JA*, p. 281). Poor Beau Didapper. The world as it is portrayed in the book is simply unequipped to deal with Adams, just as Cervantes' world was unable to accommodate Don Quixote. And yet however ridiculous he may be made to appear, he retains tremendous and at times moving integrity. One of Fielding's main concerns in the narrative is to provide a Cervantic context where Adams's idealism is an incongruous feature amid the sustained bathos, and the unworldly heroism of the character is ironised further by his physical robustness and fiery temper.

But for all his prominence within the narrative, Abraham Adams is not its single hero. As the tale opens, we see residual traces of Pope's recipe for the 'Fable' of a modern epic, and indications of recognisable parodic intent, alongside a thorough-going endorsement of the 'low' concerns of the modern novel:

> Mr. *Joseph Andrews*, the Hero of our ensuing History, was esteemed to be the only Son of Gaffar and Gammer *Andrews*, and Brother to the illustrious *Pamela*, whose Virtue is at present so famous. As to his Ancestors, we have searched with great Diligence, but little Success: being unable to trace them farther than his Great Grandfather, who, as an elderly Person in the Parish remembers to have heard his Father say, was an excellent Cudgel-player . . .   (*JA*, p. 17)

As the 'Hero' is brought upon the scene, the epic invocation of the past rubs up against the bathetic ordinariness of the present. The effect is clearly comic, making fun of epic pretensions, of the failure of the narrator to discover the truth of Joseph's lineage, and introducing scepticism about the reputation of his famous sister. Furthermore, it creates a virtually self-parodying and ironised author, who embarks on an oddly abrasive relationship with the interpellated reader, throwing the audience off guard by the oscillation between styles, addressing him or her in different voices, and constantly destabilising the terms of the engagement. In the terms used by Barthes, discussed earlier, *Joseph Andrews* cannot make up its mind whether to be a 'readerly' text, friendly and accessible to its potential consumers, or a 'writerly' one, prepared to be 'difficult' by deliberately and systematically drawing attention to the processes of its own manufacture and frustrating the conventions of verisimilitude.

One of the most vexing problems facing the author of a 'comic Epic-Poem in prose', as Fielding sees it, lies in choosing an appropriate form of address. As we have seen, the author occasionally enjoys the epic sweep, introducing elevated style both for its own sake and as an exercise in the mock-heroic. At other times, he exploits the grand epic simile to give his reader ridiculously heightened experience, as in the first episode of bedroom comedy between Joseph and Mrs Slipslop:

> As when a hungry Tygress, who long had traversed the Woods in fruitless search, sees within the Reach of her Claws a Lamb, she prepares to leap upon her Prey; or as a voracious Pike, of immense Size, surveys through the liquid Element a Roach or Gudgeon which cannot escape her Jaws, opens them wide to swallow the little Fish: so did Mrs. *Slipslop* prepare to lay her violent amorous Hands on the poor *Joseph*, when luckily her Mistress's Bell rung, and delivered the intended Martyr from her Clutches. (JA, p. 29)

The terms of engagement between author and reader presented here seem reasonably secure. In order to elevate the episode to greater heights of drama, the participants are conventionally metamorphosed into predator (Tygress/Pike) and prey (Lamb/Roach/Gudgeon). The conventions of epic discourse are observed, even if the transformation of Joseph into a number of carefully identified small freshwater fish lacks persuasive heroic dignity, and the familiar genre of the mock-heroic embraces the event. An epic perspective is being brought to bear on a comic episode, reinforcing the incongruity of Joseph's chastity without creating generic instability or introducing confusion. The reader is informed about the (in)significance of the event, while being offered a passage of isolated 'fine writing'. Similar episodes are dispersed throughout the text, culminating in Book III, Chapter VI, where Joseph's behaviour is so extraordinarily magnanimous and heroic that it leads Fielding simply to throw up his hands and abandon his responsibilities: 'we could find no Simile adequate to our Purpose' (JA, p. 213).

The epic invocations are thus part of the mock-heroic and 'writerly' fabric of the narrative. However, immediately after the 'Tygress' apostrophe, the author seems to slacken the reins, to become uncertain of his position, and his next claim to epic authority seems altogether less convincing:

> It is the Observation of some antient Sage, whose Name I have forgot, that Passions operate differently on the human Mind, as Diseases on the Body, in proportion to the Strength or Weakness, Soundness or Rottenness of the one or the other.
>
> We hope therefore, a judicious Reader will give himself some Pains to observe, what we have so greatly laboured to describe, the different Operations of this Passion on Love in the gentle and cultivated Mind of the Lady *Booby*, from those which it effected in the less polished and coarser Disposition of Mrs. *Slipslop*.
>
> Another Philosopher, whose Name also at present escapes my Memory, hath somewhere said, that Resolutions taken in the Absence of the beloved Object are very apt to vanish in its Presence; on both which wise Sayings the following Chapter may serve as a Comment.
>
> (JA, pp. 29–30)

In this passage, the author forgets a number of things conventionally understood to be of importance to the epic story-teller (as to the academic writer of scholarly articles), and yet he seems blithely unconcerned about it. Later, he repeats his casual attributions – '*Plato* or *Aristotle*, or somebody else hath said . . . I would quote more great Men if I could: but my Memory not permitting me . . . ' (JA, pp. 152–3). Given the nature of his audience, he seems to feel that such lapses of memory need not be troublesome, or detract from his authority. After all, he suggests, what does the reader know? The author has 'greatly laboured', and in return hopes that 'a judicious Reader will give himself some Pains to observe'. Fielding seems to be creating a relationship of unequal partners, with himself as the repository of wisdom, when he can be bothered, and the reader devoid of knowledge. Fielding may well forget the names of these philosophers, but, he hints, at least he knew them some time, and could find them again if he really felt he had to, which is more than the ignorant and lazy reader could ever claim.

The lethargic and insensitive reader has to be cajoled into observing what has been so strenuously created, and to be led by the nose through all the meanings of the episodes. Fielding holds absolute power over the reader, as long as that reader is prepared to keep turning the pages. But, of course, the reader also has the power to stop turning the pages. At times, Fielding flaunts his power by withholding information germane to the plot (Joseph's real identity, for example), and at other times he simply sports with the audience: 'Indeed, I have often been assured by both, that they spent these Hours in a most delightful Conversation: but as I never could prevail on either to relate it, so I cannot communicate it to the Reader' (JA, p. 151). As well as exploiting and ironising those conventions of authorship associated with the style of verisimilitude, such references are all part of the continuing process of putting the reader in his or her place. Whatever else Fielding may be up to, he is seeking a mode of address which will enable the uninformed reader to recognise the authority of his or her guide and mentor, and enable the author to express his exasperation at the ridiculous extent he must go to to be understood.

The author of *Joseph Andrews* constantly throws down such challenges to the reader, suggesting that the relationship thereby created is much more combative and abrasive than the more edifying and affable one described by Wolfgang Iser mentioned earlier. Fielding is constantly teasing and provoking his reader to deny what he says – 'If there be anyone who doubts all this, let him read the next Chapter' (JA, p. 32) – engaging in fitful contest with those ill-qualified and credulous consumers of popular writing who were taken in by the preposterous *Pamela* and by Colley Cibber.

At times, the narrator seems to be rejoicing in the power he holds over his bemused and befuddled audience:

> It is an Observation sometimes made, that to indicate our Idea of a simple Fellow, we say, *He is easily to be seen through*: Nor do I believe it a more improper Denotation of a simple Book. Instead of applying this to any particular Performance, we chuse rather to remark the contrary in this History, where the Scene opens itself by small degrees, and he is a sagacious Reader who can see two Chapters before him.   (JA, p. 42)

Such a 'sagacious Reader', of course is nowhere to be found, and Fielding has to make do with the ill-qualified public provided. At times, he seems almost reduced to despair by his reader's lack of preparation or imaginative competence:

> Those who have read any Romance or Poetry antient or modern, must have been informed, that Love hath Wings; by which they are not to

understand, as some young Ladies by mistake have done, that a Lover can fly .   (JA, p. 44)

At others, he recognises and relies on the differing experiences of his differing readers:

> This shyness therefore, as we trust it will recommend her Character to all our Female Readers, and not greatly surprize such of our Males as are acquainted with the younger part of the other Sex, we shall not give our selves any trouble to vindicate.   (JA, p. 129)

And eventually, he realises that however much he might seem to be in a despotic position within the narration, he has no *real* control over his reader's interpretation of events:

> I shall refer it to my Reader, to make what Observations he pleases on this Incident.   (JA, p. 153)

The problem of communication becomes more insistent as the narrative progresses. Ill-prepared and unimaginative these readers may be, but there may be no others to be found. In an all-too-obvious sense, the customer is always right. However incompetent the contemporary reading public might appear to be, that is the readership with which the author is inevitably in dialogue, so for communication to be even possible he has to find some common points of contact with them. And there are moments when the author seems to have lost all confidence in the possibility of fruitful contact. Towards the end of the novel, the shadow of indeterminacy seems to hang over events, and at one point Fielding seems to relinquish control of his readers totally. He expresses these anxieties most clearly when he entitles Book III, Chapter viii 'Which some Readers will think too short, and others too long' (JA, p. 224).

In seeking for a range of reference which will help these readers make sense of the episodes in the narrative, or at least make the *kind* of sense in which the author believes, Fielding gradually abandons the traditional scope of the epic and turns instead to the more immediate vocabulary of contemporary popular culture:

> You have heard, Reader, Poets talk of the *Statue of Surprize*; you have heard likewise, or else you have heard very little, how Surprize made one of the Sons of *Croesus* speak tho' he was dumb. You have seen the

Faces, in the Eighteen-penny Gallery, when through the Trap-Door, to soft or no Musick, Mr. *Bridgewater*, Mr. *William Mills*, or some other of ghostly Appearance, hath ascended with a Face all pale with Powder, and a Shirt all bloody with Ribbons; but from none of these, nor from *Phidias*, or *Praxiteles*, if they should return to Life – no, not from the inimitable Pencil of my Friend *Hogarth*, could you receive such an Idea of Surprize, as would have entered in at your Eyes, had they beheld the Lady *Booby*, when those last Words issued out from the Lips of *Joseph*.

(JA, p. 35)

The key phrase here may be '. . . or else you have heard very little . . .', which seems to reinforce Fielding's recurrent uncertainties over the possibility of successful communication. After all, perhaps (or, he seems to hint, *probably*) his reader has indeed heard 'very little', putting the author in the position of having to spell everything out very carefully, in words of no more than one syllable.

In pursuit of some suitable frame of reference in which to understand the specific episode, the inexperienced and unimaginative reader is here given more accessible literary contexts to help him or her recognise what is going on, pointers to contemporary acting practice, mythological allusions, as well as the ever-instructive example of Hogarth. By offering these different parallels, Fielding is creating a range of interpretive possibilities, from the noble to the farcical. But even if all these really were to be recognised, Fielding still wants to go one better, and claim that this outstanding example of surprise expressed by Lady Booby, invented by himself alone, outdid every other example available, and so alas cannot be adequately recreated by readers anyway.

Significantly, and entertainingly, this hyperbole actually serves to excuse the author from a detailed description of whatever happened. The reader is instructed to think of the most graphic representation of surprise he or she can imagine, then think of an even more extraordinary one. As Wolfgang Iser sees it, the reader has to fill in the gap left in the text, even while Fielding speculates on the impossibility of doing so successfully. As I see it, Fielding's dialogue with his reader has become increasingly antagonistic, setting deliberate traps and asking the impossible. Iser's commentary on this passage suggests a relatively supportive and productive relationship between author and reader:

The result is an opportunity for discovery, and the more the reader brings to life himself, the greater the discovery.[10]

But surely the passage requires both the 'mere *English* reader' and the 'classical reader' merely to confirm their relative ineptitudes. The first will recognise only the theatrical reference, yet remain unable to visualise what has happened. The second will feel empowered by the classical and mythological comparisons, just as Adams so regularly does, yet even then will be equally unable fully to comprehend or visualise the event. To see it properly, the passage announces, you had to be there. And since this was a product of Fielding's imagination, you couldn't be. The mimetic principle behind both popular and classical fiction – a repeated point of satiric attack in Fielding's fiction – is here shown to be especially inadequate, and the background against which different readers interpret both the events and the narration remains uncertain.

As Fielding simultaneously empowers and disenfranchises his readers, we see him exploring the limits of the contemporary novel. Sometimes, as Iser suggests, he leaves literal 'gaps' for the reader to fill in. In one of the stylish pieces of 'high' writing, a space is quite deliberately left:

> That beautiful young Lady, the *Morning*, now rose from her Bed, and with a Countenance blooming with fresh Youth and Sprightliness, like Miss *——, with soft Dews hanging on her pouting Lips, began to take her early Walk over the eastern Hills.   (JA, pp. 200–1)

In an explanatory footnote, the asterisked young woman is to be identified as 'Whoever the Reader pleases'. Such freedoms of the pen are made more prominent in *Tom Jones* (and later still, of course, in Sterne's *Tristram Shandy* and *A Sentimental Journey*), but here they create the sense of frustrated interaction between reader and writer, revealing, but not quite dispelling the arcane mysteries of the 'science of *Authoring*'.

As Fielding intrusively and extravagantly draws the tale to its conclusion, feeling free to exploit plotting devices of lost babies, pedlars and strawberry birthmarks more ridiculous and implausible than any in contemporary romance fiction, he constantly stresses the enjoyable unreality of the book. For instance, he introduces complications about incest only to enjoy his skill in dispersing them.

He casually relocates Joseph Andrews in the social hierarchy, and at last marries him off to Fanny – the ending of this 'comic Epic' being, as Pope suggested, 'fortunate'. Continuing his enjoyment of the conventions of verisimilitude, he talks of receiving letters from Mr Wilson, apprising him of events subsequent to those related. And he ends the book finally by reversing the customary terms of address, and denying all possibility of a sequel:

> . . . what is particularly remarkable, he declares he will imitate them in their Retirement; nor will be prevailed upon by any Booksellers, or their Authors, to make his Appearance in *High-Life*.   (JA, p. 312)

The parodic impulse is thus momentarily over, with the suggestion that an equivalent to Richardson's relatively unsuccessful *Pamela II* is not even worth the effort.

Joseph Andrews is thus a highly self-conscious book, fully aware of its own story-telling devices, conscious of its dialogic relation with other books. Even more prominent than the intertextuality, however, is the constant dialogue with the audience, the sustained examination of their literary qualifications and their fitness to read the book so carefully made for them. Inside the narrative, the comic potential of dialogic story-telling is exploited when Adams and the others constantly interrupt the account of 'Leonora, the Unfortunate Jilt' or the tale of Mr Wilson, trying to make sense of it within the restrictive and inadequate frameworks of their own experience. As Adams repeatedly groans when Wilson tells his version of fashionable London life, so Fielding acknowledges his awareness of the audience's capacity to intensify or misconstrue anything an author offers.

In the terms offered by the semiotician and novelist Umberto Eco – appropriate if again anachronistic – Fielding is constantly fighting with the 'closed' nature of his text. Eco talks of the relationship between a text and its reading communities in the following way:

> In the process of communication, a text is frequently interpreted against the background of codes different from those intended by the author. Some authors do not take into account such a possibility. They have in mind an average addressee referred to a given social context. Nobody can say what happens when the actual reader is different from the 'average' one. Those texts that obsessively aim at arousing a precise response on the part of more or less empirical readers (be they children, soap-opera addicts, doctors, law-abiding citizens, swingers, Presbyterians,

farmers, middle-class women, scuba divers, effete snobs, or any other imaginable sociopsychological category) are in fact open to any possible 'aberrant' decoding. A text so immoderately 'open' to every possible interpretation will be called a *closed* one.[11]

Eco's concern with the role of the reader in creating a text and the possibilities of controlled and aberrant readings is clearly useful in discussing *Joseph Andrews*. Having produced a commercially successful foray into the private lives of his readers, Fielding remains deeply uncertain about what use they may subsequently make of his book. Unfortunately for him, his readers do not fall into the manageable categories of scuba divers or swingers, or any such knowable interpretive community. The procedures and reading practices of the reading community his book is compelled to address are at the time of his writing still unclear. Yet in order to explain the 'science of *Authoring*', he has to be confident that he is addressing *someone* and he has to impose some constraints on that person's responses. His text may be open to many readings, in Eco's sense (which means it is 'closed', if I follow the argument correctly), but it goes well beyond the self-referential and uses the literary debate about the competence of its readers to set an agenda of social and political concerns. In the next section, we can examine the substance of the narrative: after all, amid all this rhetorical dexterity and playfulness, what *is* Fielding talking about? How is he trying to act upon his readers?

Roasting examples

What the Female Readers are taught by the Memoirs of Mrs. *Andrews*, is so well set forth in the excellent Essays or Letters prefixed to the second and subsequent Editions of that Work, that it would be here a needless Repetition. The authentic History with which I now present the public, is an Instance of the great Good that Book is likely to do, and of the Prevalence of Example which I have just observed: since it will appear that it was by keeping the excellent Pattern of his Sister's Virtues before his Eyes, that Mr. *Joseph Andrews* was chiefly enabled to preserve his Purity in the midst of such great Temptations . . .

(JA, p. 16)

As to the Character of *Adams*, as it is the most glaring in the whole, so I conceive it not to be found in any Book now extant. It is designed a Character of perfect Simplicity; and as the Goodness of his Heart will recommend him to the Good-natur'd; so I hope it will excuse me to the

Gentlemen of his Cloth; for whom, while they are worthy of their sacred Order, no Man can possibly have a greater Respect. They will therefore excuse me, notwithstanding the low Adventures in which he is engaged, that I have made him a Clergyman; since no other Office could have given him so many Opportunities of displaying his worthy Inclinations. (JA, p. 9)

My reading of *Joseph Andrews* so far has concentrated on seeing it as maintaining and developing a literary and ideological debate about 'the science of *Authoring*', conducted at a moment of peculiar intensity. Until now, I have presented the book as being an adversarial and combative attempt to find a space in the contemporary literary market-place, which had been recently transformed by the development of more sophisticated printing technology and distribution methods, for the traditionally learned author, without undue compromise or dilution of standards. By appropriating the form of the emergent novel to his own self-aggrandising ends, Fielding was eager to legitimise a certain kind of erudite and polished comic writing in the face of what he saw as a marked deterioration in the aesthetic standards of his culture, the speed and severity of this decline being epitomised for him by the popularity and currency of the meretricious work of Samuel Richardson, Colley Cibber, Conyers Middleton and many others.

To begin to reconstruct his literary culture by a decisive act of personal intervention, or at the very least to diagnose properly its failings and simultaneously find a secure place for himself as an author, Fielding enters into dialogue with existing forms of narrative and with their interpellated readers. Through the direct address of his narrative style, he scrupulously examines the credentials of readers, and questions their qualifications, while taking great pains to emphasise his own expertise and superiority. The author's aim is thereby to create a more sophisticated and authoritative version of the contemporary novel, which will retain the legitimate status and meaning of more traditionally dignified writing by negotiating between the comic and the satiric. And at the same time, the author has to be engaged on a quest to discover whether or not there still exist any readers who can interact fruitfully with him, while remaining conscious that the marketing and production and distribution of works of fiction inevitably lead to the disquietingly 'closed' (Eco's term) nature of the book he has written, with the possibility of 'aberrant' readings always lurking behind the narrator's attempts at control.

This reading of the text makes it primarily a book about books and about the social practice of reading, as constructed within a particular social context. From such a point of view, *Joseph Andrews* becomes a text which interrogates and ironically reproduces the forms and procedures of other texts, particularly the mimetic conventions of contemporary popular novels and their stylised modes of address. But I want to argue that *Joseph Andrews*, as well as engaging in polemical agitation on behalf of properly qualified authors, is dialogic and intertextual in a wider social sense, negotiating not only with the literary conventions and expectations of other recent and contemporary books, but also with their moral and ideological assumptions and the meanings they disseminated.

After all, Fielding's novel is not just an intertext, an ironised compilation of citations from other literary texts – what Julia Kristeva calls 'a mosaic of quotations' – it is also emphatically and obviously directive and judgemental.[12] As well as being a dialogue with other popular novels, *Joseph Andrews* is an interventionist project, designed to take issue with and contest both the form and ideology of these widely read rival texts. By framing the content of his novel in terms of the positive examples of the Bible and *Don Quixote* (however ironised), as well as the negative examples of *Pamela* and Cibber's *Apology*, Fielding seeks access to a more overtly ideological re-reading of the state of contemporary culture, to a way of examining the moral values and social priorities of early eighteenth-century Britain as well as its more favoured literary techniques and styles.

The moral values Fielding chooses to examine in *Joseph Andrews* are those of personal and social conduct, principally concerning the issues of individual behaviour as they had been encoded in recent popular writing. However, the question of Fielding's own personal point of view on these issues, of the authorial priorities or allegiances which lie at the heart of the book, remains persistently difficult to determine, cloaked as it is by successive layers of irony and deliberate confusion. In pursuit of a perennially elusive certainty, a great deal has already been written on the recoverable religious and ethical background of Fielding's work, and, following the initial research of James A. Work in the 1940s, Martin C. Battestin has demonstrated to the satisfaction of many critics and scholars the prevailing influence of such 'latitudinarian' thinkers as Isaac Barrow, Robert South, John

Tillotson, Samuel Clarke and Benjamin Hoadly on the novelist's social and moral views.[13]

Battestin argues that in opposition both to the materialist cynicism of Thomas Hobbes or Bernard Mandeville, and to the concentration on 'faith' and 'enthusiasm' vehemently advocated by the great 'Methodist' evangelists George Whitefield and John Wesley, the broad base of latitudinarian thinking held firmly to its belief in the essential goodness and nobility of human nature, however corrupted that might often be in practice through bad habits or influences or through weakness of the will. Heavily in debt to these thinkers, claims Battestin, Fielding the novelist and pamphleteer thus becomes both an ethically motivated and principled commentator on the depravity of his own times and a more universally applicable figure: he describes Fielding as 'a Christian censor of the manners and morals of his age, and of ours as well' (Battestin, p. x).

Although Battestin's hugely influential presentation of these beliefs and their influence on the novels is persuasively coherent and schematic, it has attracted mounting criticism from a variety of directions over the last thirty years, and it no longer holds the undisputed sway in Fielding studies it once did. To begin with, even the most sympathetic of subsequent scholars have come to believe that there may actually be no single creed or system of belief which can exactly be called 'latitudinarianism', and that it might be better seen as a loose affiliation or allegiance, emphasising the positive moral possibilities of benevolence with greater or less conviction, advocating the importance of 'works' rather than 'faith' in living a good life, and holding in the highest moral esteem the 'good man' who manages to combine personal chastity and public charity.

There can be no doubt that these ideas or priorities or allegiances infiltrate Fielding's non-fictional work regularly, and no one could deny that even the author of the novels strives to endorse them where he can. Battestin cites copious and persuasive examples of the representation of such 'latitudinarian' views from the novels and periodical writings, but he then goes on more contentiously to argue that Fielding adhered to a fully coherent, self-conscious moral and religious position, in which the positive forces of active good nature and charity are consistently given their due prominence. In this reading, the novels become deliberate and confident demonstrations of the moral and religious beliefs seen to be held by the author, in this particular case illustrated by the twin examples of Joseph himself and his friend and mentor Parson Adams. In contrast, then, to the insignificant antique figure dismissed by F.R. Leavis, or the great designer praised by R.S. Crane, Henry Fielding thus becomes once again a novelist of ideas, and a writer of developed moral sensitivity.

However, while accepting the incontrovertible evidence of its influence, I take the case about the 'latitudinarianism' in Fielding to be more volatile and complex than Battestin suggests, especially when dealing with the novels. In wrestling with the forms of comic and satiric fiction that were available to him, Fielding had to inflect his views, whatever they might have been, and they may thus acquire a wholly different emphasis and status within the confines of the narratives, no matter what personal importance they may have had outwith them. However much Fielding the man may or may not have wanted to believe in a benevolist reading of human nature, and however much these notions can be recovered from his diverse literary productions, he nonetheless had to confront the overwhelming evidence of human selfishness and hypocrisy which contravened the latitudinarian position, and these points of stress become particularly prominent in the dramatised peripatetic narratives of his fiction.

As a result, I believe that much of Fielding's writing shows a more dialectic (or even dialogic) rendering of latitudinarian principles, where they are voiced in opposition to equally important episodes which seem to contradict them. In the comic novels especially, the structuring device of the episodic journey constantly introduces evidence of malice, envy, hypocrisy, affectation and greed, rather than of benevolence or fellow feeling, and the sermonising reading which Battestin looks for in the books becomes obscured in the complexities and confusions of the internal debate. As I see it, the novels then offer at best an adversarial account of 'latitudinarian' affiliations, where such beliefs have to participate in dialogue with other contending and contradictory notions, the narrative offering a series of dynamic confrontations rather than the unmediated processional expression of one particular point of view.

Even in Fielding's non-fictional works, the case for 'good nature' is often represented adversarially, in contest with the evidence which seems to confute it. In his *Essay on the Knowledge and Characters of Men*, for instance, published in the first volume of his *Miscellanies* (1743), and referred to extensively by Battestin, Fielding dialectically defines 'Good-Nature' in opposition to the opposing quality of 'Good-Humour':

> Good-Nature is that benevolent and amiable Temper of Mind which disposes us to feel the Misfortunes, and enjoy the Happiness of others; and consequently pushes us on to promote the latter, and prevent the former; and that without any abstract Contemplation on the Beauty of Virtue, and without the Allurements and Terrors of Religion.[14]

The definition of 'Good-Nature' is clear, and seems to be confidently voiced. But however noble and humane this quality might be, Fielding remains in no doubt that it is rare, a remarkable feature of the human personality rather than a representative one. Even in this essay, he is prepared to surround 'Good-Nature' with all the customary obstacles and impediments to its operations:

> Thus, without asserting in general, that Man is a deceitful Animal, we may, I believe, appeal for Instances of Deceit to the Behaviour of some Children and Savages. When this Quality therefore is nourished and improved by Education, in which we are taught rather to conceal Vices, than to cultivate Virtues; when it hath sucked in the Instruction of Politicians, and is instituted in the *Art of thriving*, it will be no Wonder that it should grow to that monstrous Height to which we sometimes see it arrive.   (*Misc I*, p. 154)

The evidence for the very existence of 'Good-Nature' has to be weighed up against the copious evidence for all the contrary and contending qualities, and it may be that within the confrontational and ironised structure of his novels, Fielding comes up with an assessment of the relative possibilities radically different from the one that he offers in his non-fiction.

But even in the *Miscellanies*, he is eager to show both sides of the coin. In his elegant and confident poem *Of Good-Nature*, also taken by Battestin as persuasive evidence of the strength of Fielding's commitments, the author examines the meaning and possibility of natural goodness, at first giving the most optimistic account of its existence:

> What by this Name, then, shall be understood?
> What? but the glorious Lust of doing Good?
> The Heart that finds it Happiness to please,

Can feel another's Pain, and taste his Ease.
The Cheek that with another's Joy can glow,
Turn pale, and sicken with another's Woe;
Free from Contempt and Envy, he who deems
Justly of Life's two opposite Extremes.
Who to make all and each Man truly blest,
Doth all he can, and wishes all the rest?

(*Misc* I, p. 31)

This new sermonising and pious Fielding may be a rather surprising figure for us to encounter, given the abusive and vitriolic satirical energies we have identified earlier and elsewhere in his career. But the initially assertive presentation of 'good nature' is complicated by the ensuing awareness of its fragility. The existence of 'good nature' may not entirely be in doubt, but neither is it given a completely free run. Even in this confident poem, the power of good nature is seen to be limited and contested by the strongest contrary urges, its existence figured only tentatively:

Who wonders that Good-nature in so few,
Can Anger, Lust, or Avarice subdue?
When the cheap Gift of Fame our Tongues deny,
And risque our own, to poison with a Lie.

(*Misc* I, p. 34)

There are a number of similar passages in *The Champion* and *The Covent-Garden Journal*, as well as in many of Fielding's later pamphlets about crime, most notably in his *Enquiry into the Causes of the Late Increase of Robbers* (1753), in all of which the possibility of benevolence is, as it were, put on trial, and no unanimous verdict about its power or its efficacy is reached. The benevolent comedy of good nature in Fielding is always beset and jeopardised by powerful contending ironies and satire, as if the author had a much clearer idea of the complex problems besetting his society than of any simple or universal solution to them. To accept part of Battestin's case, there can be no doubt that Fielding thought 'good nature' or benevolence to be valuable. However, despite the confidence with which Battestin asserts Fielding's beliefs, there must be room to doubt whether the author thought it was possible, in a world as corrupt as this one, to enact any such qualities.

In the comic novels, this dialectical tension between 'good nature' and its many adversaries is expressed dialogically. That is to say, Fielding as novelist does not offer a programmatic or proselytising account of 'good nature', arguing wholly on its behalf. Rather, the representation of the two main examples in the novel (Joseph and Adams) shows him preferring to introduce, with the appearance of disinterest, the evidence for and against its prevalence. But that evidence is always personalised and dramatised, conducted through different voices and characters and attitudes, rather than remaining contained within a monoglot argument. As stated in the opening sentence of *Joseph Andrews*: 'It is a trite but true Observation, that Examples work more forcibly on the Mind than Precepts' (JA, p. 15). And by concentrating on the creation of many such 'Examples', Fielding relies heavily on interruption and inconsistency, eventually producing a multi-faceted, heteroglot account of his society in which complication and confusion take precedence over clarity and precision.

To take just one obvious example, it is clear that one idea recurrently debated in *Joseph Andrews* is the power of sexual attraction, conventionally associated with the moral issue of the possibility of living a virtuous life of chastity – an issue already formulated in one way in *Pamela*. As we have seen, Fielding's contemporary reputation was not one which would suggest a firm personal commitment to the ideal of chastity, or to any easy equation of virtue and sexual inexperience. But, whatever Henry Fielding's private views on this subject might or might not have been, there is no simple homiletic sermon to be found inside this narrative. As it expresses itself through sexual desire and restraint, the power of 'good nature' is characteristically rendered in *Joseph Andrews* through dramatised paradoxes and antimonies, fully encompassed by ironies, rather than through shining examples given unequivocal endorsement by the narrator.

We have already seen how Fielding re-read Pamela's version of chastity in *Shamela* to make it seem self-serving and covetous, the very opposite of the pious restraint it pretended to be. In his own later novel, he returns to this question again, and further ironises the issue of chastity by turning the helpless female victim of the original into a rather robust young man, brother of the revered Pamela Andrews, and by making the main sexual predators women of a certain age. Indeed, after extracting familiar bawdy comedy from the pursuit of Joseph by Lady Booby and Mrs Slipslop, making the sexual desires of unattractive middle-aged women an easy and obvious subject for ridicule, the book compiles a compendium of sexual possibilities. These range from the prolonged chaste courtship of the astonishingly constant Joseph and his beloved (and equally robust) Fanny, through to the casual promiscuity of the more urban high-life characters, dramatised further in the story of 'Leonora the Unfortunate Jilt' and the version of fashionable London life recounted by Mr Wilson.

The traditionally understood comic features of relations between the sexes are heightened intermittently, particularly in the contrast between the antagonistic marriage of the Tow-wouses, and the more relaxed sexual standards of Betty the Chambermaid. However, even within the overall comic structure, the book does not neglect to recognise the potentially dangerous intensities of sexual passion in the much more disturbing threats of rape and sexual coercion which surface from time to time in the narrative, usually when Fanny is menaced by various assailants.

Time and again throughout the novel, Fielding returns to the ironist's fundamental notion that in all human affairs things are not as straightforward as they seem, or as we might like them to be, and he intensifies this general principle by showing that sexual attraction (like avarice or the desire for self-preservation or other 'intuitive' features of the human personality) has a splendidly reliable way of revealing the fundamental hypocrisy or ridiculousness of most people's conduct. The basic urges associated with sex cut across artificial distinctions in rank or social standing and make even the most coy and polite behaviour seem like affectation.

In the Preface, that revelation of affectation is announced as the satiric basis of his *exposé*:

> The only Source of the true Ridiculous (as it appears to me) is Affectation. But tho' it arises from one Spring only, when we consider the infinite Streams into which the one branches, we shall presently cease to admire at the copious Field it affords to an Observer. Now Affectation proceeds from one of these two Causes, Vanity, or Hypocrisy: for as Vanity puts us on affecting false Characters, in order to purchase Applause; so Hypocrisy sets us on an Endeavour to avoid Censure by concealing our Vices under an Appearance of their opposite Virtues . . .   (JA, p. 6)

The book then compiles a user's guide to the 'true Ridiculous', itemising the stealthy workings of affectation, vanity and hypocrisy in everyday life as they are particularly provoked by sexual desire and by our contact with the misfortunes of others, dramatised through a gallery of recognisable separately voiced social types rather than a more abstract range of argumentative positions.

In the early episodes concerning Joseph and Lady Booby, Fielding offers another derisive parody of *Pamela*, reappraising the sexual politics of the servant–employer relationship by switching the genders of the protagonists. However, at the same time, he broadens the intertextual range of his narrative by ironically naturalising and rewriting the story of Joseph and Potiphar's wife from the Book of Genesis (37: 7–20). The biblical Joseph is a servant sexually tempted by his master's wife. He refuses to accede to her advances, out of a sense of duty to his master and to God, provoking fury in the woman, who then contrives to have him imprisoned. So, too, in Fielding's version, the dashing young Joseph spurns the advances of the dowager Lady Booby, barely one week into her widowhood, as well as those of her grotesque attendant Mrs Slipslop, through a combination of an immediate sense of distaste, not a little naivety, the shining awareness of his famous sister's exemplary conduct, and his deep sense of duty to and devotion for his beloved Fanny. Joseph thus triumphantly displays a remarkable example of personal integrity and 'good nature'. In consequence, inevitably, he is dismissed from his post without future prospects of employment.

As Fielding ironically represents the episode, the question of personal morality cannot be considered entirely in isolation. Lady Booby moves through a squalid world of gossip and insinuation, to which Joseph is more or less blind. In the context of the comic novel, his resolute refusal to respond to her advances may well be understood as an amusing revelation of his rustic naivety and incomprehension as much as a definite act of moral principle. He does indicate in his first letter to his sister that he entertains certain suspicions about Lady Booby's intentions:

> Don't tell any body what I write, because I should not care to have Folks say I discover what passes in our Family, but if it had not been so great a Lady, I should have thought she had had a mind to me. Dear *Pamela*, don't tell any body: but she has ordered me to sit down by her Bed-side, when she was in naked Bed; and she held my Hand, and talked exactly as a Lady does to her Sweetheart in a Stage-Play, which I have seen in *Covent-Garden*, while she wanted him to be no better than he should be. (JA, p. 27)

Joseph may well have his suspicions, later to be graphically confirmed. Nonetheless it has already been made clear that, even if he passes for a young man of fashion in London society, at once more masculine and more feminine than his fellows, he is to remain at heart incorruptible – 'they could not teach him to game, swear, drink, nor any other genteel Vice the town abounded with' (JA, p. 22).[15] In the representation of Joseph, then, as so often in this book, the comic celebration of extreme innocence jostles alongside the satiric exposure of the iniquities of contemporary life. The dramatic interaction of the characters complicates any simple sermonising, and 'good nature' exists in the book as a device to enable the satiric revelation of prevailing contrary qualities as much as a privileged moral point of reference or shining example to readers.

So part of Joseph's function in the narrative is to act as the conventional 'innocent abroad' whose extraordinary combination of integrity and naivety allows Fielding the novelist to reveal what seems to him to be the more normal and prevailing attributes of humanity – self-interest and lust – and to dramatise the comic consequences of what he sees as the notion of 'male chastity'. This notion may well be taken to represent some kind of positive moral force in the predominantly seamy world of the novel, endorsed and advocated by an extra-diegetic authorial 'Christian censor', as Battestin would have it, but it is also quite clearly a notion with extensive comic potential, introducing ridiculous possibilities which the narrative is more than eager to realise and exploit. Joseph fights off the comic advances of Lady Booby and Mrs Slipslop, just as Fanny tries to fight off the more violent and dangerous advances of Beau Didapper's servant and others. But although chastity is here seen as active resistance, a more empowering quality than its passive equivalent in Richardson, as a preservation of the self against unwelcome encroachment, Fielding complicates the sexual politics of his book by showing the serpentine confusions of sexual attraction, and the moral confusions and turbulence which one person's chastity can provoke in a world where such selfless restraint is exceptionally rare.

As Joseph and Abraham Adams are resting up at the Tow-wouses' inn, they (and we) encounter the splendidly vivid character of Betty the Chambermaid:

> She had Good-nature, Generosity and Compassion, but unfortunately, her Constitution was composed of those warm Ingredients, which,

though the Purity of Courts or Nunneries might have happily controuled them, were by no means able to endure the ticklish situation of a Chamber-maid at an Inn, who is daily liable to the Solicitations of Lovers of all Complexions, to the dangerous Addresses of fine Gentlemen of the Army, who sometimes are obliged to reside with them a whole Year together, and above all are exposed to the Caresses of Footmen, Stage-Coachmen, and Drawers; all of whom employ the whole Artillery of kissing, flattering, bribing, and every other Weapon which is to be found in the whole Armory of Love, against them. (JA, p. 75)

The military imagery here is jocular and mock-heroic, but the notion of sexual attraction being a kind of combat between unequal forces lies deep at the heart of this novel, just as it does of *Pamela*. However, unlike Pamela's strength of character, Betty's 'good nature' in this context becomes weakening, enfeebling her resistance to the many sexual advances she receives, and it is successively overcome by 'an Ensign of Foot', who infects her with some venereal disease, 'the Rhetorick of *John* the Hostler, with a new Straw Hat, and a Pint of Wine', '*Tom Whipwell* the Stage-Coachman, and now and then a handsome young Traveller' (JA, pp. 75–6).

Good-natured Betty thus selectively accommodates only those males who have the appropriate qualifications, even though we may be invited to see these qualifications as rather undemanding and easily gained. The 'Rhetorick' of John the Hostler sounds unimpressive, and can in any case be easily enhanced by the right kind of gifts, and in the splendidly ambiguous final phrase it is left tantalisingly uncertain as to whether youth and handsomeness are the attributes of one lover or the qualifications of many. The fact that she accommodates these suitors 'now and then' is perhaps yet a further indication of a rather relaxed sense of sexual selectivity.

As we have already seen from the Lady Booby and Mrs Slipslop episodes, Joseph himself clearly has these appropriate personal qualities of youth and handsomeness in abundance, so his arrival on the scene is immediately welcomed by the 'warm', temporarily unattached Betty:

Ever since *Joseph's* arrival, *Betty* had conceived an extraordinary Liking to him, which discovered itself more and more, as he grew better and better; till that fatal Evening, when, as she was warming his Bed, her Passion grew to such a Height, and so perfectly mastered both her

Modesty and her Reason, that after many fruitless Hints, and sly Insinuations, she at last threw down the Warming-Pan, and embracing him with great Eagerness, swore he was the handsomest Creature she had ever seen.

Joseph in great Confusion leapt from her, and told her, he was sorry to see a young Woman cast off all Regard to Modesty: but she had gone too far to recede, and grew so very indecent, that Joseph was obliged, contrary to his Inclination, to use some Violence to her, and taking her in his Arms, he shut her out of the Room, and locked the Door.

How ought Man to rejoice, that his Chastity is always in his own power, that if he hath sufficient Strength of Mind, he hath always a competent Strength of Body to defend himself: and cannot, like a poor weak Woman, be ravished against his Will.   (JA, p. 76)

The narrative presentation of this boisterous episode is worth considering. Although this entire passage is, of course, fundamentally controlled by the narrator, it moves its local centre of attention around. The narrating 'voice' may always be Fielding's (or, remembering Wayne C. Booth's more cautious account, that of his authorial personality), but the point of perspective moves from character to character.

It is invariably the narrator who speaks, but it is varying characters who see the events, and from whose point of view they are rendered. In the first paragraph, the 'focalizer' is Betty: in the second it is Joseph. Her experience is first given priority, to be replaced by his, before eventually both of the participants are replaced by the ironic and controlled voice of the moralising narrator. The effect of this dispersal of focus is to create and articulate confusion, to show how one episode can be differently experienced and understood by the separate participants in it, reinforcing the indeterminacy of the 'closed' text and surely putting in serious doubt the solemnity or universal applicability of the concluding moral assessment.[16]

At this point, my disagreement with Battestin's serious and single-minded reading is sharpened. If Fielding, writing as a 'serious man', was seeking to articulate 'latitudinarian' thinking, without inter-ference, offering an unqualified endorsement of good nature and the practical good life, he would surely have to assess and convey the moral complexities of this event. In fact, Battestin sees him as doing so, and he argues that Betty's good nature and other generous qualities 'more than atone for her indiscretions' (Battestin, p. 111). Yet the episode as it is represented in the novel seems to me to be more complex both in significance and perspective than Battestin allows. There is no unambiguous indication within the text itself that Betty has in fact anything to 'atone' for – the religious language of 'atonement' does not figure anywhere in the novel's representation of the episode. In a more worldly, more ironic reading of the passage, Betty simply is what she is. And Joseph's stout resistance to her 'warmth', rather than acting as a bright moral beacon in a murky world, actually introduces further complications and makes life more difficult for the other characters.

As the episode is developed, we see the ramifications of one man's remarkable chastity in a complex world where such qualities are rare and lead to frustation. After being violently ejected by Joseph, the vulnerable and scorned Betty seeks her consolation elsewhere:

Betty was in the most violent Agitation at this Disappointment. Rage and Lust pulled at her Heart, as with two Strings, two different Ways; one moment she thought of stabbing Joseph, the next, of taking him in her Arms, and devouring him with Kisses; but the latter Passion was far more prevalent. Then she thought of revenging his Refusal upon herself: but whilst she was engaged in this Meditation, happily Death presented himself to her in so many Shapes of drowning, hanging, poisoning, &c. that her distracted Mind could resolve on none. In this Perturbation of Spirit, it accidentally occured to her Memory, that her Master's Bed was not made, she therefore went directly to his Room; where he happened at that time to be engaged at his Bureau. As soon as she saw him, she attempted to retire: but he called her back, and taking her by the hand, squeezed her so tenderly, at the same time whispering so many soft things into her Ears, and, then pressed her so closely with his Kisses, that the vanquished Fair-One, whose Passions were already raised, and which were not so whimsically capricious that one Man only could lay them, though perhaps, she would have preferred that one: The vanquished Fair-One quietly, submitted, I say, to her Master's Will, who had just attained the Accomplishment of his Bliss, when Mrs. Tow-wouse unexpectedly entered the Room, and caused all that Confusion which we have before seen, and which it is not necessary at present to take any farther Notice of: Since without the Assistance of a single Hint from us, every Reader of any Speculation, or Experience, though not married himself, may easily conjecture, that it concluded with the Discharge of Betty, the Submission of Mr. Tow-wouse, with some things to be performed on his side by way of Gratitude for his Wife's Goodness in being reconciled to him, with many hearty Promises never to offend any more in the like

> manner: and lastly, his quietly and contentedly bearing to be reminded of his Transgressions, as a kind of Penance, once or twice a Day, during the Residue of his Life.   (JA, pp. 76–7)

This long passage brings together many of what I see as the most salient narrative and ideological features of the text. Its delight in the convolution of sexual attraction and the emotional disturbances that passion can create, and its reliance on the role of coincidence and complication, surely aligns it with exuberant and uproarious sexual comedy rather than with a judgemental moral attitude, however relaxed or tolerant that moral attitude might be thought to be.

Yet at the same time as it celebrates comic effects of sexual desire, the episode is also trying to make a satiric point about the sterility of contemporary marriages, through the awful Tow-wouses, and to maintain its dialogue with 'every Reader of any Speculation, or Experience'. In short, Fielding uses this example to reveal the complications of a world in which there is very little honest affection, and very little opportunity for decisive and successful moral intervention, rather than one in which there might be momentary triumphs for the well-intentioned and benevolent. Despite the authority with which Battestin speaks, it is surely very difficult to locate the strong voice of a 'Christian censor' anywhere in this extract.

In this particular episode, as in many others, the author experiments with the confusions of perspective created by multiple characterisation, and his presiding role ironises the whole event. There is little evidence here that he is primarily seeking to turn it into a useful parable offering coherent advice to his readers about how they might maintain good nature in a corrupt world. And this exposure of the misdirections and confusions surrounding sexuality in the contemporary world does not stand in isolation. It is further dramatised in the interpolated tale of Bellarmine and Leonora, and the history of Mr Wilson, as well as in the other complex trysts within the main narrative, which reappraise the misunderstandings involved in sexual attraction through a range of literary forms and moods.

Another episode where comedy and satire jostle each other is in the famous rewriting of the biblical parable of the good Samaritan (Luke, 10: 30–7). Joseph, travelling to be reunited with his beloved Fanny, has been cruelly set upon by a pair of highwaymen, robbed, beaten, and finally left naked in a ditch. As he begins to recover, initiating the series of deep groans that reverberate throughout the novel, a stage-coach passes by. Like the coach full of the spirits of the recently deceased in the second chapter of A Journey from This World to the Next (1743), this conveyance turns out to be a miniature version of the contemporary social world, containing a number of representative figures.

As the vehicle passes by, the postillion hears Joseph's groan, assumes for some reason that the groaner is therefore dead, and asks the coachman to stop. The coachman is reluctant to delay, since he is running late, but eventually he does agree to pull up. Once the naked and abused Joseph is discovered, the passengers respond as they think fit. An 'old Gentleman' urges them to hurry on, lest they are robbed too. A younger man 'who belonged to the Law' counsels caution, suggesting that, having been foolish enough to stop, they should now save Joseph, not out of fellow-feeling or altruism, but just in case by leaving him they are accidentally incriminated in his death. A 'Lady' expresses horror at the prospect 'for she had rather stay in that Place to all Eternity, than Ride with a naked Man'. The coachman wonders who would be responsible for Joseph's fare if they did take him up. Then, as the lawyer explains the legal implications of leaving Joseph to die, and as the old Gentleman sees in the naked figure 'frequent Opportunities of shewing his Wit to the Lady', a majority decision is reached to assist Joseph after all. It is even boldly suggested that the coachman may have been 'a little moved with Compassion at the poor Creature's Condition'.

So far, the laconically expressed rewriting of the biblical parable seems to heighten the topicality of its social satire. But a further complication remains. Inspired by the 'spotless Example of the amiable Pamela, and the excellent Sermons of Mr. Adams', Joseph refuses to enter the coach until he is decently covered, and this presents a problem:

Though there were several great Coats about the Coach, it was not easy to get over this Difficulty which Joseph had started. The two Gentlemen complained they were cold, and could no spare a Rag; the Man of Wit saying, with a Laugh, that Charity began at home; and the Coachman, who had two great Coats spread under him, refused to lend either, lest they should be made bloody; the Lady's Footman desired to be excused for the same Reason, which the Lady herself, notwithstanding her Abhorence of a naked Man, approved: and it is more than probable, poor Joseph, who obstinately adhered to his modest Resolution, must have perished, unless the Postillion (a Lad who hath been since transported for robbing a Hen-roost) had voluntarily stript off a great Coat, his only Garment, at the same time swearing a great Oath, (for which he was rebuked by the Passengers) 'that he would rather ride in his Shirt all his Life, than suffer a Fellow-Creature to lie in so miserable a Condition'.   (JA, pp. 46–7)

The serpentine confusions and complexities of this episode are worth lingering over. Clearly, and most importantly, the fact that the only act of spontaneous generosity comes from the 'lowest' character on the scene introduces a conventional satiric perspective on the events, and the sceptical social analysis is given great prominence.

The assorted representatives of contemporary high life in the coach are uniformly mean-spirited and egocentric, concerned only with their own well-being and self-interest. The intermediary figure of the coachman may possess some tiny spark of compassion, but he has little avenue through which to express it, being more concerned with money and the requirements of his job. And, in a further sardonic twist, the generous postillion is in no way exalted by his generosity. Not only do the passengers immediately rebuke him for swearing, he suffers a grimmer fate at some unspecified later date. In an unusual and chronologically disruptive extra-diegetic intrusion, the narrator provides us with evidence of an event taking place long after this episode, known to none of the other participants in it – 'a Lad who hath since been transported for robbing a Hen-roost'. The biblical injunction 'Go thou and do likewise', with which the 'Good Samaritan' parable is concluded, seems to be markedly absent from this recounting of the original, and it is made singularly unattractive. The rewards for such spontaneous generosity in the world of *Joseph Andrews* as the narrator tells us, are typically nothing more than abuse and transportation.

So it looks at first as though this episode is couched in a reasonably familiar satiric language, exposing to ridicule and thereby condemning the affectations of the wealthier characters, and paradoxically showing how basic human decency may be found in the most surprising places, overlooked and unrewarded. This point is reinforced immediately afterwards, when the coach is held up by those very highwaymen who attacked Joseph, and the travellers instantly behave in an even more hypocritical and cowardly way, once again revealing their true selves. Even when they reach the eventual safety of an inn, normal service resumes as soon as possible with all the characters looking out only for themselves. By rewriting the parable of the good Samaritan in these contemporary terms, Fielding finds a perspective from which to castigate his own society for its failures of generosity and compassion, and from which to discover the virulence of affectation and hypocrisy.

But even that is not the whole story. This passage clearly does satirise the sanctimonious behaviour of the wealthy, and it does ironically aggrandise the humble postillion, but we cannot overlook what it does with the nominal exemplary hero, Joseph himself. By concentrating on his embarrassment rather than on his pain, and by making such a spectacle of the naked figure awkwardly trying to hide himself from the curious eyes of the fine lady, the episode carnivalises the whole experience. In the original biblical parable, the poor victim is not personalised in any way, although he is 'stripped . . . of his raiment' and Fielding's incorporation of the uncomfortable, modest Joseph, anxious 'to prevent giving the least Offence to Decency' (JA, p. 47) seems to redirect the passage away from single-minded orthodox corrective satire (away, that is, from the operation of a 'Christian censor') towards a more anarchic comedy of errors. Apart from the postillion, everybody in this episode behaves farcically, and no clear point of judgemental perspective is offered either by the narrator or by any privileged participant.

Similar ironic undercutting and destabilisation of perspective is persistent throughout the portrayal of the book's other principal character, Abraham Adams. Again, the biblical parallels are prominent and unmistakable, if at times difficult to interpret. As the name so obviously suggests, Abraham Adams is a version of both Abraham the law-giver, and Adam the original of all humanity. Not only is he the devoted father of a large family, inconsolable with grief when mistakenly told of the death of his son, he also arbitrates in disputes with learned argument, broad fist, and stout crabstick, and all the time he strives to lay down the law in a resolutely Old Testament manner.

At the same time, of course, Adams represents the contending figure of the knight errant Don Quixote in this narrative, living on illusions gleaned not from chivalric romance but from the Bible and the classics. Just as the Don tries to live a heroic life in a resolutely unheroic world, Adams tries to live an austere Christian life in a secular world of conspicuous consumption. Also like Don Quixote, Adams seems at times too large a figure for the book he inhabits, and

Fielding makes efforts to install him in the popular imagining of his culture by citing him elsewhere. In 1743, it is Adams's authority which is ironically used to attest to the authenticity of *A Journey from This World to the Next*, and in 1748, the parson takes to writing letters to Fielding's *Jacobite's Journal*.

Fielding may have come to see in Adams the possibility of what we would now call a 'serial' character, a recurring and recognisably affiliated figure like 'Isaac Bickerstaffe' of *The Tatler* or 'Sir Roger de Coverly' of *The Spectator*. As he is first introduced, in Book I, Chapter iii, both his undoubted moral integrity and his obvious comic potential are immediately made clear:

> Mr. *Abraham Adams* was an excellent Scholar. He was a perfect Master of the *Greek* and *Latin* Languages; to which he added a great Share of Knowledge in the Oriental Tongues, and could read and translate *French, Italian* and *Spanish*. He had applied many years to the most severe Study, and had treasured up a Fund of Learning rarely to be met with in a University. He was besides a Man of good Sense, good Parts, and good Nature . . .   (JA, p. 19)

In this ringing character reference, Adams is praised for his extraordinary and unrewarded learning – which may partly explain why he seems sympathetic and heroic to so many academic critics – as well as for his fundamental goodness. Even this early in the novel, however, experienced readers of Fielding will be awaiting the appearance of one significant little word, and it arrives immediately:

> . . . but was at the same time as entirely ignorant of the Ways of this World, as an infant just entered into it could possibly be. As he had never any intention to deceive, so he never suspected such a Design in others. He was generous, friendly and brave to an Excess; but Simplicity was his Characteristic . . . His Virtue and his other Qualifications, as they rendered him equal to his Office, so they made him an agreeable and valuable Companion, and had so much endeared and well recommended him to a Bishop, that at the Age of Fifty, he was provided with a handsome Income of twenty-three Pounds a Year; which however, he could not make any great Figure with: because he lived in a dear Country, and was a little encumbered with a Wife and six Children.   (*ibid.*)

As the reservations about Adams's complete lack of worldliness are presented, the oscillation between comedy and satire reappears. The simplicity of Adams is not only a way of reappraising the implausible protestations of innocence offered throughout Cibber's *Apology*, it also introduces yet another robust naive figure to be set loose on the contemporary world, whose integrity and lack of embarrassment can be used to show up the affectations of others within the text.

Internally, as many critics have shown, Adams is used to examine the moral and social state of the contemporary clergy, and demonstrate the power of money. Subsisting on his meagre annual income of £23 with his large family – it works out at approximately one shilling (five pence) per head per week – Adams in his torn cassock follows the proper biblical models in refusing to pile up treasures upon earth, and stands as a model by which we may judge his fellow professionals in the tale. Unlike the money-oriented inn-keepers, surgeons, coachmen, lawyers, justices of the peace, and all the other stoutly materialist citizens of the novel, Adams in his obvious poverty represents an honourable contempt of worldly riches, although it is a contempt problematised by his continual inability to pay his bills or come to the assistance of the needy or even look after himself properly.

The recurrent emphasis on Adams's poverty is both part of the general satiric fabric of the book, and a more intense topical allusion. Specifically, the subject of the distressed clergy and their dependents was prominent in public discussion at this time, and it appeared in a number of Fielding's non-fictional texts as well as in all three of his novels, receiving particular attention in *The Champion* in 1740 and *The Jacobite's Journal* in 1748. As Battestin argues, it is clear from these that the author was extremely well versed in the contemporary controversies about how the clergy should conduct themselves, and that he saw this issue as representative of many of the failings of his contemporary society, making it a more important concern in *Joseph Andrews* than, say, the equally frequent contemporary discussion about how lawyers should properly conduct themselves, or inn-keepers for that matter (Battestin, pp. 130–6).

In the narrative of *Joseph Andrews*, the travellers encounter six different clergymen, all of whom are disfigured by vanity, hypocrisy or affectation in ways that dignify the honest poverty and spiritual integrity of Adams, especially the vain and worldly figures of the port-drinking Parson Barnabas and the pig-keeping Parson Trulliber. In comparison with these two high-living figures, Adams emerges as not quite of this world, but as nonetheless noble and genuinely devout, as he does in his extended dialogue with the small-spirited lawyer, Peter Pounce. Yet, of course, Fielding is equally at pains to make his model clergyman seem absent-minded, misguided and hopelessly gullible, his trust in the wisdom of Providence seeming at once entertainingly naive and impressively Stoic. In a complex negotiation with its readers, reminiscent of 'the Manner of Cervantes', the book invites laughter at Adams's persistent ridiculousness as he gets into scraps 'partly owing to his Goodness, and partly to his Inadvertency' (JA, p. 298), while intermittently insinuating moments of disquiet at the scornful basis of that laughter.

The key episode here, central to any full reading of Adams's role in the narrative, is Book III, Chapter vii, 'A Scene of Roasting very nicely adapted to the Present Taste and Times' (JA, p. 216), in which a country squire and his mocking 'Curs', comprising 'an old Half-pay Officer, a Player, a dull Poet, a Quack Doctor, a scraping Fidler, and a lame German Dancing-Master' (JA, p. 218) attempt to 'roast' Adams by playing coarse practical jokes on him, rendering him ridiculous. These jokes are no more subtle or dangerous than spilling soup on the Parson, pulling his chair from beneath him as he tries to sit on it, and tumbling him in a tub of water. No real harm comes to the parson, although his dignity suffers badly. Yet although Adams is in danger only of brief humiliation, the slapstick humour seems deliberately coarsened, forcing us to confront our own responses to Adams's more ridiculous moments.

The narrator positions himself in relation to these events, and to his readers, when he divulges his sources of information about the goings-on. His informant is not the roaring squire, but Adams himself:

> Mr. Adams, from whom we had most of this Relation, could not recollect all the Jests of this kind practised on him, which the inoffensive Disposition of his own Heart made him slow in discovering; and indeed, had it not been for the Information which we received from a Servant of the Family, this Part of our History, which we take to be none of the least curious, must have been deplorably imperfect . . .
>
> (JA, p. 218)

As Adams is chased by dogs, forgets his sermons and his horse, gets punched on the nose by an inn-keeper, has a pan full of hog's blood thrown over him, finds himself in the wrong bed, and suffers all manner of indignities, Fielding challenges his readers to respond appropriately. The obvious response is surely to see Adams as the object of laughter, as a rather absurd tatterdemalion figure, at best as another example of the incongruities of a noble innocence. However, the presence of the coarse mockery of the 'Curs' within the narrative, possibly voicing the laughter of readers, introduces a caricature of a certain kind of response, satirising a certain kind of simple-minded reading, and a certain kind of laughter.

In fact, any derisive laughter generated by Adams's propensity for misadventure has to be balanced against the constant evidence of his 'worthy Inclinations'. Like Joseph's chastity, Adams's charity is often spontaneous and never anything other than genuine. Yet time after time his unworldly idealism leads him into ridiculous positions, stripping him of dignity more often than it ennobles him. Through the presentation of these two characters, the narrative seems to be offered at first as an opportunity for readers to feel comfortably superior, while then more surreptitiously chastening and correcting any tendency to ridicule the hypocritical and the impolitic equally. Adams occasionally fails to live up to the standards he sets himself – his highly emotional response to the apparent loss and recovery of his son contradicts and unveils the elevated trust in Providence he has been preaching. But nonetheless within the narrative it is his idealism, and not its impracticality, which is presented as an example, in contrast to the small-spirited surroundings he inhabits.

Adams, then, although offered as full of 'worthy Inclinations', is no more of an exemplary paragon in the novel than the single-minded Joseph. His constant mishaps and failures to recognise what is happening render him a comic figure, just as his nobility of purpose satirises the smaller visions of those around him. Neither Joseph nor Adams is a fully realised hero, and in each case the reader is challenged to discover within himself or herself the awareness and sophistication which the characters lack. For all the narrative's apparent simplicity, Fielding does not seek to produce a reductive parable of the good life, but rather to offer an incomplete version of it, only to be realised through the active participation of the appropriately intelligent reader. Through the intertext of *Joseph Andrews*, Fielding is able not only to renegotiate his literary terms, but also to use them in pursuit of more intelligent readers. The complex negotiations between the comic and the satiric, the controlled and the anarchic, the erudite and the credulous – all of which are prominent in the text of this novel – become the recurrent traces of

Fielding the *auteur*, sometimes facilitated by the material being presented, and sometimes not. As we shall now see, such points of tension are discernible in very different texts.

Notes and references

1. Henry Fielding, *The History of the Adventures of Joseph Andrews etc.* (1742), ed. Douglas Brooks-Davies (Oxford, 1970), p. 3. Further references will be incorporated in the text.
2. The amusing story about Millar offering Fielding the money is quoted in Martin C. Battestin with Ruthe R. Battestin, *Henry Fielding: A Life* (London, 1989), p. 325.
3. John Dryden, Preface to *An Evening's Love* (1671), in *Of Dramatic Poesy and Other Critical Essays*, ed. G. Watson (London, 1962), I, 146.
4. See Mikhail Bakhtin, *Rabelais and his World* (1965), trans. Helene Iswolsky (Cambridge, Mass., and London, 1968), pp. 27, 36, 97.
5. See Ronald Paulson, *Hogarth: His Life, Art and Times*, abridged edn (New Haven, 1971), p. 205.
6. Henry Fielding, *The Covent-Garden Journal*, ed. Bertrand A. Goldgar (Oxford, 1988), p. 73. Further references will refer to this edition.
7. John Dryden, *Heroic Poetry and Poetic Licence* (1677), in *Of Dramatic Poetry and Other Essays*, ed. G. Watson 2 vols, (London, 1962) vol. I, p. 199.
8. Alexander Pope, *Peri Bathous* in *Selected Prose of Alexander Pope*, ed. Paul Hammond (Cambridge, 1987), p. 206.
9. Michael McKeon, *The Origins of the English Novel 1600–1740* (Baltimore and London, 1987), p. 385.
10. Wolfgang Iser, *The Implied Reader* (Baltimore and London, 1974), p. 39.
11. Umberto Eco, *The Role of the Reader: Explorations in the Semiotics of Texts* (London, 1979), p. 8.
12. See Julia Kristeva, *Desire in Language: A Semiotic Approach to Literature* (1969, 1977), ed. L.S. Gouriez, trans. T. Gora, A. Jardine and L.S. Gouriez (New York, 1980), p. 66.
13. See Martin C. Battestin, *The Moral Basis of Fielding's Art: A Study of 'Joseph Andrews'* (Middletown, Conn., 1959), pp. 3–85. Further page references will be incorporated in the text.
14. Henry Fielding, *Miscellanies* (1743), ed. Henry Knight Miller (Oxford, 1972), p. 158. Further references will be incorporated in the text.
15. See the discussion of 'masculine' and 'feminine' in Angela J. Smallwood, *Fielding and the Woman Question* (New York, 1989), pp. 109–12.
16. See the discussion of 'focalizer' and 'focalization' in Steven Cohan and Linda M. Shires, *Telling Stories: A Theoretical Analysis of Narrative Fiction* (London and New York, 1988), pp. 83–112.

CHAPTER 4
The sublime and the ridiculous

This world (and the next)

GREAT. Applied to a Thing, signifies Bigness; when to a Man, often Littleness, or Meanness.[1]

But now, when party and prejudice carry all before them, when learning is decried, wit not understood, when the theatres are puppet shows and the comedians ballad singers, when fools lead the town, would a man think to thrive by his wit? If you must write, write nonsense, write operas, write entertainments, write *Hurlothrumbos*, set up an *Oratory* and preach nonsense, and you may meet with encouragement enough. If you would receive applause, deserve to receive sentence at the Old Bailey; and if you would ride in your coach, deserve to ride in a cart.[2]

Despite the great popular success of *Joseph Andrews* in Britain and, by virtue of its many translations, throughout Europe in the eighteenth century, its author was not immediately showered with either riches or esteem, and Fielding spent the financially difficult years following its publication casting around for new literary projects which would allow him to live in the manner to which he was eager to become accustomed. However, given the material conditions of authorship at the time, the nature of publishing and the composition of the literary audience, Fielding's attempts to 'thrive by his wit' in the 1740s were not at first conspicuously dignified or obviously fruitful.

We must remember that his actual income from the huge sales of his novel was, to say the least, modest. In a straightforward cash transaction, he is believed to have received the sum of £200 for the copyright of his book from the entrepreneurial and unusually honest Scottish publisher Andrew Millar. Although this was seen as an uncharacteristically substantial payment for a first novel, and was thought by Fielding himself at the time to be remarkably generous – it is said that he had been previously offered no more than £25 for the manuscript and the copyright – it was also a shrewd business move on the publisher's part and it represented nothing like enough to enable its recipient to be a man of independent means.

After all, thanks to the bookseller's apparent act of *largesse*, Fielding might have suddenly been £200 better off, and able at least temporarily to satisfy the pressing demands of his many creditors, but as a conventional part of the arrangement he received no subsequent royalties whatsoever from the sales of his book, however enormous these might be, or from the various translations and adaptations. From the moment of the agreement onwards, *Joseph Andrews* was Andrew Millar's property, not Henry Fielding's, and he could do with it more or less whatever he wanted. And although the author retained the right to renegotiate with his publisher when he revised the original text for any subsequent editions, as Fielding did quite extensively later in 1742 and again in 1743, he was helpless to prevent or capitalise upon the appearance of the many corrupt and inaccurate piracies, serialisations, chapbook editions and other unauthorised redactions of his book, for which he would receive nothing at all.[3]

Fielding's persistent and pressing need for cash throughout the early 1740s led him to continue to 'write entertainments', to turn out political pamphlets and other occasional pieces to order, and it even brought him once again to write for the theatre. His first public work after the publication of *Joseph Andrews* was not another novel, but the largely forgotten oppositional pamphlet *A Full Vindication of her Grace the Dutchess Dowager of Marlborough* published on 2 April 1742. After some other squibs, he tried to capture an audience with the revamped stage farce *The Wedding Day*, a relatively unsuccessful piece which, despite its author's theatrical reputation, barely lasted six nights at Drury Lane in February 1743, bringing the author (according to his own account) no more than £50.

However, of more interest here is his simultaneous work on the compilation of his *Miscellanies*, eventually to be published in three volumes in April 1743. The new project may have been discussed among Fielding's close circle for some time previously but it was first made public in the pages of the *Daily Post* on 5 June 1742, just over three months after the first publication of *Joseph Andrews*, in an advertisement calling for subscribers. After a brief description of the proposed contents of the volumes, the announcement quickly gets down to its real business of drumming up trade:

The Price to Subscribers is One Guinea; and Two Guineas for the
Royal Paper. One Half of which is to be paid at Subscribing, the other
on the Delivery of the Book in Sheets. The Subscribers Names will be
printed.[4]

This method of publication by advance subscription may now seem
unfamiliar, but it was by no means unusual at the time for prestigious
editions of classical works or for more expensive and lavishly produced
texts. For example, John Dryden's handsome edition of Vergil in 1697
had been published by this method, and prospective subscribers to
Fielding's project would already have been familiar with the procedure
through such diverse works as Alexander Pope's massively successful
translations of Homer, which came out in many volumes by
subscription between 1715 and 1726, and John Gay's play *Polly*, the
suppressed sequel to *The Beggar's Opera*, not performed on stage but
successfully published for subscribers in 1729. Possibly inspired by the
enormous financial success of Pope's undertaking, many such
proposals were put before the readers of newspapers and periodicals at
this time, and the eventual appearance or non-appearance of the text
would depend on the enthusiasm of the public's response. That
Fielding chose this method for his *Miscellanies* is not wholly surprising,
but the implications for our understanding of his authorial position
and of his relationship with the audience are worth examining.

First of all, from the subscriber's point of view, taking part in the
publication of a literary project by direct personal sponsorship offered
an opportunity to stand out publicly as a magnanimous patron of the
arts at relatively little expense. When Fielding's advertisement
announces that 'The Subscribers Names will be printed' the promise is
made that the sponsorship would be made public, and that the
subscribers would be given due recognition for their generosity. Thus,
the opportunity to become involved in such a project quite simply
flattered the vanity of the subscribers. In more controversial episodes,
as in the case of the sponsored publication of Gay's suppressed play,
where the subscribers' names were not originally printed in the text,
an act of subscription allowed more cautious dissidents to make a
stealthy yet self-conscious statement of oppositional political
alignment or support for the author without undue personal risk, and
the published text helped create and consolidate an oppositional
community. Rather like the present-day T-shirt printed with an
ideologically impeccable slogan about dolphins or rain forests, the

subscribed book in the eighteenth century could provide its
subscribers and consumers with both an avenue for public statement
and a desirable fashion accessory, an opportunity to display an
affiliation or make a gestural stand without actually having to put
anything uncomfortable or disturbing (or dangerous) into practice.

The attractions of subscription publication did not end there. For
publishers, even if the eventual revenue from a particular subscribed
title or series might not be great, it was more or less foolproof. In the
eyes of the bookseller, the subscription had something of the charm of
the modern 'vanity press', where the main expenses of printing and
distribution were guaranteed in advance, and the elements of venture
capital and risk associated with more popular publishing were kept
more or less under control through a guaranteed print run. From the
author's point of view, too, publishing by subscription held a number
of obvious advantages. The author working with a list of subscribers
was a more powerful and authoritative figure than the author who had
sold his copyright, in that he (or, infrequently, she) could then
relegate the bookseller to a secondary position, simply employing him
as an agent to carry out a particular printing and distribution job.

When copyright was sold outright, as it more usually was, the
author seemed to be working on behalf of the publisher: with
subscriptions, that relationship was reversed. In Fielding's case, such
an assumption of proprietorial control over his work was clearly an
important issue. Unlike the unusually fortunate Samuel Richardson,
who was able to print and publish his own novels, Fielding was forced
into negotiation with middle-men to organise the distribution of his
books, and ensure the proper recognition for his authorship of them.
As his career developed, Fielding's authorial role became more central
to the presentation of his texts, but it never obliterated the presence
of the publisher entirely. Leaving *Shamela* aside as a one-off spoof, we
can see the relationship between author and publisher changing from
text to text. Where the title page of *Joseph Andrews* omitted the
author's name entirely and announced that the book was 'Printed for
A. MILLAR', the title page of the *Miscellanies* gave Fielding's name
great prominence and announced that it was 'Printed for the
AUTHOR; And sold by A. MILLAR'. After the success of *Joseph
Andrews* and the *Miscellanies*, Fielding's name became more visible
again, and it appeared prominently on the title-pages of *Tom Jones*
and *Amelia*, both of which carried the suggestion of greater
partnership between author and publisher. Each of these two title

pages ascribed authorship of the novel to 'Henry Fielding, Esq.' while at the same time acknowledging the persisting role of the copyright-holder – 'Printed for A. MILLAR'.

The subscription for the *Miscellanies* thus gave Fielding the greatest degree of control and the most exalted authorial status he achieved at any point in his publishing career. However, not all authors secured Fielding's degree of public recognition, and only a few could capitalise on the lucrative and ego-boosting possibilities of subscription. For the relatively unknown or hack author, the call for subscriptions was unlikely to be successful, unless the project itself was unusually compelling. But for the author who had established an identity or a 'name' with the more affluent sections of the public, like John Dryden or John Gay, and who could address them confidently, subscriptions could be highly remunerative, as they most famously were with Pope's edition of Shakespeare and his translations of Homer. With the success of Fielding's pre-1737 plays still in living memory, with the prominence of such periodicals as *The Champion* in the preceding three years, and with the recent commercial triumph of *Joseph Andrews*, this author was clearly 'marketable' in this way in the second half of 1742.

By the 1740s, the conventional system of payment associated with this method of publication was that the author kept the bulk of the subscription money (after the deduction of printing, advertising and distribution expenses) and the publisher received the revenue from the subsequent sale of other sets to members of the public. Furthermore, and even more to the author's immediate advantage, half the subscription money came in before publication, indeed in many cases probably even before final composition. The time elapsing between the payment of the subscription and the delivery of the copies could be variable, allowing for minor revisions and even larger editorial efforts, but longer-term projects (for example, Samuel Johnson's massive 1755 *Dictionary of the English Language*) seemed inappropriate for this kind of sponsorship, and they had to rely on the increasingly rare and persistently problematic method of direct individual aristocratic patronage.

From the literary point of view, it must be added, subscription publication not only changed the economic relationship between author and publisher, it also altered the terms of address between author and readers. Unlike the writer of a novel, a poem or a play offered for sale in the orthodox way, an author working in subscription publication had the unusual advantage of knowing precisely who at least some of his readers would be before completing the text, and might then choose to hail these multiple patrons directly, or play more elaborate games with that known reading community. That is to say, the list of names published at the beginning of the book, or, if not made public at least known to the author, empowered the writer much more than other methods of publication could. It allowed the author to fall in line with what that known audience might be expected to want, or it could give the author the opportunity to retain a position of authority and surprise or frustrate the expectations of subscribers, whose names might remain prominent nonetheless. In the present day, perhaps only those harmless drudges who write doctoral theses or monographs on academic subjects addressed to the limited community of fellow-specialists are so fortunate.

The list of subscribers appended to the first edition of a subscription volume did not usually appear formally in subsequent versions, but it could become well-known, and it is worth considering what effect the catalogue of names would have on any other readers who came across it. Other unidentified readers who purchased or gained access to the text at a later date would be positioned in an unusual way, almost as spectators or eavesdroppers, overhearing the dialogue between author and his paymasters, the named subscribers. The best analogy for this procedure comes from the contemporary Augustan playhouse, where those members of the public sitting in the most expensive boxes near (or virtually *on*) the stage could be seen as the prime audience for the drama, to be observed almost as part of the performance by the more amorphous crowd sitting out front. As Hogarth's famous picture of the staging of *The Beggar's Opera* illustrates, with the ironic pairing of figures onstage and offstage, the interconnection of the drama and the most immediate audience could be a provocative and significant part of the overall spectacle for others.[5]

In his *Daily Post* advertisement, Fielding refers to earlier delays in the appearance of the *Miscellanies*, which 'hath been hitherto retarded by the Author's Indisposition last Winter, and a Train of melancholy Accidents scarce to be parallel'd' [sic] (*Misc*, p. xlvi). Despite his claim that 'the Books will very shortly go to Press', it is clear that they were by no means complete at the time of invitation, and, after further delays, the finished sets were not eventually delivered to subscribers until the following April. However, no matter how severe the author's problems in actually preparing the texts might have been, his request for subscriptions was undoubtedly successful – from a total of 427 subscribers, there were 342 orders for the ordinary edition and a further 214 for the deluxe version – and Fielding is computed to have received in total something around 770 guineas (slightly over £800, four times the fee for his first novel) for the planned volumes, half of which came to him some time before they appeared.

The published list of subscribers in the first edition makes for very interesting reading, giving a clear indication of the elevated social status of this particular section of the reading public of the time, and containing suggestive indications of the implied dialogue between the text and its known readers. Many of Fielding's own acquaintance among the better-off classes and the political opposition are predictably lined up, with his new colleagues in the legal profession very strongly represented, but nonetheless it is hard to find any clearly defined common allegiance among those listed. Most interestingly, Robert Walpole, apparently the target of so much sustained criticism in *Jonathan Wild* in the third volume, is down for ten sets of the expensive edition under his new title as the Earl of Orford, an overlooked feature of the publication which certainly further problematises any reading of both this volume and the politics of Fielding's work as a whole, and indicates the unusually intricate difficulties involved in discussing the first audience for or the contemporary reception of his texts.

These social and political questions about the composition of the readership are worthy of greater investigation, but perhaps the financial side of Fielding's publishing is the most immediately important in this context. Given that Fielding was later to receive a cash advance of only £600 from Millar for the copyright to *Tom Jones*, and only £800 from him for *Amelia*, written when Fielding was the hottest literary property around, the financial success of the *Miscellanies* shows the author's persisting connections with a coterie of well-connected readers, existing alongside his new place within the market economy of writing novels addressed to a wider, more anonymous public. The varying methods of publication of Fielding's fiction place him on the cusp between the virtually defunct system of individual aristocratic patronage and the newer apparatus of marketing books through booksellers or publishers to a mass audience, and, as we shall see, the unease and uncertainty arising from that interim and ambivalent position affects the content of his work as much as its method of dissemination.

The effects of the methods of production and dissemination can be seen to infiltrate the main texts in various ways. The complex terms of address between author and reader, for example, which vary so much in Fielding's writing, are at least partly to be explained by the relationship between coterie publishing (addressed to a known audience through subscription) and the less controlled dissemination of the major novels, launched into the down-market void. Fielding's constant challenging of the novel reader's literary competence by the ironic misdirections so prominent in *Joseph Andrews* is only one of a number of signs of his anxiety that the dialogic role of writing for a known community slips into a more monologic form within the market economy and its anonymous 'reading public'.

When the three volumes of the *Miscellanies* eventually appeared, they indicated the rather haphazard genesis of the project, the author seeming to want to 'cash in' on the new celebrity brought to him by the revelation that he was responsible for the popular *Joseph Andrews*. The first volume has a rather apologetic introduction, dismissing most of its contents as *juvenilia*, and emphasising once more the various exculpatory personal difficulties the author was under at the time of composition:

> Indeed when I look a Year or two backwards, and survey the Accidents which have befallen me, and the Distresses I have waded through whilst I have been engaged in these Works, I could almost challenge some Philosophy to myself, for having been able to finish them as I have; and however imperfectly that may be, I am convinced the Reader, was he acquainted with the whole, would want very little Good-nature to extinguish his Disdain at any Faults he meets with.
>
> (*Misc*, pp. 13–14)

Fielding here may be referring to problems arising from his first wife's deteriorating health – Charlotte Cradock Fielding was to die in 1744 after a long illness – or to the sudden death of his eldest daughter in 1742, or simply to the persistently disturbing consequences of his apparently endemic fecklessness. Whatever the particular reason, it is clear that the first volume at least is a somewhat eclectic gathering of various bits and pieces, assembled under pressure. It brings together poems previously published in magazines, epigrams, versions of classical works and longer prose essays on moral subjects, all clearly addressed to a more up-market and literate audience than that conventionally associated with the stage, the novel or even the periodical at the time.

Read in terms of Fielding's personal history, the essay *Of the Remedy of Affliction for the Loss of our Friends* seems close to the sombre concerns of the previous year, dealing as it does with the nature of consolation, the ideas presented clearly and with none of the obvious dramatic irony developed when Adams offers similar views in *Joseph Andrews* (IV, viii). In the context of the *Miscellanies*, the single voice of the essay allows for the uninterrupted presentation of an uncontested view, addressed to a predictable audience, whereas the more heteroglot and confrontational drama of the novel disrupts and challenges the main speaker's claims to authority. Furthermore, there are many passages in pieces like the *Essay on the Knowledge of the Characters of Men* and the poem 'Of Good-Nature' which by their singleness of vision and lack of internal contestation lend serviceable insight into Fielding's stated social and moral ideology, as we have already seen in the preceding discussion of the early comic and burlesque fiction. These texts are all interesting in their own way, and they have been used by such critics as Martin Battestin and Bernard Harrison to help build connections between Fielding's life and his work. However, I have already expressed doubts about that pattern of argument, and, as I see it, not until the second volume is there anything of direct relevance to Fielding's career as an author of extended narratives.

The unfinished prose narrative *A Journey from This World to the Next*, which, along with the texts of *The Wedding-Day* and the 1737 play *Eurydice*, comprises the second volume of the *Miscellanies*, moves away from the innovative forms of contemporary fiction and draws instead on certain classical traditions of satire and story-telling to establish and maintain Fielding's literary authority. Whereas *Joseph Andrews* engaged in dialogue with the antecedent models provided by Richardson, Cervantes, Cibber, the Bible and a host of recent and contemporary texts in its attempt to legitimise (and problematise) the new form of prose fiction, the *Journey* looks for the scant classical precedents for the novel, offering an allegoric journey through the afterlife, and negotiating most extensively with the work of the second-century Syrian satirist and rhetorician, Lucian, whom Fielding in 1752 called 'the Father of True Humour' (*CGJ*, p. 285).

Two of Lucian's works in particular seem to lie behind Fielding's invention, *Dialogues of the Dead* (*Mortuorum dialogi*) in which the great names of the ancient world discuss affairs in the underworld, revealing thereby the vanities and follies of all humankind and the illusory nature of human greatness, and *The Voyage to the Underworld* (*Kataplous*) where a boat filled with the recently deceased is the scene for a debate about the nature of the world that the spirits have just left. In this case, then, Fielding was attempting to achieve the authority he persistently sought in his writing by means of an alignment with the conventional neo-classical ideal of imitating or adapting the ancients, trying to find an acceptably dignified version of his own contemporary literary enterprise in what so many eighteenth-century writers saw as the greater and more authoritative precedent literary culture of Greece and Rome.

The idea that imitation of the ancients was the approved path to good writing and literary authority was familiar to more literate eighteenth-century readers through the influential earlier work of John Dryden, Alexander Pope and many others, but by Fielding's time it was beginning to change its emphasis. The strongest neo-classical case, that *only* by imitating the ancients could anyone learn to write successfully, was most clearly put through the voice of Crites in Dryden's *Essay of Dramatic Poesy* (1668) and it still emerges forcefully over forty years later in parts of Pope's *An Essay on Criticism* (1711):[6]

> Be *Homer's* works your *study* and *delight*,
> Read them by day, and meditate by night,
> Thence form your judgement, thence your maxims bring,
> And trace the muses *upward* to their *spring*;
> Still with *it self compar'd* his *text* peruse;
> And let your *comment* be the *Mantuan muse*.

The rigorous campaign of study and imitation encouraged by Pope in this early poem is based on the notion that classical writing not only did everything first, it also did everything better: 'To copy *Nature* is to copy *them*.' Even though Pope's own later imitations of Horace involve much greater imaginative freedom and much less reliance on their sources than this manifesto seems to allow, the neo-classical idea of the artist's need for sustained reverential involvement with the superior culture of Greece and Rome is fundamental to his thinking, and to the thinking of many of his like-minded contemporaries, who were also predictably unanimous in their hostility to 'modern' literary innovations.

The idea of imitation and reverence for the past maintained great currency in the earlier part of the eighteenth century, surfacing intermittently in Swift as well as in Pope, and surviving through to its moment of culmination and dispersal in Sir Joshua Reynolds' *Discourses* (1769). Although Reynolds comes out strongly against what he calls 'the drudgery of copying', he extols the need for any aspiring artist to respect and to learn from the recognised great masters of the past:

> On whom then can he rely, or who shall show him the path that leads to excellence? The answer is obvious: those great masters who have travelled the same road with success are the most likely to conduct others. The works of those who have stood the test of ages, have a claim to that respect and veneration to which no modern can pretend.[7]

Reynolds' more pragmatic version of 'imitation' is clearly much less rigid and more dialogic than Pope's, at least as it is formulated in *An Essay on Criticism*, even if Reynolds is reluctant to recognise the difficulties involved in this continuing unquestioned reverence for the past. In Fielding's time, the notion of the authority of 'imitation' was modulating under the pressure of the unauthorised and largely unprecedented new literary forms of the novel and the periodical from being a prescriptive programme into a more flexible recommendation. After all, since there were no 'great masters' from the past to offer suitable precedents for the novel, how was an author of such a work to proceed?

Representative of the less restrictive account of imitation which was beginning to be offered in the mid-century is a passage from Edward Young's *Conjectures on Original Composition* (1749):

> Yet let not assertors of classical excellence imagine that I deny the tribute it so well deserves. He that admires not ancient authors betrays a secret he would conceal, and tells the world that he does not understand them. Let us be as far from neglecting, as from copying, their admirable compositions: sacred be their rights, and inviolable their fame. Let our understandings feed on theirs; they afford the noblest nourishment: but let them nourish, not annihilate, our own. When we read, let our imagination kindle at their charms; when we write, let our judgement shut them out of our thoughts; treat even Homer himself as his royal admirer was treated by the Cynic: bid him stand aside, not shade our composition from the beams of our own genius; for nothing original can rise, nothing immortal can ripen, in any other sun.[8]

As expressed here, Young's views are clearly moving away from the earlier Augustan certainties towards what we might see as a more 'Romantic' emphasis on individuality, imagination and creativity. But at the same time, Young, like Reynolds, is still at pains to retain the importance of classical models, and he is unwilling to discard the authority of the ancients without recognising a sense of loss. For Edward Young, the ancients are not simply to be copied, but to be creatively remade, according to 'our own genius'. If understood properly, the great writers of the past may provide the basis for intelligent adaptation or appropriation, for the beginnings of dialogue, rather than offering unchangeable templates for slavish imitation.

In this complex and nuanced aesthetic debate, Fielding's declared position seems more opportunist than theorised, lying somewhere between Pope's early prescriptiveness and Young's looser advocacy of the classics. When, in *The Covent-Garden Journal* in 1752, Fielding proposed a new translation of Lucian – the proposal went no further, probably because not enough subscribers were forthcoming – he described the classical author not as someone to imitate strictly, but as someone to learn from and to adapt to current needs:

> And as I am thus unwilling to think that Lucian was the Imitator of any other, I shall not be much more ready to grant, that others have been the Imitators of him. The Person whom I esteem to be most worthy of this Honour is the immortal Swift. To say the Truth, I can find no better Way of giving the English Reader an Idea of the Greek Author, than by telling him, that to translate Lucian well into English, is to give us another Swift in our own Language.   (CGJ, p. 286)

Similar enthusiasm for Lucian penetrates *Tom Jones* (XIII, i), *Amelia* (VIII, v) and *The Journal of a Voyage to Lisbon*, and the comparison of the earlier writer with Jonathan Swift also recurs elsewhere in Fielding's work.

Fielding's version of the reverence for the ancients is interesting here because his formulation seems to emphasise some kind of ideological congruity or imaginative affinity between the imitated and the imitator, rather than any precise mimetic following of prior stylistic procedures or techniques – a congruity which might equally be found between Pope and Horace, or Johnson and Juvenal. Fielding, it is true, seems occasionally to take his resemblance to Lucian very seriously, and he even described himself as one 'who hath formed his Stile upon that very Author' (CGJ, p. 289). But in making this rather imprecise and implausible claim, he seems to be offering an alignment to the line of satiric and ironic imagination which he sees running through Lucian, Erasmus, Rabelais and into Swift, rather than defending any fully developed imitative strategy.

For Fielding, working in the largely unprecedented form of extended prose fiction, the search for proper lineage and authority was never likely to be easy. The copious prose writing of the previous half-century seemed altogether too down-market and shabby for Fielding, and no doubt for his subscribers, and yet the search for more legitimate models for imitation or adaptation was not especially fruitful. In the prefatory chapters to *Joseph Andrews*, there were complicated and deeply ironised versions of the past offered, and lines of imitation satirically indicated. Although it was a subject he returned to frequently in his periodical writing, Fielding wrote most clearly about this problem of precedent in the preface he contributed to the second edition of his sister Sarah Fielding's novel *The Adventures of David Simple* (1744). In a rather slippery argument, he seeks classical authority for comic fiction while simultaneously seeming to deny its availability:

> I have attempted in my Preface to *Joseph Andrews* to prove, that every Work of this kind is in its Nature a comic Epic Poem, of which *Homer* left us a Precedent, tho' it be unhappily lost.
>
> The two great Originals of a serious Air, which we have derived from that mighty Genius, differ principally in the Action, which in the *Iliad* is entire and uniform; in the *Odyssey*, is rather a Series of Actions, all tending to produce one great End. *Virgil* and *Milton* are, I think, the only pure Imitators of the former; most of the other *Latin*, as well as *Italian*, *French*, and *English* Epic Poets, chusing rather the History of some War, as *Lucan* and *Silius Italicus*; or a Series of Adventures, as *Ariosto*, &c. for the subject of their Poems.
>
> In the same manner, the Comic Writer may either fix on one Action, as the Authors of *Le Lutrin*, the *Dunciad*, &c. or on a Series, as *Butler* in Verse, and *Cervantes* in Prose have done.[9]

Fielding's account of the possibilities of comic fiction here seems remarkably loose and non-specific, drawing on a great many names and saying little about any of them, showing how awkward it has become for the mid-eighteenth-century prose writer to seek alignment with an authoritative past which has provided insufficient models for guidance.

When he offered his own extended updated version of Lucian's narratives in the second volume of the *Miscellanies*, it was hedged around by ironic uncertainties and disclaimers, as Fielding thought any such enterprise must inevitably be in the degenerate modern world. To emphasise this fragility, the text of *A Journey from This World to the Next* is carefully and playfully offered as no more than a fragment, serendipitously discovered in highly unusual and slightly ridiculous circumstances:

> Mr. *Robert Powney*, Stationer, who dwells opposite to *Catharine-street* in the *Strand*, a very honest Man and of great Gravity of Countenance; who, among other excellent Stationery Commodities, is particularly eminent for his Pens, which I am abundantly bound to acknowledge, as I owe to their peculiar Goodness that my Manuscripts have by any means been legible: this Gentleman, I say, furnished me some time since with a Bundle of those Pens, wrapped up with great Care and Caution, in a very large Sheet of Paper full of Characters, written as it seemed in a very bad Hand. Now I have a surprizing Curiosity to read every thing which is almost illegible; partly perhaps from the sweet Remembrance of the dear *Scrawls, Skrawls,* or *Skrales* (for the Word is variously spelt), which I have in my youth received from that lovely part of the Creation for which I have the tenderest Regard; and partly from that Temper of Mind which makes Men set an immense Value on old Manuscripts so effaced, Bustoes so maimed, and Pictures so black that no one can tell what to make of them. I therefore perused this Sheet with wonderful Application, and in about a Day's time discovered that I could not understand it. I immediately repaired to Mr. *Powney*, and inquired very eagerly whether he had not more of the same Manuscript. He produced about One Hundred Pages, acquainting me that he had saved no more: but that the Book was originally a huge Folio, had been left in his Garret by a Gentleman who lodged there, and who had left him no other Satisfaction for nine months' Lodging . . . hearing the Gentleman was gone to the *West-Indies*, and believing it to be good for nothing else, he had used it as waste Paper.[10]

According to the so-called 'editor', Powney had tried unsuccessfully to interest various booksellers in this discovered text, and he had met with an equally frosty reception from that perennial target of Augustan satire, the Royal Society – 'they shook their heads, saying, there was nothing in it wonderful enough for them'. Fielding, though, claims to be intrigued by what he has found, and he has taken the advice of none other than his distinguished fellow-author Abraham

Adams in authenticating the manuscript. Acting as an unquestionable authority, Parson Adams rather testily verifies its author's knowledge of Greek, and with Fielding's own endorsement of the 'moral' of the tale, it is thus offered for the reader's entertainment and edification.

Fielding's ironic pose as merely an editor of someone else's words, negotiating with a character from one of his own books, confirms the contemporary uncertainties about authorship and about the writer's responsibility for fiction, which can also be found in Defoe and Richardson. For those earlier novelists, who must have inherited a broadly Puritan distaste for falsehood and imposture, pretending to be no more than the editor of texts by other people allowed a space free from contamination by the mendacity of fiction, even if they simply intensified the deception by claiming it.

In this case, though, Fielding very self-consciously adopts the satirical inflection of Swift's voice, most audible in the prefatory sections where he simultaneously distanced himself from and orchestrated *Gulliver's Travels*, taking opportunities to ridicule the illiteracies of women and the general inadequacies of the reading public, as well as reiterating the stubborn materiality of writing. The rigmarole of the discovered fragmentary manuscript was very much to Fielding's advantage here for a number of reasons both material and literary. Most simply, it allowed him to pass off as complete a work which he had not managed to finish, while at the same time offering an attractive penumbra of antiquity and ironic distance to his text.

Later in the century, a similar strategy of pretended discovery was more forcefully (and perhaps rather more deceitfully) adopted in James Macpherson's *Fragments of Ancient Poetry Collected in the Highlands of Scotland and Translated from the Gaelic or Erse Language* ['*Ossian*'] (1760), to great effect. Later still, the same kind of incomplete and intermittent narrative was exploited in Henry Mackenzie's *The Man of Feeling* (1771), where the original manuscript is said by the 'editor' to have been discovered in pieces of wadding used in guns. In each of these two subsequent examples, the reification of the text is used to absolve the named author (James Macpherson and Henry Mackenzie, respectively) from complete responsibility for the offered work, and at the same time it operates to convey an air of unquestionable authenticity and materiality to the printed word – the 'editor' may not be able to attest to the truth of the narrative, but in a very obvious way he can vouchsafe its genuineness.

In Fielding's case, the pretence of the manuscript's discovery is simply tossed into the *Miscellanies* as an off-hand comic reminder of the haphazard nature of this particular account, and its absurdities are quickly acknowledged. A similar device had already been thrown into the first published edition of his play *The Tragedy of Tragedies* (1731), as part of its overall parodic project. All the same, however casual the convention may be, this playfulness and desire for distance from the text of the *Journey* shows again Fielding's continuing uncertainties about his authorial role, his doubts about the extent of his responsibilities as a literary producer, and his persistently awkward relationship with his audience.

Fielding's use of the fragmentary narrative in this text allows him to compile a series of short essays, which are reminiscent of some of the concerns of *The Champion*, under one broad heading. It also allows him the opportunity to make a number of familiar Swiftian jokes about the limited attention-span of modern readers, and about the way literature has recently been devalued by its introduction into the market-place. When the tale breaks off, in the middle of Anna Boleyn's account of her life, the 'editor' takes the opportunity to chasten his readers and remind them of how little they really value the written word:

> Here ends this curious Manuscript; the rest being destroyed in rolling up Pens, Tobacco, &c. It is to be hoped, heedless People will henceforth be more cautious what they burn, or use to other vile Purposes; especially when they consider the fate which had likely to have befallen the divine *Milton*, and that the Works of *Homer* were probably discovered in some Chandler's Shop in *Greece*.   (*Journey*, p. 128)

Fielding's concern with the impermanence of literature, with its increasing disposability and its ephemeral nature, is here actualised in a playful way – to our relief, the 'vile Purposes' to which fugitive papers might be put are not painstakingly spelled out, as they no doubt would be in Swift. In the tale itself, however, similar notions of impermanence and the fleeting nature of human achievement become increasingly prominent, and the main story becomes a series of inquiries into the constantly frustrated human desire to make some lasting mark on history, to rise to 'greatness'.

In a very arresting opening, dismissing at once the allegedly dominant conventions of formal realism, the first sentence of the main text actualises the death of the author: 'On the first of *December* 1741 I departed this Life at my lodgings in *Cheapside*' (*Journey*, p. 7). That this sad event had happened so recently might seem surprising, given the previous account of the discovered manuscript, but Fielding has little time for such precision, and in a footnote he casually throws away all the paraphernalia he has previously erected:

> Some doubt whether this should not be rather 1641, which is a Date more agreeable to the Account given of it in the Introduction: but then there are some Passages which seem to relate to Transactions infinitely later, even within this year or two. To say the truth, there are Difficulties attending either Conjecture; so the Reader may take which he pleases.   (*Journey*, p. 7)

That the interpellated reader may do as 'he' pleases is always a source of both security and jeopardy to Fielding. To his obvious relief, the author may not always be held responsible for his reader's activities, but yet nor can he exercise his due authority and control over his audience. In *Joseph Andrews*, as we have seen, the reader's freedom of interpretation was used at various times to show the limits and the extent of authorial power – indicated in the chapter entitled 'Which some Readers will think too short, and others too long' (III, viii). In this text, the author seems to be unwilling to engage in full dialogue with the audience, preferring to hint and suggest, to display his conventions, and to ignore the cumbersome constraints of realism or plausibility. Because of the nature of the project, Fielding has a clearer idea of whom he is addressing than he had in *Joseph Andrews*. Also, the sense that he can rely on their acumen and literary sophistication more heavily than he could rely on the very limited responsiveness of anonymous novel-readers allows the text greater allusiveness, and less of the exasperated description and explanation which so regularly interrupts the comic fictions.

The form of the *Journey* is sketchy and unsystematic, but the picture of the world it offers is as ironic and unsentimental as that in either of the earlier narratives, particularly reminiscent of the coach scene in *Joseph Andrews*. After the death of the central figure, the newly departed narrator describes the reaction of his loved ones:

> My Friends and Relations had all quitted the Room, being all (as I plainly overheard) very loudly quarrelling below-stairs about my Will; there was only an old Woman left above to guard the Body, as I

apprehend. She was in a fast Sleep, occasioned, as from her Savour it
seemed, by a comfortable Dose of Gin.   (*Journey*, pp. 7–8)

The narrator thus leaves behind him a world without any vestiges of
true greatness, composed exclusively of self-seeking imperceptive
individuals, an idea reinforced by the accounts offered by other spirits
of the shabby and dishonourable ways in which they met their own
deaths. The cumulative effect is to confirm 'the Vanity, Folly and
Misery of the lower World' (*Journey*, p. 15). As the narrator meets
other spirits in the City of Diseases and then at the Gate of Elysium,
further examples of the meanness of the world and the vanity of
human wishes from monarchs to commoners are allowed to
accumulate, with the presence of Alexander the Great and Charles
XII of Sweden being introduced, as they so regularly were, to point
the moral and adorn the tale.

In the distribution of rewards and punishments to the spirits as
they seek entry to Elysium, we see again the implied social critique of
Joseph Andrews in the unveiling of the hypocrisy of more exalted
members of society, including such 'great men' as generals and
politicians, and in the discovery of the relative worthiness of the
humble. The world is seen to offer little proper reward for virtue, and
little appropriate punishment for vice. Yet, apart from offering
sustained commentary, the writer can do little to rectify this sorry
state of affairs. As the analysis continues, Fielding's characteristic
irony and scepticism about the reformative role of literature become
obvious:

> . . . a spirit . . . told the Judge he believed his Works would speak
> for him. What Works? answered *Minos*. My Dramatic Works, replied
> the other, which have done so much Good in recommending Virtue
> and punishing Vice. Very well, said the Judge, if you please to stand by,
> the first Person who passes the Gate, by your means shall carry you in
> with him: but if you will take my Advice, I think, for Expedition sake,
> you had better return and live another Life upon Earth. The Bard
> grumbled at this, and replied, that besides his Poetical Works, he had
> once lent the whole Profits of a Benefit Night to a Friend, and by that
> Means had saved him and his Family from Destruction. Upon this, the
> Gate flew open, and *Minos* desired him to walk in, telling him, if he
> had mentioned this at first, he might have spared the Remembrance of
> his Plays.   (*Journey*, pp. 32–3)

The self-reflexive joke about the uselessness of writing (made within a manuscript originally used to wrap pens) is deftly turned against the author, and it sits alongside the ironic treatment of the upper classes, many of whom find appropriate counterparts in the list of subscribers appended to the first edition, creating a familiar satire on the vanity of human wishes, recognisable in outline without being unduly discomforting.

Fielding's ironies next move towards the dramatised confrontation of the ancient world and the modern world previously exploited by Swift in *The Battle of the Books* and in the episode of the sorcerers in Glubbdubdrib in Book III of *Gulliver's Travels*. The narrator encounters the spirits of the very greatest ancients, accompanied by some of their rather less impressive modern counterparts, with predictable results: 'VIRGIL then came up to me, with Mr. *Addison* under his Arm' (*Journey*, p. 38). There are clear moments of personal satire in these passages, where the narrator makes Virgil admire those translations of his work offered by Fielding's allies, and where particular venom is directed at familiar Scriblerian targets. However, amid this conventional business, Fielding is also engaged again on the pursuit of true greatness, to be defined in opposition to false greatness, and it is to be found here exclusively in the noble spirits of great writers long gone.

The venerable ancients, and the greatest English writers such as Shakespeare and Milton, express genial curiosity about their fate in the contemporary world, but as well as showing the relative tawdriness of recent writing, Fielding adapts this episode to show how little really important authors need to care for the reception of their work. Homer and Shakespeare, genuinely 'great' men, exhibit indifference to the trappings of fame, displaying a lordly disdain for the petty squabbles of translators and actors over the correct interpretation of their texts. As Shakespeare is made to say, after watching Betterton and Booth, two eminent eighteenth-century actors, dispute the reading of a line from *Othello* by torturing the most obscure emphases from it:

> Faith, Gentlemen, it is so long since I wrote the Line, I have forgot my Meaning. This I know, could I have dreamt so much Nonsense would have been talked, and writ about it, I would have blotted it out of my Works; for I am sure, if any of these be my Meaning, it doth me very little Honour.   (*Journey*, p. 40)

For the greatest authors, then, the squabbling of pedantic readers is no more than an amusing distraction, but for the minor and small-minded critics themselves, such disputes are vital. Like Shakespeare and Milton, with whom he quite clearly aligns himself, Fielding seems to want to view the scene with detached amusement rather than outrage. Although the whole episode is designed to denigrate the modern world, the satire remains relatively easy-going, avoiding the greater cynicism of Lucian or the savagery of Swift.

At this point, the account abruptly shifts focus, and after brief encounters with Oliver Cromwell and Tom Thumb (who corrects some of the misconceptions of his portrayal in Fielding's play *The Tragedy of Tragedies*), Fielding's narrative authority is further displaced. Responsibility for the remaining conduct of the narrative is handed over to the spirit of Julian the Apostate, the fourth-century Roman emperor, self-confessed pagan and occasional satirist, who acts as yet another projection of Fielding himself. Julian is presented as worldly, experienced, and harbouring no illusions about human folly, and far removed from the commercially motivated figure really lurking behind the book.

In order to gain access to Elysium, Julian the Apostate has had to live several subsequent lives

> in the different Characters of a Slave, a Jew, a General, an Heir, a Carpenter, a Beau, a Monk, a Fidler, a wise Man, a King, a Fool, a Beggar, a Prince, a Statesman, a Soldier, a Taylor, an Alderman, a Poet, a Knight, a Dancing-Master, and three times a Bishop, before his Martyrdom, together with his other Behaviour in this last Character, satisfied the judge, and procured him a Passage to the blessed Regions.
>
> (*Journey*, pp. 45–6)

As the book goes on, Julian completely takes over the responsibility of story-telling, and recounts events from several of his lives throughout Europe over a thousand years, a nimble narrative device for the representation of persisting character-types throughout the ages.

After many brief and inconsequential anecdotes recounted by Julian, the narrative simply breaks off. 'Here Part of the Manuscript is lost, and that a very considerable one' (*Journey*, p. 111) announces Fielding in a laconic footnote, blithely relinquishing all previous claims to narrative authority. The book resumes with an account of the life of Anna Boleyn, written in the first person, which the main narrator disavows as being 'writ in a Woman's Hand'. Like the interpolated tale of Horatio and Leonora in *Joseph Andrews*, it develops a note of the pathetic, contesting the ironic voice of the main narrative, and some commentators have argued that it is actually the work of Fielding's novelist sister, Sarah, brought in to swell the pages as Fielding himself ran out of ideas or time. If this is true, then the text becomes heteroglot in yet another sense, quite literally having been composed by more than a single author.[11]

The narrative is thus incomplete, and has every appearance of simply being unfinished, no matter what protestations the 'editor' may make. And not all readers have been able to enjoy the lack of resolution of the *Journey*. As the Victortian critic George Saintsbury rather wittily put it, 'as the author was to leave it unfinished, it is a pity that he did not leave it unfinished much sooner than he actually did'.[12]

From this brief account of *A Journey from This World to the Next*, it will be clear that Fielding is using this fragmentary narrative to reinforce his own authority in a variety of ways. Within the overall publishing context of the *Miscellanies*, it maintains his self-presentation as a 'name', as an author whose very scraps are worth serious attention. Within the *Journey* itself, he develops this self-presentation in various ways. By engaging in dialogue with a classical text, he is aligning himself with the 'Ancients' in their contemporary cultural contest with the 'Moderns', reviving Swiftian or Scriblerian satiric forms and anatomising the contemporary world in an unsympathetic but perhaps eventually resigned way – the text may reveal that the world is a corrupt and unjust place, but it offers no comforting alternative, and has no corresponding confidence in the human capacity to reform. Other alignments within the text place Fielding within the pantheon of great writers, and wise men, while showing the compromises forced on him by his place in the modern world. The saga of Julian the Apostate serves to anatomise the world of Christendom from a secular classical point of view close to what seems to have been Fielding's own, drawing out the persistent and recurrent folly of humankind.

Unlike *Joseph Andrews*, this narrative does not contextualise its satire in the immediate world of contemporary England, and prefers a broader historical sweep. Yet as Fielding addresses his affluent and influential audience, he contrives to make similar points about injustice and vice, without adopting any accusatory stance. Even in the more personal moments, his account of 'greatness' remains generalised, and need not unduly trouble even those subscribers who have been recently prominent in affairs of state. But with the third volume of the *Miscellanies*, and the elaborately ironic biography of *Jonathan Wild*, Fielding's satiric energies are given much more direct focus, and his writing encounters once again the madness of contemporary society.

Puppets and prompters

. . . the stage of the world differs from that in Drury Lane principally in this – that whereas, in the latter, the hero or chief figure is almost continually before your eyes, whilst the under-actors are not seen above once in an evening; now, on the former, the hero or great man is always behind the curtain, and seldom or never appears or doth anything in his own person. He doth indeed, in this GRAND DRAMA, rather perform the part of the prompter, and doth instruct the well-drest figures, who are strutting in public on the stage, what to say or do. To say the truth, a puppet-show will illustrate our meaning better, where it is the master of the show (the great man) who dances and moves everything, whether it be the King of Muscovy or whatever other potentate *alias* puppet which we behold on the stage; but he himself keeps wisely out of sight: for, should he once appear, the whole motion would be at an end. Not that anyone is ignorant of his being there, or supposes that the puppets are not mere sticks of wood, and he himself the sole mover; but as this (though every one knows it) doth not appear visibly, i.e. to their eyes, no one is ashamed of consenting to be imposed upon; of helping on the drama, by calling the several sticks or puppets by the names which the master hath allotted to them, and by assigning to each the character which the great man is pleased they shall move in, or rather in which he himself is pleased to move them.[13]

The circumstances of publication and the nature of the identifiable audience for the *Miscellanies* encouraged many of the formal conventions and narrative procedures of *A Journey from This World to the Next*. That tale's casual allusiveness and its neo-classical concern with the nature of history align it firmly with up-market allegoric and aristocratic literature, and away from the more mundane or progressivist concerns of the down-market contemporary novel. The only exception to this move in the direction of the essay might be the interpolated tale of Anna Boleyn, which seems to indicate a different, more recognisably 'novelistic' conception of plot and character.

Reachable through the procedures of subscription publishing, the upper-class audience which the narrative self-consciously addresses is assumed to be familiar with the strategies and demands of traditional rhetoric, even though they may be largely (and happily) ignorant of the rough and ready flashiness of novelistic or 'realist' prose. The fact that this narrative is incomplete and sketchy, however, indicates Fielding's lack of confidence in the sustainability of this authorial role at this time, and makes the text itself internally inconsistent and often puzzling. After the ingenuity and playfulness of *Joseph Andrews*, energetically and combatively redefining the contemporary novel and challenging its audience in Fielding's own terms, his attempt to return to the narrative procedures of the classics, and thereby to address a known community of well-qualified readers through authorised rhetorical conventions, seems relatively retrograde and unsuccessful.

For the final volume of the *Miscellanies*, Fielding offered an even more curious narrative, clearly devised in opposition to the prevailing mimetic and diegetic assumptions of the emergent novel, again involving complex contextual and intertextual negotiation, and once more playing with the perceived expectations of his readership. *The Life of Mr. Jonathan Wild the Great* at first looks like a reasonably familiar exercise in the mock-heroic style, ironically reversing the conventional terms of biographical panegyric along the lines of his earlier burlesque play *The Tragedy of Tragedies* (1731), and drawing on many theatrical conventions of representation, but on examination it can be seen to be much more complex than that.

In recounting the life of Jonathan Wild, the text deals with a 'real' character known to his audience, however marvellously transfigured by Fielding. We shall make connections between Fielding's Jonathan Wild and the legendary historical figure of that name a little later, but for the moment it is worth dwelling on the terms of address exploited by this text. Employing an ironically inappropriate vocabulary, the narrative purports to celebrate the unscrupulous eponymous master criminal as the real representative hero of early eighteenth-century England, while simultaneously undercutting even that presentation by showing the quasi-heroic figure to be preyed on by the operations of fear and the activities of a fearsome wife and faithless friends. Amid bizarre Swiftian digressions about false learning, hats and the maritime adventures of Mrs Heartfree, Fielding conducts another sceptical examination of the principles of 'greatness' through the extraordinary conduct of his central character.

As Claude Rawson has pointed out, it is not difficult to isolate passages in the tale where the inversion of heroic or epic language is being quite straightforwardly carried out for the purposes of parody, just as it was in the opening chapters of *Joseph Andrews* charting the hero's unheroic genealogy.[14] The introduction of the unworldly Heartfree, for instance, closely echoes the similar presentation of Abraham Adams:

> Mr Thomas Heartfree, then (for that was his name) was of an honest and open disposition. He was of that sort of men whom experience only, and not their own natures, must inform that there are such things as deceit and hypocrisy in the world, and who, consequently, are not at five-and-twenty so difficult to be imposed upon as the oldest and most subtle. He was possessed of several great weaknesses of mind, being good-natured friendly, and generous to a great excess. He had, indeed, too little regard to common justice, for he had forgiven some debts to his acquaintance openly because they could not pay him . . . He was withal so silly a fellow that he never took the least advantage of the ignorance of his customers, and contented himself with very moderate gains on his goods . . .   (*JW*, p. 84)

The honest bourgeois tradesman – thought by some to be based on Fielding's friend, the dramatist George Lillo – is here presented in a luxuriant ironic wrapping, alerting readers to the conventional strategies of inversion in the tale, to the refusal of verisimilitude, and polarising responses between the 'good' man (Heartfree) and the 'great' man (Wild).

⌐Conscious of the sophistication of his audience, Fielding feels able throughout this tale to mingle irony and allusiveness quite freely, engaging in dialogue with a number of other recognisable literary forms.⌐When Wild visits the apartment of his future sister-in-law Miss Theodosia Snap, for instance, the narrator offers a conventional mock-heroic invocation of the *Odyssey*, thereby providing a clearly ironic and bathetic frame of reference for the related events:

> Mr Wild, on his arrival at Mr Snap's, found only Miss Doshy at home, that young lady being employed alone, in imitation of Penelope, with her thread or worsted, only with this difference, that whereas Penelope unravelled by night what she had knit or wove or spun by day, so what our young heroine unravelled by day she knit again by night. In short, she was mending a pair of blue stockings with red clocks; a

circumstance which perhaps we might have omitted, had it not served
to shew that there are still some ladies of this age who imitate the
simplicity of the ancients.   (JW, p. 92)

This recognisable satire on the threadbare pretensions of the modern
world echoes many Swiftian procedures, best found in such parodic
mock-epic pieces as the 'Description of Morning' or the 'Description
of a City Shower'. In juxtaposing the heroic (and perhaps rather
absurd?) fidelity of Odysseus's wife Penelope with the less elevated
concerns of her modern counterpart, Fielding also offers a parodic
account of the emergent novel's mimetic precision by so carefully and
so uselessly itemising those memorable 'blue stockings with red
clocks'.

     Although the mock-heroic or mock-epic technique exploited in
this passage is familiar, the effect is at least as complex as in Swift's
poems, with what Michael McKeon calls a 'double critique' operating
– 'first of aristocratic ideology by progressive, then of progressive
ideology by conservative'.[15] Throughout the tale, the cynical ideology
of Wild is interrogated by the purity of the Heartfrees, but in turn
their simplicity is seen as the gullibility by which Wild can thrive. In
the passage above, representative of the multifocal nature of this text,
the orthodox conservative critique of the down-market 'ladies of this
age' jostles against the more modern and sceptical interrogation of the
antique classical references.

     Each of these critical activities recurs throughout the text, but
neither achieves uncontested dominance, and the narrator eventually
assumes an unstable position, casting ironic aspersions on both the
modern world and the ancient, without a clear point of view emerging
unscathed. When compared with the flickering glimpses of the
genuine heroic and epic lying behind Pope's Dunciad, Fielding's
authorial position seems less grandiose, more exasperated and
disaffected. Although the central figure seems to be offered at first as a
demonic personification of evil, Wild turns more and more into a
desperate figure driven by uncontrollable urges, reminding this reader
at least of the wonderful Wile E. Coyote of Chuck Jones's Road
Runner cartoons, whose constant ingenuity and single-mindedness
lead only to repeated humiliation and disaster. Indeed, through
Fielding's manipulation of events, Wild may be represented as a rather
absurd figure, belittled by his desire for greatness, easily out-
manoeuvred by various women (including the guileless Mrs Heartfree,

whom he tries unsuccessfully to rape in a rapidly sinking boat). But at the same time Heartfree himself, the pillar of goodness in the tale, is also periodically subjected to indignities, and is no more of a spotless paradigm in this narrative than Adams was in the earlier book.)

As it continues, the narrative of *Jonathan Wild* is replete with many such examples of disorientation, undercutting and mock-heroic contrast, designed to show up the contemporary world as one with little dignity and no heroism, yet without offering the compensations of any corresponding refuge in a classical fixed point of judgement. If it were no more than that, no more than a formal exercise in the burlesque or the mock-heroic, Fielding's parodic biography of Jonathan Wild could then be located within the overall ideological territory of the *Miscellanies* as yet another attempt to identify or dismember the meaning of 'greatness' within contemporary culture, a concern which permeates many of the poems and essays of the first volume as well as the *Journey* itself, and which appears regularly throughout Fielding's journalism.

Such a generalised and thematic reading of the text initially looks attractive, giving Fielding the Swiftian (or perhaps the Lucianic) role of authoritative ironic commentator on the follies of the times, using a biographical narrative as a way of chronicling and demonstrating the dynamics of personal behaviour, developing the intertwined stories of Jonathan Wild and his gang, rival 'prigs', the Snap sisters and the Heartfree family into a fantasia upon both contemporary and more timeless notions of greatness. But as Fielding indicates at the beginning of the *Miscellanies*, the book remains more complex in its perspectives and more difficult to identify than this. As it is offered to its readers, Fielding's account of Wild's life disrupts the normal categories of biographical representation, being deliberately and unapologetically more fanciful and imaginative than accurate:

I now come to the Third and last Volume, which contains the history of *Jonathan Wild*. And here it will not, I apprehend, be necessary to acquaint my Reader, that my Design is not to enter the Lists with that excellent Historian, who from authentic papers and Records, &c. hath already given so satisfactory an Account of the Life and Actions of this Great Man. I have not indeed the least intention to depreciate the Veracity and Impartiality of that History; nor do I pretend to any of those Lights, not having to my Knowledge, ever seen a single Paper relating to my Hero, save some short Memoirs, which about the Time of his death were published in certain Chronicles called Newspapers, the Authority of which hath been sometimes questioned, and in the Ordinary of *Newgate* his Account, which generally contains a more particular relation of what the Heroes are to suffer in the next World, than of what they did in this. (*Misc*, pp. 8–9)

As an introduction to a new biography, hoping to attract purchasers, this is most odd. Fielding, by his own admission, has nothing authentically new and unprecedented to impart about his subject. Even by modern journalistic standards, his research looks unimpressive, and he does not offer any extensive revision of the existing material. Nor will he seek to contest the many previous biographies of Wild. And even if he is prepared in passing to question once again the 'Authority' of newspapers in general, Fielding claims he has no reason to be particularly sceptical about their versions of his hero's life.

Furthermore, at the beginning of the text proper, Fielding ironically disassociates himself from 'a set of simple fellows, called, in derision, sages or philosophers' (*JW*, p. 40), who have misconstrued the true barbarity of the 'great' ancient figures of Alexander and Julius Caesar, and wrongly complimented them for their occasional acts of clemency amid lives of consistently repressive savagery. By confusing 'greatness' and 'goodness', these chroniclers have sentimentalised their figures, turning them into acceptable role-models for an ill-informed readership. The narrator of this new life reprimands his predecessors for their failures of discernment, and offers in their place a thorough-going and unflinching examination of a truly 'great' individual, softened only to the extent that he is 'partaker of the imperfection of humanity' (*JW*, p. 41).

In a developed vein of oblique and disorientating irony, the author seems to be intervening in the public domain here, reminding his subscribers of recent history quite some time after the fuss has died down. In this belated version of Wild's life – the hero had after all been executed no less than eighteen years earlier – Fielding shows history repeating itself, this time as farce. The author's subjects in this volume are no longer as remote from his readers as were Homer or Julian the Apostate or Anna Boleyn of the *Journey*, but nor are they the virtually contemporary figures found in *Joseph Andrews*, *Tom Jones* and *Amelia*.

Despite the archness of his description and the air of antiquity it suggests, we must remember that the main figure Fielding is chronicling was one of the most celebrated and notorious personages of the 1720s. The utterly unscrupulous Jonathan Wild, self-appointed 'Thief-Taker General of Great Britain and Ireland', first attracted widespread public and literary attention as the scourge of London's criminal gangs and the apparently untouchable enemy of villains, informing on offenders and, for a fee, sending many to the gallows. However, it gradually became apparent that this lucrative traffic was nothing more than an elaborate front for an even more ruthless and extensive criminal regime of his own, specialising in extortion and blackmail.

According to the extensive contemporary reports, often very lurid in tone, Wild was an organizer of professional criminals, acting as the instigator of thefts and the clearing-house for stolen property. As well as using the law to his own advantage by turning in unprofitable members of his entourage for a reward of £40 a conviction, Wild's most flagrant strategy of extortion was to arrange the theft of valuable articles, or buy stolen property from other thieves. Then, pretending to be the bereft owner, he would advertise their loss in the press, and nominate the sum to be paid on their return. For a consideration, these items would then be restored to their actual owners, who seem to have understood such coded communications, and who would be criminalised and implicated by their complicity in Wild's schemes, ensuring their silence. Operating with one foot in the legal world and one in the criminal, Jonathan Wild's slippery allegiances and policies attracted great public interest, culminating in a sensational court case at the Old Bailey in 1724, where he was attacked by an aggrieved gang-member and stabbed, and finally leading to his eventual execution on 24 May 1725, an event attended by thousands and covered extensively by the contemporary press.[16]

Not only did Jonathan Wild use newspapers to publicise his thefts, the press used him to present and epitomise their often sensationalist accounts of rampant organised crime being carried on in the midst of the prosperity of London. Stories about Wild appeared regularly in most papers, and there were copious accounts of his career in ballads, songs, and broadsheets.[17] However, although Wild was the focus of an enormous amount of contemporary literary attention, there was no unanimity of interpretation of his career, and his exploits quickly became the site of intense ideological contest.

For many writers at the time, the case of Wild challenged conventional assumptions about the integrity of the city, as well as about the aetiology of crime, and even provoked scepticism about the wholesome basis of mercantile society. For a few others, the 'Thief-Taker General' (like his glamorous contemporary and escape artist Jack Sheppard, and like the later highwayman Dick Turpin) briefly became a romantic outlaw, flouting the hypocritical conventions of bourgeois society and living instead by his own ingenious rules. For still more, Wild demonstrated the darker side of modern life, using the developing apparatus of commerce paradoxically to foster vice and cruelty. And for a few, Jonathan Wild was no more than a terrifying monster, atavistically challenging the network of agreements and considerations by which modern life was made tolerable, eventually over-reaching himself to be brought to a properly humiliating end on the gallows at Tyburn in 1725.

As he was invented and reinvented in the press, presented as the criminal within us all, as a daring brigand, as the quintessentially 'modern' man, or as a frightening throwback to pre-civilized society, Wild became a national celebrity, his trial and execution being perhaps the first major 'media event' in modern British culture, extensively covered by newspapers and pamphleteers. Between 1724 and 1726 he was even more prominent in print than in the 'real' world and those writers who offered biographies strove to make their particular work seem like the last word on the subject, the definitive version of their hero's life. In order to do so, they found ways of authenticating their accounts, often dismissing the equally outspoken claims to authority made by their rivals. Daniel Defoe, for instance, who probably wrote two separate accounts of Wild's life, offered this testimony to his own accuracy and reliability in A *True and Genuine Account of the Life and Actions of the Late Jonathan Wild, etc.* (1725):

> We have the advantage in this account to come at the particular of his story from unquestioned authority, for he was sensible wrong accounts would be published of him, he was not backward to give materials from his own mouth which nobody can contradict, and others fully conversant with him, having given the same stories and accounts of the same facts, we have the satisfaction to see them agree fully together, and thereby be assured of the truth of both.[18]

By vouchsafing the accuracy of his version in this way, Defoe is clearly working within the conventional paradigms of empiricism and verisimilitude, just as he does in the prefatory testimonies to the truth of his works of fiction. He goes even further in a sub-title, assuring readers that his pamphlet is 'not made up of fiction and fable, but taken from his own mouth, and collected from papers of his own writing'. By strenuously claiming that his work on Wild is attested and verifiable, straight from the horse's mouth, Defoe is accommodating its challenges to plausibility, and naturalising its capacity to astonish.

In so doing, Defoe is operating once again within the context of an important recognisable literary tradition whereby such 'Wonders' could be accommodated – a tradition to which Fielding's multiple subversive ironies and deliberate paradoxes can be opposed. As J. Paul Hunter puts it:

> Many texts between 1680 and 1720 participate in the tradition of Wonder, whether or not they use the term itself as a lure. Other terms that express the rarity of what is to be described – 'awful,' 'astonishing,' 'strange,' and 'surprizing' – often tumble over each other in the titles and in the accounts themselves, but such words are yoked with terms that certify actuality and truth. 'News' is one term that tries to anchor the accounts in reality (the Wonders books really are journalism), and 'True' is another. Accounts are often said to be 'strange but true,' the basic formula of the tradition indicative of the motives behind it.[19]

Defoe's personalised testimony to the truthfulness and genuineness of his account of Wild (whether we choose to believe it or not) becomes a way of handling the narrative's extraordinary nature, a way of managing and perhaps normalising a life which seemed to threaten these very categories.

At the same time, of course, the author's testimony becomes a way of privileging this particular text over others suggested to be fraudulent and misleading. The author's role in such a work is to act as a witness to remarkable events, not as an instigator or orchestrator. As so often in the 'undifferentiated matrix' of early eighteenth-century narrative, where the contending discourses of fact and fiction were intermingled, 'truth' is said to be stranger than fiction, for solidly material as well as any more rarefied epistemological reasons.[20]

When Fielding offered his own commentary on Wild's life eighteen years later, it was clearly no longer of much interest as 'news', and the author makes little effort to 'anchor the accounts in reality'. Indeed, in his prefatory remarks Fielding continues his dialogue with these precedent texts, but assumes an entirely different authorial role. He resolutely refuses to take on the truth-telling responsibilities of the historian, conventionally made prominent by Defoe and other journalistic writers, and instead he goes out of his way to deny any claims to strict accuracy. The forensic precision and the statistical exactness which distinguished Fielding's later writings on crime, such as A *True State of the Case of Bosavern Penlez* (1749) or *An Enquiry into the Causes of the Late Increase of Robbers, &c.* (1751), are here abandoned in favour of greater inventive licence, and a much more sportive attitude towards illusion and reality.

Whereas Defoe opens his account of Wild's life by flaunting his journalistic credentials, Fielding relies on his imaginative and inventive capacities:

> To confess the Truth, my Narrative is rather of such Actions as he might have performed, or would, or should have performed, than what he really did; and may in Reality, as well suit any other such great Man, as the Person himself whose name it bears.   (*Misc*, p. 9)

So the episodes in Fielding's text are not, as they are alleged to be in Defoe's account and in its contemporary rivals, the incontestably genuine events of Wild's life, to which the genuine historian is enslaved. Instead, Fielding treats Jonathan Wild as a legendary figure, comparable to Robin Hood or Dr Faustus or Tom Thumb or any other inhabitant of the hinterland between fact and fiction, whose life might be continued and developed by the story-teller, in whatever direction he sees as appropriate for his immediate purposes.

Throughout the tale, the high black comedy of Wild and the Heartfrees is heavily stylised and the process of its invention is constantly made prominent. The main narrative is as full of references to 'the custom of all biographers' (*JW*, p. 41), and self-conscious references to the activities of the narrator, as it is to the exploits of the nominal hero. The narrator constantly makes references to his role as puppet-master and impresario, expressing pride in his achievements, engaging in dialogue with the readers, and all the time positioning himself as the dominant figure 'always behind the curtain'. The role is perhaps less dignified than that of the historian or the Homeric orator, but it is the only one available to him. In this 'GRAND DRAMA', as stated in the passage quoted at the opening of this section, Fielding offers his Jonathan Wild as an imaginative exploration of possibilities under the control of the narrator, as a self-conscious literary device rather than as a verifiable person – a move which effectively displaces the criminal and his colourful cohorts from the centre of the narrative and puts the selective and inventive mediating narrator there instead.

Like the bizarre figures animated by 'Harry Luckless' in Fielding's earlier play *The Author's Farce* (1731), and like those under Fielding's control in his Panton Street theatre in 1748, the characters in *Jonathan Wild* are best seen as no more than life-size puppets, a contextualised version of the knock-about Punch and Judy show, taken to clear satirical ends. The world within the narrative is described early on as 'this great theatre' (*JW*, p. 45), and the events are uncovered in separate scenes, as though in a theatrical pageant. But although the form of the narrative is stylised and non-naturalistic, drawing attention to its own processes and laying bare its conventions, competent readers should be untroubled by its artificiality:

> It would be to suppose thee, gentle reader, one of very little knowledge in this world, to imagine thou hast never seen some of these puppet-shows which are frequently acted on the great stage; but though thou shouldst have resided all thy days in those remote parts of this island which great men seldom visit, yet, if thou hast any penetration, thou must have had some occasions to admire both the solemnity of countenance in the actor and the gravity in the spectator, while some of those farces are carried on in every village in the kingdom. He must have a very despicable opinion of mankind indeed who can conceive them to be imposed on as often as they appear to be so. The truth is, they are in the same situation with the readers of romances; who, though they know the whole to be one entire fiction, nevertheless agree to be deceived; and, as these find amusement, so do others find ease and convenience in this concurrence. But, this being a sub-digression, I return to my digression.   (*JW*, p. 155)

With deeply disorienting irony, Fielding digresses from his digression to raise the question of whether or not people are 'imposed on as often as they appear to be so'. His suggestion that their deceptions are voluntary has important ramifications throughout the tale, and it is clear that the narrator enjoys the paradoxical position of using the most artificial, most theatrical of literary forms to examine the darkest of truths. Once again, the powerful self-projection of Fielding lurks behind the curtain as the grand master of these ceremonies, simultaneously bamboozling and speaking plainly to his readers.

There is further indication in the prefatory passages that Wild's life is to be interpreted as exemplary, as though Fielding was writing a species of ironic hagiography, that the events related might well be applied to 'any other such great Man' as to the named hero. For contemporary readers, the key phrase 'great Man' was often understood to be a coded reference to the current or recent Prime Minister, Sir Robert Walpole, a figure as controversial and difficult to interpret as Wild himself. In many oppositional texts from earlier in the century, that great man's career and the career of the master criminal Jonathan Wild were surreptitiously or openly linked, with derogatory connections being made between Wild's extensive criminal network and the equally corrupt 'Robinocracy' of Walpole's regime.

In each of these cases, the one dominant and charismatic figure was taken as representative of the growth of 'politics' in the contemporary world, of the triumph of manipulative ingenuity over statesmanship or altruism. Furthermore, to return to one of the recurrent motifs of Fielding's fiction, the success of Wild and Walpole showed once again how a smiling face and an apparently candid demeanour might disguise the hardest of hearts. In many ways, Fielding's *Jonathan Wild* is the climactic and most exuberantly carnivalised version of a connection between high life and low life of long standing, and its meanings had become almost stale and conventionalised by the time of Fielding's revitalising and defamiliarising intervention.

In John Gay's enormously popular play *The Beggar's Opera* (1728), for instance, which can be seen as a point of particular intensity in the body of Wild literature in the 1720s as well as a mock-heroic inversion of Italian opera and many other things, Walpole's points of contact with the criminal underworld are referred to both directly and indirectly. The central ideas of the drama are announced at the very beginning in a song by that master bourgeois manipulator and spokesman for eighteenth-century enterprise culture, the thief-taker and 'fence', Peachum:

> Through all the Employments of Life
>   Each Neighbour abuses his Brother;
> Whore and Rogue they call Husband and Wife:
>   All Professions be-rogue one another.
> The Priest calls the Lawyer a Cheat,
>   The Lawyer be-knaves the Divine;
> And the Statesman because he's so great,
>   Thinks his Trade as Honest as mine.[21]

Peachum, clearly echoing Wild, is a wholly unscrupulous thief-taker and dealer in stolen property, whose presentation of the world is as unromantic and mercenary as that offered elsewhere in the play by Lockit the gaoler, who gives an even clearer indication of the competitiveness of modern life – 'Every one of us preys upon his Neighbour, yet we herd together' (Gay, II, 46).

These bleak visions of rivalry and contest are accommodated within the play, and exploited towards enjoyably ironic ends, but there is no reason to think that they are either simply endorsed or denied by the main body of the text. Even though the drama does not seem to involve any authoritative narrator-figure 'behind the curtain', its confrontational procedures force us to see the seamy world of the play as an ironised and stylised discovery of our own world, the connections between the two being both disturbing and amusing. In an anticipation of Fielding's ambivalence, it is as though we are to be left suspended between believing that the world outside the play is as bleak as it seems inside the play, and simultaneously remembering that the whole thing is an elaborate illusion, a contrivance designed to entertain and amuse more than to outrage or horrify.

Clearly, both Peachum and Lockit offer versions of the cynicism associated with Wild, and contemporary audiences would no doubt have been expected to see the links between them without further prodding. However, the connection with Walpole is introduced more stealthily. When Peachum gives a catalogue of members of his gang, he fondly mentions one 'Robin of Bagshot, alias Bluff Bob, alias Carbuncle, alias Bob Booty' (Gay, II, 6). This unappealing multi-faceted figure never actually appears on stage (although in a pleasing intertextual connection he is heavily involved in the plot of Fielding's *Jonathan Wild*) but the names would be recognised by competent and well-informed members of the audience as a version of Walpole, who is thus infiltrated into the play, but dispersed over several characters. He is not represented or symbolised entirely by any single figure in the drama, any more than Wild is, but his abundant 'greatness' is attested to by the way it takes so many different figures to produce a composite version of him, and his substantial shadow hangs over the whole drama.

Like Peachum, Walpole was at the centre of power in his community, but was thought by many unsympathetic commentators to be prepared to be wholly unscrupulous in the maintenance and articulation of that power. Like Lockit, he was the manager and

custodian of his domain, notoriously and almost exclusively concerned
with the 'garnish' it could offer him – an equation made even easier
for the audience to recognise by having Lockit played at the early
performances in Lincoln's Inn Fields by an actor as corpulent as
Walpole himself. And even like Macheath, the more romantic
highwayman hero of the piece, the Prime Minister had widely known
embarrassing problems with women. Where the highwayman has to
negotiate between the contending demands of his two lovers, Polly
Peachum and Lucy Lockit, not to mention the others who clamour
outside his cell as he awaits death, Robert Walpole famously had to
arbitrate between the competing and exhausting claims of his wife,
Lady Walpole, and his mistress, Molly Skerrett. As Fielding
subsequently reappraises these exploits through the complex and
farcical interactions of Wild, Laetitia Snap and Fireblood, the 'great'
figure at the centre of his narrative gradually turns from elevated and
terrifying hero to pathetic victim.

The ability to make these identifications and cross-references was
within the competence of any reasonably well-informed spectator of
the play in the year of its first production in 1728, and Walpole's
response to this challenge was to suppress Gay's sequel, the
unperformed *Polly* (1729). For duller viewers or readers, assistance
could be sought from *A Compleat Key to the Beggar's Opera*, which
systematically spelt out the connections, published in *The Craftsman*
in February 1728, and from Hogarth's famous picture of a scene from
the play painted the following year which pictorially gives even more
tantalising hints of the immediate social context of the action.[22]

That the links between politicians and thieves were not difficult to
make at this time can further be seen in a paper by Swift published in
The Intelligencer later in the same year:

> My Reason for mentioning *Courts*, and *Ministers*, *(whom I never think
> on, but with the most profound Veneration)* is, because an Opinion
> obtains, that in the *Beggar's Opera*, there appears to be some Reflection
> upon *Courtiers* and *Statesmen*, whereof I am by no Means a Judge.
>
> It is true, indeed, that Mr. Gay, the Author of this Piece, hath been
> somewhat singular in the Course of his Fortunes; for it hath happened,
> that after Fourteen Years of attending the *Court*, with a large Stock of
> real Merit, a modest and agreeable Conversation, a *Hundred Promises*,
> and *five Hundred Friends*, he hath failed of Preferment; and upon a very
> weighty Reason. He lay under the Suspicion of having written a Libel,
> or Lampoon against a great Minister. It is true, that great Minister was

demonstratively convinced, and publickly owned his Conviction, that
Mr. Gay was not the Author; but having lain under his Suspicion, it
seemed very just, that he should suffer the punishment; because in this
most reformed Age, the Virtues of a Prime Minister are no more to be
suspected, than the Chastity of *Caesar's* Wife.[23]

With unmistakable and characteristic irony, Swift contrives to mean
the very opposite of what he says here, confident that his readers will
be able to tune into the genuine message through the distracting
crackle of ironic interference. While protesting a vehement denial, he
affirms that the play deals with politicians, and that Gay was
personally slighted by Walpole, reiterating the overall theme of *The
Beggar's Opera* that rewards and punishments are not justly allocated
in contemporary society, and that, as ever, it's the rich what gets the
pleasure, the poor what gets the blame.

As the Beggar himself says at the end of his play, anticipating
ironic perceptions we have already seen in *Joseph Andrews*:

> Had the Play remain'd, as I at first intended, it would have carried a
> most excellent Moral. 'Twould have shown that the lower Sort of
> People have their Vices in a degree as well as the Rich: And that they
> are punish'd for them.   (Gay, II, 64)

Although *The Beggar's Opera* complicates this 'message' in its
performance by the multiple ironies of its celebratory ending, and
although the Beggar's statement is left as no more than a
'might-have-been', it is nonetheless clearly made and left largely
unquestioned.

In this pervasive climate of irony and satire, identifiable
throughout the 1720s, communication between writers and at least
some of their readers or audiences could be successfully achieved
through nuance and obliquity rather than through the more direct
means of unambiguous statement. Yet irony is always a form of
restricted code, and can only be used effectively if it is a shared code,
if the audience addressed are aware of the strategies of decoding, if
they are prepared to accept irony's playful distortions of language and
meaning, and if they can be confidently expected to see what lies
under the surface. When an author misreads the audience's abilities to
decode irony, terrible misunderstandings can take place, as when
Daniel Defoe's intended ironies at the expense of the government's
handling of non-conformists in *The Shortest-Way With Dissenters*

(1702) were drastically misread, taken simply at their face value, and he was pursued for the severity of his remarks.

But such mistakes show a mismatch between audience and author, and happen relatively rarely, in print at least – no doubt every reader can recall personal examples where a coruscating shaft of irony has been understood literally, to the embarrassment of all parties. The statement 'I was being ironic' is always a deeply humiliating one to make, both for speaker and listener. More often, though, the ironic project works within its understanding of its audience's competence, and tries to achieve its communications indirectly. Indeed, it can be argued that much of the ironic writing of the 1720s worked within these constraints to consolidate an oppositional community of readers who shared a body of attitudes and commitments, and could present themselves as the rightful custodians of authority, while at the same time recognising their exclusion from power. Whereas satire surrounds itself with the language of correction and amendment, legitimately or not, irony merely encourages solidarity among its users, while recognising an inability to exert influence over events.

The ideological purpose of using irony in a popular success like *The Beggar's Opera* was at least partly to develop an oppositional community and enfranchise theatre audiences within it. Like Fielding's subsequent account of Wild, Gay's play conveys little sense that things might be changed by the interventions of writers, and encourages an exasperated but fatalistic recognition that the world will go on in its ridiculous ways no matter what poets and playwrights might have to say. More often, though, ironic writing of this kind narrowed down its audience, and acted to consolidate its readership by its own acts of exclusion, its adversarial relationship with a wider audience, and by developing a complex and partly inaccessible restricted code, heavily dependent on the dropping of hints, casual allusions, and enigmatic deformations of conventional meaning, only comprehensible to those 'in the know'.

I have already argued that such acts of inclusion and exclusion are operating in the way the audience is addressed at the beginning of *Joseph Andrews*, and Fielding clearly draws on what he saw as the earlier heydays of irony, acutely conscious that the ease of address achieved by Swift and Gay in the 1720s was no longer possible for an author working in the later period. By the early 1740s, the ironic community was felt to have been dispersed, and many commentators clearly thought that the lunatics had taken over the asylum. In Pope's final version of the *Dunciad,* first made public in 1742, where the prominent figure of Colley Cibber rather than the much less well-known Shakespearean editor Lewis Theobald is made the focal point, the dream that 'universal Darkness covers all', only glimpsed in the 1728 version, is now presented as a reality. The possibilities of saying one thing and being recognised by an intelligent public as meaning another were perceived as diminishing. As a result, in Fielding's version of the life of Wild, the ironies do not offer themselves up for any simple decoding or reversal, and the connections between the criminal and the statesman are made both obvious and elusive, organised around the sceptical and exasperated interrogation of 'greatness'.

Even the conventional identification of Wild with Walpole is made unusually problematic in this text. We may choose to accept that the main text of *Jonathan Wild* had been begun around 1737, as some scholars suggest, but we must still remember that at the time of its first publication in 1743 Walpole had been removed from office, and had retired to private life as the first Earl of Orford, where he had the leisure to follow quieter pursuits, such as subscribing to Fielding's *Miscellanies.*[24] By 1743, too, the frenzy of interest in Wild seemed to belong to the past, and the interaction between these two powerful figures was no longer so immediate or so sharply controversial. Fielding thus seems to be reappraising an older connection, knowing of course that Walpole is part of his audience, nursing and cultivating his sense of outrage in order to interrogate its meanings and simultaneously to confront his audience with a network of references and implications which they might or might not still recognise.

In fact, although earlier satirists had reason to be more assured of their terms of address, Fielding's deeply felt uncertainties about the competence of his audience were nothing new. Even in the 1720s many satirical writers were losing confidence in their audience's abilities to identify or decode ironised meaning, and the notion of the ironic community was never fully stable. In discussing the first version of the *Dunciad,* where the names of the dunces were not included in the text, Swift advised Pope that an unadorned or unannotated poem would be largely incomprehensible to the public at large, however accessible it might be to an enlightened coterie of fellow-thinkers:

> . . . I have long observed that twenty miles from London nobody understands hints, initial letters or town-facts and passages; and in a few

years not even those who live in London. I would have the names of
those scribblers printed indexically at the beginning or end of the
poem, with an account of their works, for the reader to refer to. I would
have all the parodies (as they are called) referred to the authors they
imitate.[25]

It is interesting here that Swift's advice about the need to name
names does not depend on the integrity of the author or the superior
moral authority of the outspoken and direct style. Rather, he
encourages Pope to spell his message out because of his anxiety about
the basis of communication. The audience these days, he says, is
simply not up to the demands of more complex allusive satire.

A problem then emerges about the legitimacy of the whole satiric
project. Without an intelligent readership to address, satire loses any
persuasive claim to moral authority or reformative zeal, becoming
virtually indistinguishable from invective or vituperation or reprisal. If
satirists are to be the chorus leaders of the riotous laughter which
accompanies each act of world history, as Mikhail Bakhtin puts it,
they must share the dominant assumptions of their audiences. If the
satirist feels alienated from that audience, as Pope and Swift
increasingly came to feel, and as Fielding clearly felt, then his laughter
loses its festive elements and becomes instead hollow, solitary and
disturbing.[26]

We have already seen how this anxiety about the receptiveness of
the audience was articulated by Fielding in both *Joseph Andrews* and
the *Journey*, and it has its effects on the terms of reference established
in *Jonathan Wild*. As Fielding looked back, the tantalisingly elusive
ironic community of the 1720s was best epitomised for him by the
work of the Scriblerus Club. An informal and occasional gathering
which met during the last days of Queen Anne in 1713 and 1714, this
grouping drew on writers like Pope, Swift, Gay, Arbuthnot and
Thomas Parnell, as well as involving political creatures like Harley
and Bolingbroke. Its aim was to produce collaborative work, exerting
pressure on the holders of political office, and although very little of
this appeared until the much later publication of *The Memoirs of
Martinus Scriblerus* (1743), the label 'Scriblerian' nonetheless became
well known as representing an erudite combination of social
commentary, irony and sceptical wit, and it has become associated
with most of the major satiric projects of the 1720s. That Fielding
wanted to perpetuate this identity and align himself with authoritative

earlier satirists is obvious in his repeated statements of admiration for the work of Pope and Swift, as well as in the way he signed many of his Haymarket plays of 1730 and 1731 'Scriblerus Secundus'.

The Lucianic text A Journey from This World to the Next represented an involvement with certain traditional satiric forms previously exploited by Swift, and elsewhere Fielding reappraises a number of other familiar 'Scriblerian' devices. His 'A Modern Glossary' in The Covent-Garden Journal in 1751, for instance, is linked to Swiftian satire, in showing how language has become debased, and how words needed careful redefinition to show their actual referents in the modern world. One particular example shows Fielding's continuity with the Scriblerian project, and his diminished confidence in his own role:

> AUTHOR. A laughing Stock. It means likewise a poor Fellow, and in
> general an Object of Contempt.   (CGJ, p. 35)

It is clear that Wild develops this theme of redefinition, examining the meanings of 'Greatness' and 'Goodness' in a darkly Swiftian way, where the 'great' figure is reduced to an automaton and the 'good' is wholly ineffective, both acting as puppets under the control of their prompter.[27] Yet the audience addressed is no longer communal or intimate, and Fielding instead reaches out to individual readers, seeking to make connection with the private feelings of his addressees, whoever and wherever they may be:

> If there are any Men of such Morals who dare to call themselves Great,
> and are so reputed, or called at least, by the deceived Multitude, surely
> a little private Censure by the few is a very moderate Tax for them to
> pay, provided no more was to be demanded: But I fear this is not the
> Case. However the Glare of Riches, and Awe of title, may dazzle and
> terrify the Vulgar; nay, however Hypocrisy may deceive the more
> Discerning, there is still a Judge in every Man's Breast, which none can
> cheat nor corrupt, though perhaps it is the only uncorrupt Thing about
> him. And yet, inflexible and honest as this Judge is (however polluted
> the Bench be on which he sits), no Man can, in my Opinion, enjoy
> any Applause which is not thus adjudged to be his Due.   (Misc, p. 10)

The concentration on privacy here, on self-examination, and the apparent confidence in 'the judge in every man's breast' show both a continuing reliance on the reformative power of satire and a move away from the communal or festive public side of the display of follies.

In place of the scathing exposure of the madness of a few, addressed to the many, Fielding is left with the more disturbing and unfocused exposure of the insanity of many, addressed only to a few, even then without confidence. And as he does so he reiterates his recurrent theme of imposture, looking again at the basis for human gullibility and the reasons for the continuing triumphs of the crafty over the well-intentioned. In contrast to the public life of 'greatness', Fielding looks for a more private life of 'goodness', yet he remains every bit as aware of its particular imperfections and its unlikeliness as he is of the dangers of 'greatness'.

When he describes the episodes in Wild's life, he constantly returns to the notion that Wild is more at the mercy of events than in control of them:

> . . . the two friends sat down to cards, a circumstance I should not have mentioned but for the sake of observing the prodigious force of habit; for though the count knew if he won ever so much of Mr Wild he should not receive a shilling, yet he could not refrain from packing the cards; nor could Wild keep his hands out of his friend's pockets, though he knew there was nothing in them.   (JW, p. 56)

The 'prodigious force of habit' turns the character into no more than a puppet, with that rigidity of motion thought by Henri Bergson to be at the basis of comedy, at the mercy both of the notion of 'greatness' he exemplifies and the commanding power of the narrator. The world in the text is seen as wholly predictable, surprising only in its capacity to run true to expectations, with no persuasive sense that any change is possible, and Wild exists as a kind of clown figure at the centre of the blackest of comedies.

In keeping with this very dark vision, seen by some critics as close to the absurdist view of Alfred Jarry and others, a kind of nihilism increasingly comes to dominate Fielding's representation.[28] And though he strives to keep his distance from his creatures, the narrator is unable fully to keep free of contamination by the absurdity of the events related. Towards the end, Wild puts forward fifteen maxims of 'priggism' – 'the certain methods of attaining greatness'. These are Machiavellian mottoes, designed to ensure the survival and flourishing of the wholly materialist politician. Wild's overt cynicism here interacts with the naive faith of Mrs Heartfree, who despite everything still believes 'THAT PROVIDENCE WILL SOONER OR LATER

PROCURE THE FELICITY OF THE VIRTUOUS AND INNOCENT' (JW, p. 203). The double critique is thus disquietingly sustained even through to the disorientating end, with these two views left in dialectical opposition. The cynical survivor, Wild, goes off to be hanged, and the naive Mrs Heartfree struggles on, and with this deep structural irony left wholly unresolved the narrative steadfastly refuses to turn into a morality play.

Among the maxims left behind by Wild is a piece of advice addressed as much to would-be authors as to fellow-thieves:

> Never to communicate more of an affair than was necessary to the person who was to execute it.   (JW, p. 216)

Fielding, too, seeks to curtail and define his communicative processes, telling his audience only what he thinks it fit for them to know. The author flits through the text, bulging the curtain, pulling the strings, being neither fully frank nor fully misleading, ironising the whole text to such a degree that his own views remain elusive. Although the list of maxims at the end describes Wild's personal code, many of them also seem applicable to the principles which the ironist sees at work in the world. But in this text, Fielding simply lurks behind the scenes, present but not prominent. He refuses to impose authority on the representation of events, preferring to adapt theatrical forms of confrontation into prose narrative, leaving readers with little sense of guidance or security. By ironising the 'great man' to such an extent that the text veers from the anarchic to the sentimental and back again, drawing on allegory, incongruous parallels and bravura exercises in literary sleight-of-hand, Jonathan Wild remains a miscellany of its own amid the Miscellanies. It shows Fielding's persisting engagement with the personal problems of hypocrisy and affectation, alongside the social problems of corruption, but does not choose to organise its examinations around a composing authorial figure. To see the redemptive move from this scathing nihilistic satire towards a more architecturally aware comic form, we need to leave the Miscellanies alone, and begin our inspection of the experiments with shape and ideology in Tom Jones.

Notes and referenes

1. Henry Fielding, 'A Modern Glossary', *The Covent-Garden Journal*, (14.1.1752), ed. Bertrand A. Goldgar (Oxford, 1988) p. 36.

2. Henry Fielding, *The Author's Farce* (1730), ed. Charles B. Woods (London, 1967), p. 16.

3. For an account of Millar's role, see Martin C. Battestin with Ruthe R. Battestin, *Henry Fielding: A Life* (London, 1989), pp. 324–6.

4. Henry Fielding, *Miscellanies*, ed. Henry Knight Miller (Oxford, 1972), p. xlvi. Further references will be incorporated in the text.

5. See the discussion of this picture and its significance in my *Literature and Crime in Augustan England* (London, 1991), pp. 84–6.

6. Alexander Pope, *An Essay on Criticism* (1711), in *The Poems of Alexander Pope*, ed. John Butt (London, 1963), p. 148.

7. Sir Joshua Reynolds, *Discourses* (1769), ed. Pat Rogers (Harmondsworth, 1992), p. 92.

8. Edward Young, *Conjectures on Original Composition* (London, 1749), pp. 19–21.

9. Sarah Fielding, *The Adventures of David Simple* (1744), ed. Malcolm Kelsall (Oxford, 1969), p. 6.

10. Henry Fielding, *A Journey from This World to the Next*, in *Miscellanies, Volume Two* ed. H. Amory, intro. B.A. Goldgar (Oxford, 1993), pp. 3–4. Further references will be incorporated in the text.

11. For an elaborate discussion of this possibility, as well as the possibility of greater collaboration between Henry and Sarah Fielding in *Joseph Andrews* and elsewhere, see J.F. Burrows and A.J. Hassall, 'Anna Boleyn and the Authenticity of Fielding's Feminine Narratives', *Eighteenth-Century Studies* 21 (1988), 427–54.

12. George Saintsbury, *The Works of Henry Fielding*, 12 vols (London, 1902), XI, xiii.

13. Henry Fielding, *The Life of Mr. Jonathan Wild the Great*, ed. David Nokes (Harmondsworth, 1982), p. 154. Further references will be incorporated in the text.

14. See C.J. Rawson, 'Epic *vs.* History: *Jonathan Wild* and Augustan Mock-Heroic', in *Henry Fielding and the Augustan Ideal Under Stress* (London, 1972), pp. 147–70.

15. Michael McKeon, *The Origins of the English Novel 1600–1740* (Baltimore and London, 1987), p. 385.

16. The fullest account of Wild's life will be found in Gerald Howson, *It Takes a Thief: The Life and Times of Jonathan Wild* (London, 1987).

17. Detailed accounts of the extensive body of 'Wild' literature, and on the specific interpretive emphases of Fielding, can be found in W.R. Irwin, *The Making of Jonathan Wild* (New York, 1941).

18. Daniel Defoe, *A True and Genuine Account of the Life and Actions of the*

Late Jonathan Wild, etc. (1725), in *The Shakespeare Head Edition of the Novels and Selected Writings of Daniel Defoe: Colonel Jacque II* (London, 1928), pp. 232–3.

19. J. Paul Hunter, *Before Novels: The Cultural Contexts of Eighteenth-Century English Fiction* (New York and London, 1990), pp. 215–16.

20. For a discussion of the 'undifferentiated matrix', see Lennard J. Davis, *Factual Fictions: The Origins of the English Novel* (New York, 1983), pp. 45–70.

21. John Gay, *The Beggar's Opera*, in *Dramatic Works*, ed. John Fuller, 2 vols (Oxford, 1983), II, 4. Further references will be incorporated in the text.

22. For discussions of the Hogarth painting, see my *Literature and Crime in Augustan England* (London, 1991), pp. 84–5, and Ronald Paulson, *Hogarth: His Life, Art and Times*, abridged edn (New Haven, Conn., 1971), pp. 75–84.

23. Jonathan Swift, *The Intelligencer* (1728), in *The Prose Works of Jonathan Swift*, ed. H. Davis (Oxford, 1955), xii, 34–5.

24. See Henry Knight Miller's introduction to the *Miscellanies*, pp. xlii–xlvi.

25. Jonathan Swift, *The Correspondence of Jonathan Swift*, ed. Harold Williams, 5 vols (Oxford, 1963–5), III, 293.

26. See Mikhail Bakhtin's comments on Rabelais as 'coryphaeus' in his *Rabelais and his World* (1965), trans. Helene Iswolsky (Cambridge, Mass., and London, 1968), p. 474.

27. See the extensive discussions of Fielding's critique of language in G.W. Hatfield, *Henry Fielding and the Language of Irony* (Chicago, 1968).

28. See C.J. Rawson, 'The World of Wild and Ubu', in *Henry Fielding and the Augustan Ideal Under Stress* (London, 1972), pp. 171–228.

CHAPTER 5
Great Tom

'Hushed be every ruder Breath'

Tho' we have properly enough entitled this our Work, a History, and not a Life; nor an Apology for a Life, as is more in Fashion; yet we intend in it rather to pursue the Method of those Writers who profess to disclose the Revolutions of Countries, than to imitate the painful and voluminous Historian, who to preserve the Regularity of his Series thinks himself obliged to fill up as much Paper with the Detail of Months and Years in which nothing Remarkable happened, as he employs upon those notable AEras when the greatest Scenes have been transacted upon the human Stage.

Such Histories as these do, in reality, very much resemble a News-Paper, which consists of just the same Number of Words, whether there be any News in it or not . . . Now it is our Purpose in the Ensuing Pages, to pursue a contrary Method. When any extraordinary Scene presents itself (as we trust will often be the Case) we shall spare no Pains nor Paper to open it at large to our Reader; but if whole Years should pass without producing anything worthy his Notice, we shall not be afraid of a Chasm in our History; but shall hasten on to Matters of Consequence, and leave such Periods of Time totally unobserved. [1]

Amid all the diversity of Fielding's earlier fiction, the adversarial relationship between the story-teller and the audience was invariably made prominent and problematic within the texts themselves, acting always as a challenging and teasing sub-plot, mirroring and mediating more discursive thematic concerns with authority developed within the main narratives. In his various one-sided dialogues with the heterogeneous reading public for fiction, Fielding appeared in various disguises. As well as taking on the satirist's grave mantle when he thought he could get away with it, he also exploited the less austere roles of quasi-theatrical impresario and master of ceremonies, intermittently flattering his audience, and intermittently abusing them, while visibly operating behind the scenes as a grand puppeteer to his characters.

At the same time as he was interrogating his own status as an author, Fielding was also subjecting to severe examination the various conventions of contemporary fiction. Each of his works inhabited an acknowledged literary context, which imposed pressure on its form and on its abilities to represent its author. The dialogic and intertextual relation of any one of those works with selected precedent or contemporary texts infiltrated the more conventional procedures of narration, showing them up as being nothing more than rather arbitrary conventions behind which only the small imaginations of Colley Cibber or Samuel Richardson lurked, ready to be parodied or derided or ridiculed as the more deliberate and self-conscious author demanded.

Such self-reflexive literary devices and extravagant self-parody have so far been identified as fundamental to Fielding's occasionally uncomfortable engagement with the authorship of prose fiction. His persistent uncertainties about the composition and competence of his audience, his frequently combative relationship with rival contemporary writers and his heightened awareness of the occasional absurdities of his own literary activities all contrive to make him appear unusually self-conscious of the making of his literary work. Like so many of his 'Augustan' predecessors and contemporaries, both in literature and in other adjacent areas of creative endeavour, Fielding was concerned with the dynamics of literary form, with the problems and opportunities involved in the creation of a shape and a spectacle for an admiring and well-informed audience – or, failing that, in the consequences of having to put just such a carefully crafted spectacle before a disparaging, inattentive, incompetent and ill-informed readership.

Until now, these features have been mainly embedded within the texts, subsidiary to more immediate concerns, and compromised by Fielding's uncertainties about the aesthetic validity of prose fiction and his scepticism about the intelligence of its readers. In *The History of Tom Jones, a Foundling,* first published in six volumes by Andrew Millar in February 1749, the constant chattering and chafing dialogue with the audience which goes on alongside the 'history' of the central figure, and the persistent engagement with the conventions and procedures of authorship which it reveals, take on such prominence that they spasmodically overwhelm any other concerns the novel might have. As a result, it is no simple matter to decide which of these two plots – the history or what might be called the historiography – is to be recognised as the central one.

Indeed, to put the case as strongly as possible, it is now more or less standard critical practice to place *Tom Jones* alongside *Joseph Andrews* or *Roderick Random* or *The Adventures of David Simple* as another 'readerly' mid-eighteenth-century comic interrogation of the contemporary social world and its values, revealed through a narrative account of particularly dramatic moments during the peripatetic adventures of the eponymous hero. The account of these exploits more or less conforms to the current expectations and precedent literary experience of its audience, while also recognising the need to acknowledge in passing the fictionality of the whole enterprise, and so by these reassuring recognitions of familiarity and similarity the text as a whole is made comfortable and accessible to its prospective readers.

However, it is no less possible, and in some ways it might even be better for the purposes of the present analysis, deliberately to remove the book from its immediate and local historical context, and to place it between the earlier *Don Quixote* and the later *Tristram Shandy* as an innovative and 'writerly' experimental fiction, to see it as a novel above all eager to explore the limits of its narrative possibilities and its form, thereby to agitate and perplex and astonish its complacent, habituated readers. Looked at in this light, *Tom Jones* is less interested in continuing the projects of earlier prose writers and novelists, and more interested in defamiliarising them, in forcing us to confront those very conventions which are not usually made visible by authors.

Talking of the novel in this way may at first seem excessively formalist – and as we shall see it will not serve to articulate *all* the book's ideological concerns – but such a move nonetheless effectively brings to the surface the unusually developed self-consciousness and 'literariness' of Fielding's massive novel, revealing its sustained reflexive concerns with the making of fiction, its constant questioning of the appropriate literary form for extended narrative, and its sceptical examination of the sensitivity and competence of its own readership. At the same time as it looks out to anatomise the turbulent world of Britain in 1745, it also looks inwards, gazing at its own navel in a developed consideration of how any story is to be told.

It is clear that as well as being a narrative vehicle for recognisable and traditional thematic concerns with hypocrisy or integrity or the possibilities of living a good life in a rotten world or whatever, *Tom Jones* is also a 'state of the art' investigation of the possibilities of the panoramic novel in the late 1740s. Just as the earlier *Joseph Andrews* sought to appropriate the down-market forms of contemporary prose fiction for more venerable and sophisticated literary activities, *Tom Jones* tries to find a place in the prevailing understanding of the novel for the urbane and commandeering author, for the controlling and orchestrating hand of the skilled artist, who seems in this case to be struggling *against* the mimetic conventions of his chosen medium just as much as he works within them.

The book's concern with artifice becomes obvious simply by looking at its extraordinary plot, seeing it primarily not as the vehicle of meaning, but as an elaborately created mechanism. In comparison with the unself-consciously haphazard plotting of Daniel Defoe or Eliza Haywood, the intensely detailed but often uneventful style of Samuel Richardson, and the ramshackle edifice of Tobias Smollett's *Roderick Random* (1748), Fielding's earlier fiction looks at once opportunist and erudite, seizing on the moment-by-moment possibilities of the novel but encompassing them more or less seriously within an authoritative editorial voice. *Tom Jones*, however, seems to offer a reinvigorated belief in the importance of design and elaborate plotting, and an imaginative investment in the aesthetic value of formal finesse, once again drawing on quasi-Aristotelian or neo-classical theatrical notions of 'unity', which set the literary work apart from the much less ordered world it (mis)represents. Even if the events described in the novel are fortuitous and apparently random, their incarnation in a controlled and shaped work of fiction need not be, and by means of the orchestrating figure of the narrator, Fielding seeks to impose an informative grid over the episodes, in order that they might take their rightful place within a microcosmic and coherent literary world.

It becomes clear on a close reading that the ordering of events in *Tom Jones* is very carefully wrought, and that the whole narrative articulates a complex but coherent plan. Although it would be wrong to expect every sentence or every line to contribute directly to some larger scheme of organisation, and even though the narrator takes the freedom to digress whenever he thinks it appropriate, there nonetheless remains an encompassing architecture to the narrative, which allocates a subordinate place to every one of its components. Indeed, the whole book has often been taken as another literary enactment of the surface confusion and latent clarity of human life seen by Fielding's favourite poet Alexander Pope in *An Essay on Man* (1733–4), where amid all the baffling haste of experience and the misconceptions that beset individuals, there yet remains the stealthy orchestrating hand of the divine Creator, who ensures that despite everything the world remains 'A mighty maze! but not without a plan.'[2]

Pope's account of this idea of the concealed coherence of apparently incoherent experience was only one of many circulating at the time, the argument from 'Design' (as it was known) being predominant in contemporary philosophy and theology. By analogy, the comparison between the manifest confusions of the world and those of a complex literary plot was regularly employed to illustrate the immanent role of the author/creator.[3] In this light, *Tom Jones* can be seen as the mightiest of mazes, a disconcertingly convoluted ramble through a world that cannot make sense to participants within it. And yet at the same time, by prioritising and keeping faith with the stealthy providential work of the author/creator, the narrative can be looked on as a superbly designed, symmetrical and unified artistic whole, whose internal consistency of shape imposes a pattern on the apparently haphazard internal events, and gives them significance.

In fact, the intricate plot or plan of *Tom Jones* has consistently attracted more critical acclaim than the book's thematic meanings or its values. Samuel Taylor Coleridge was famously quoted in his *Table Talk*, grouping together *Oedipus Tyrannus*, *The Alchemist* and *Tom Jones* as 'the three most perfect plots ever planned' and many have followed his lead, culminating in R.S. Crane's famous neo-Aristotelian demonstration of the novel's formal coherence.[4] Fielding, of course, also sought to emphasise (if not always to demonstrate) the importance of deft and unobtrusive plotting, using it at times simultaneously to reassure and to intimidate the reader:

> . . . we warn thee not too hastily to condemn any of the Incidents in this our History, as impertinent or foreign to our main Design, because thou dost not immediately conceive in what Manner such Incident may conduce to that Design. This Work may, indeed, be considered as a great Creation of our own; and for a little Reptile of a Critic to presume to find Fault with any of its Parts, without knowing the Manner in which the Whole is connected, and before he comes to the final Catastrophe, is a most presumptuous Absurdity.   (*TJ*, pp. 524–5)

In defending his 'great Creation' against the insensitivities of the 'little Reptile', Fielding here takes on the mantle of the immanent creator (or Creator) inherent in many of those philosophical and religious arguments about the hidden 'design' of the world, albeit in a heavily ironised form. And, as we shall see, such an aggressive and combative combination of lordly reassurance and reprimand is characteristic of the exasperation with which he addresses his audience throughout the book.

On a number of occasions in the prefaces and in the main narrative, he draws our attention to the surreptitiously 'designed' nature of the world, letting its resemblance to the created work of literature speak for itself:

> Though this Incident will probably appear of little Consequence to many of our Readers, yet, trifling as it was, it had so violent an Effect upon poor *Jones*, that we thought it our Duty to relate it. In reality, there are many little Circumstances too often omitted by injudicious Historians, from which Events of the utmost Importance arise. The World may indeed be considered as a vast Machine, in which the great Wheels are originally set in Motion by those which are very minute, and almost imperceptible to any but the strongest eyes.   (*TJ*, p. 225)

Happily endowed with the required 20/20 vision, Fielding's own uncovering of these tiny cogs in the 'vast Machine' of *Tom Jones* enables him to turn apparently trivial episodes, like the moment here where Sophia pulls her muff from the flames, into telling and significant ones, effecting great changes in the direction of events. But such acumen is rare, and it is not always easy to sort out what Barthes calls the 'cardinal functions' of a tale from the less important 'catalysers', to sift the essential turning points of the narrative from the incidental felicities which surround them.[5]

Part of the constant challenge to the 'little Reptile' of a critic thrown down by Fielding is to detect exactly which of these trivial events are the most important, and to allocate priority within the profusion of incidents successfully. Contrasting himself with other 'injudicious Historians', Fielding takes the responsibility for accommodating the trivial, but he often withholds his explanation of the disproportionate importance of tiny events. In the case of Sophia's muff, the author is prepared to underline the significance of the events. But the narrator of *Tom Jones* does not always offer the courteous assistance provided here, and he even goes out of his way to encourage the reader to make mistakes.

Although the plotting of Tom Jones is serpentine in its convolutions, leading to these local interpretive problems, in outline, the encompassing architecture of the book follows some simple procedures. The whole work is sub-divided into eighteen separate books, each of which contains a prefatory discussion between author and reader (or rather, a brief and apparently uninterrupted message from author to reader) and several discursive chapters of narration. Conventionally, the text is seen as comprising three distinct sections of six books. Books I–VI cover a period of approximately twenty years, internally dateable as taking place between circa 1725 and the latter part of that most important year, 1745. The events of Tom's early life are restricted to the county of Somerset, mostly around the country estates of the squires Allworthy and Western. Each book is approximately the same length, although the period of time covered varies from five years (Book III) to three weeks (Book VI). Twelve years are unapologetically omitted between Books II and III, as containing nothing the narrator considers to be worth relating.

After this historical and discursive opening section, the middle section of Books VII to XII intensifies its inspection of Tom's life, covering a crucial period of only twelve days during November 1745. Like the equivalent parts of Joseph Andrews, they take place on the road and at inns between Somerset and London, following Tom's journey after his shameful expulsion from Allworthy's Paradise Hall. Books VII, XI and XII cover three days each. Book VIII covers two days, and Books IX and X, right at the heart of the tale, each concentrate on the events of only twelve vital hours.

The final section of six books (Books XIII–XVIII) takes place mainly in various London settings, covering the high life and the low life of the metropolis, including the house of Lady Bellaston, Mrs Miller's lodgings, a masquerade, the town apartments of Fitzpatrick and Weston, and Tom's prison cell, the whole describing approximately thirty days in November and December 1745. As the narrator takes his farewell of the reader, the final two pages of the novel fill in the problematic gap between the end of the story and the point of narration, describing briefly what happened to the characters in this rather strange limbo – in this case, a period of little more than three years.

The tripartite division of the narrative into groups of books provides only the skeleton of the plot, but even this concern with shape represents a change from the practices of other contemporary novels, and a development from Fielding's own earlier efforts. Importantly, it shows a much greater awareness of the novel's capacity to prioritise certain experiences over others, by distinguishing between narrative time and the time taken by events – as when twelve years disappear between Books II and III. As indicated in the opening quotation, Fielding seems to be seizing on the novel's twin capacities for, on the one hand, capaciousness and inclusiveness, and, on the other, the interpretive pursuit of a single line of development. Within this outline, the plot itself reveals an immensely detailed interconnectedness of small events taking place within a radically disorganised larger social world, with chance meetings, accidents, coincidences and recurrences being rendered significant, even if only in retrospect, and with the most bizarre behaviour being made comprehensible by the eventual disclosure of its motivation.

Perhaps the most telling stroke in the narrator's plotting can be seen in the 'incest' scare which emerges towards the end. In Book IX, the end of the first half of the narrative, Tom sleeps with Mrs Waters, whom he has rescued from the violent entrapment of Northerton, at an inn in Upton. In Book XVIII, near the very end, Partridge belatedly recognises Mrs Waters as none other than Jenny Jones, whom he identifies as Tom's mother. Tom (and no doubt the reader) recoil in horror at the possibilities of incest having been committed by the central character.

Instead of dwelling on the significance of these complications, the narrator prefers to engage in what Gerard Genette calls 'analepsis' and, disrupting the chronological unfolding of the narrative, returns us to an earlier part of the story, so that he may display his skill at managing this melodramatic climax and point out something he assumes the reader will have overlooked:

> If the Reader will please to refresh his Memory, by turning to the Scene at *Upton* in the Ninth Book, he will be apt to admire the many strange Accidents which unfortunately prevented any Interview between *Partridge* and Mrs. *Waters*, when she spent a whole Day there with Mr. *Jones*. Instances of this Kind we may frequently observe in Life, where the greatest Events are produced by a nice Train of little Circumstances; and more than one Example of this may be discovered by the accurate Eye, in this our History.   (*TJ*, p. 916)

The reader, of course, can have nothing like the accuracy of eyesight enjoyed by the narrator, who remains firmly in charge, and able to allocate significance where he thinks fit. And, although this kind of analeptic re-ordering of events is central to the unravelling of the mysteries of *Tom Jones* – who were the foundling's parents? what happened to Dowling's letter to Allworthy? – it is asking a lot of any reader to arrive at this episode already aware of the 'nice Train of little Circumstances' which has led up to it.

After all, by retrospectively attaching such great importance to something that did *not* happen earlier – Partridge encountering or not encountering Mrs Waters, alias Jenny Jones – Fielding is asking his reader to do the impossible, and identify not only the relative importance of what is made explicit, but also the narrative and hermeneutic significance of things left unsaid. Eventually, as in *Joseph Andrews*, the incest scare is explained away by further convolutions of the plot and revelations about Tom's parentage, and the episode as a whole is more revelatory of the turbulent relation between author and reader, and of the degree of artifice and control exercised by the narrator, than it is of the behaviour or psychology of any of the intermediating characters.

Elsewhere, the narrative reveals a similarly playful concern with conventional procedures of plotting and narration. When the narrator first introduces the character of Sophia Western into the tale, he apostrophises it as 'A short Hint of what we can do in the Sublime':

> Hushed be every ruder Breath. May the Heathen Ruler of the Winds confine in iron Chains the boisterous Limbs of noisy *Boreas*, and the sharp-pointed Nose of bitter-biting *Eurus*. Do thou, sweet *Zephyrus*, rising from thy fragrant Bed, mount the western Sky, and lead on those delicious Gales, the Charms of which call forth the lovely *Flora* from her Chamber, perfumed with pearly Dews, when on the first of *June*, her Birth-day, the blooming Maid, in loose Attire, gently trips it over the verdant Mead, where every Flower rises to do her Homage, till the whole Field becomes enamelled, and Colours contend with Sweets which shall ravish her most.   (*TJ*, p. 154)

The fanfare continues for some pages, rising in intensity and becoming more and more elaborate, with no sense of strict relevance to the development of the plot, betraying instead a 'writerly' delight in operating the conventions of the heroic for their own sake. Thus, when Sophia herself does eventually appear, the effect is catastrophically bathetic – 'Sophia, then, the only Daughter of Mr. Western, was a middle-sized Woman, but rather inclining to tall' (TJ, p. 156).

The set-piece exercise in the sublime is meant as a *bravura* performance carried on for its own sake, a formal device which informs the reader that, despite appearances, Sophia is of the utmost importance, and as a further indication that the narrator can really turn it on when he wants to. But above all, it shows how the epic or the sublime style is no longer sustainable within the emergent forms of popular eighteenth-century writing. The clash of registers here between the heroic and the mundane, the elevated and the ordinary, is both a critique of the conventions of realistic description in the novel, dealing as it does with unremarkable characters, and a simultaneous critique of the archaism and pretentions of the sublime. Like the ideological 'double critique' operating in *Jonathan Wild*, this formal interaction serves to reappraise the status and authority both of the characters and the narrator, as well as raising the persistent questions about the expectations and competences of the novel's readership.

The effect of this deliberate shift of emphasis from the book's 'meaning' to its 'form', while recognising the constant interaction of these two aspects, is to introduce a different perspective on the novel. In short, it is to turn *Tom Jones* from being a predominantly mimetic fiction, representing and describing (in however stylised a form) the 'real' world of England in the recent mid-1740s in ways its readers would recognise, into what might be called a 'metafiction', a novel primarily concerned with describing itself and other novels. As well as being a text about contemporary issues, *Tom Jones* is a novel ostentatiously anxious about the possibilities of communication and the implications of the act of writing.

'Metafiction' may appear to be an excessively anachronistic term, perhaps, usually associated with those more recent writers who deliberately break the frame of verisimilitude and challenge the dominant assumptions of literary 'realism' – Samuel Beckett, Vladimir Nabokov, John Barth, Donald Barthelme, Italo Calvino, Richard Brautigan and Jorge Luis Borges are the names most frequently cited in this context. Also, the word may initially look uncomfortable and misleading in the context of Fielding's very vivid and memorable social portraits, and in the face of the various recognisable historical events from 1745 which form such an important part of the fabric of this narrative.

However, at the risk of sounding deliberately perverse, breaking the recently established frame of verisimilitude and exposing its fraudulent pretensions to knowledge are exactly what I think the author of *Tom Jones* is doing in this novel, back in 1749, driven by the contending contemporary pressures on his authorial role, and in particular by his doubts about the sophistication of his audience. The hegemony of 'realism' epitomised by the minute attention to detail found in the work of Defoe and Richardson may even then have seemed unshakeable, but it had already been challenged by Cervantes, and to an extent by Swift's devastating exploitation of the contemporary voyage narrative in his anti-novel *Gulliver's Travels*, and it would be dramatically challenged again within the eighteenth century by Sterne's *Tristram Shandy* and by Diderot's *Jacques the Fatalist*. In this context, Fielding's metafictional novel acts as a negotiating text, scrutinising the mimetic pretensions of fiction while simultaneously articulating them, laying bare the conventions by which the world had come to be described, while also using them to invent and describe his own world.

Leaving unnecessary questions about the lineage of the term aside, we can take 'metafiction' or 'metanarrative', as Gerard Genette does, as part of a descriptive lexicon covering those fictions which have different degrees or levels of story within them, which in whole or in part tell stories about other stories. As Patricia Waugh defines it, '*metafiction* is a term given to fictional writing which self-consciously and systematically draws attention to its status as an artefact in order to pose questions about the relationship between fiction and reality'.[6] Clearly, some highly wrought 'arty' works deliberately attempt to do this to the virtual exclusion of all else and to the exasperation of some readers, but self-reflection always remains a latent possibility within any narrative, written or oral, either simply for its own sake or to raise these difficult and tantalising questions about illusion and reality, fiction and fact.

We have already seen how many eighteenth-century novelists found ways of denying the fictionality of their work, of attesting to its truth by offering a novel as a 'genuine' life or presenting it as edited correspondence. But even when dealing with acknowledged works of fiction, readers may often choose to avoid confronting the issues of convention. Those narratives which seem to maintain a tactful silence over their own fictional procedures do so only with the tacit consent of their readers – we may agree not to inquire into the highly artificial conventions of, say, a classic detective story, because to do so would destroy the pleasures arising from its artifice and its mixture of predictability and surprise. In a sense, every detective story is a partial retelling of precedent detective stories, reassuringly reproducing their conventions and replicating their identifiable techniques. And it does not take much inspection to see that these conventions are operating all the time, guiding and maintaining vigilance over the reader, waiting to be recognised but not to be acknowledged. Only when we read such a deliberately self-referential and allusive text as Umberto Eco's *The Name of the Rose* does the tacit agreement between author and reader not to reveal the conventions break down, and all the literary and epistemological assumptions of the detective form are for once laid bare.

Since artifice and convention lie within the narrative procedures of all prose fiction, the possibility of revealing the mechanisms which support the text and help to sustain the mimetic illusion is always within an author's reach. Some of Fielding's predecessors and contemporaries chose to avoid this self-reflection by affiliating prose fiction to existent non-fictional forms, like the confessional or the letter, but even these conventions could be exposed, as they were in Swift's many exercises in parody. The 'metafictional' novel which so flagrantly flaunts its own fictionality is thus only doing what all novels *could* do, if they chose to. Consequently, when the Russian Formalist critic Viktor Shklovsky famously described the extraordinary *Tristram Shandy* as 'the most typical novel in world literature', he was using his outrageous paradox to state only the most banal and unchallengeable of perceptions, in my view as applicable to Fielding's novel as to Sterne's. [7]

By prioritising its concerns with authorship and story-telling to an even greater extent than any of Fielding's previous fictions, *Tom Jones* may seem to be moving away from the mimetic conventions of representation exploited and naturalised at the time, but nonetheless it is still a 'typical' novel in Shklovsky's sense, summarising these conventions and assessing them amid more stylised forms like the 'sublime', and offering a critique of their relative merits. Time and again throughout Fielding's narrative, as we have seen, the developed figure of the presiding narrator digresses to inform us of his methods, pointing out the odd 'Chasm' in the chronicle, or filling in some blanks, indicating what he takes to be the 'Matters of Consequence', advising the reader of what is about to be revealed, or reminding the audience of certain literary devices about to be brought into play, as in the title given to the stylised description of Sophia Western. And as the quotation at the beginning of this section confirms, Fielding always retains the editorial power to convey or withhold information, depending on whether he sees it as interesting or not, or, as in the 'incest' episode, on whether he can make further capital out of his decision in his continuing tussle with the short-sighted reader.

The overall effect of this sustained internal dialogue is finally to produce a text which is both a narrative and a simultaneous interpretation of that narrative, both a chronicle and a page-by-page commentary on that chronicle, identifying its procedures and recording its own conventions. Through the developed authorial presence, Fielding narrates the history and development of an ordinary character called Tom Jones, but he embeds this tale in the simultaneous narration of the history and development of an extraordinary book also called *Tom Jones*, producing a doubleness of vision which can be both disorientating and exhilarating. As we attempt to follow the career of young Jones, we are constantly thwarted by the interjection of other accounts, of the interpolated lives of the Man of the Hill, Harriet Fitzpatrick, Mrs Waters, Mrs Miller, Partridge and all the others. Yet the multivocal compendiousness (or, to use the appropriate technical term, heteroglossia), the piling of stories upon stories which frustrates the chronology of Tom Jones is at the same time the compendiousness which facilitates the chronology of *Tom Jones*, and readers are required to keep both these objects in focus during their encounter with the book.

Yet maybe even talking of a 'doubleness' of vision in *Tom Jones* is fundamentally inadequate. Mikhail Bakhtin's notion of parody as doubleness was appropriate as a way of reading the simpler concerns of *Shamela*, but in order to read Fielding's more complex narratives, a more intricate typology is required. As Umberto Eco puts it, all metafictional narratives can be seen as compilations of at least three different stories:

(i)   the story of what happens to its *dramatis personae*;
(ii)   the story of what happens to its naive reader;
(iii) the story of what happens to itself as a text (this third story being potentially the same as the story of what happens to the critical reader). [8]

That these overlapping and interwoven stories are told simultaneously, albeit to different readers, seems incompatible with Patricia Waugh's more schematic notion that they are displayed systematically. And furthermore it seems likely that the self-reflexive elements of a text might not always be quite so easy to disentangle from the other elements of a narrative, or to isolate for the purposes of analysis as both Eco and Waugh suggest. In fact, in Fielding's novel the commentary and the more orthodox 'main' story might *seem* to be clearly separated and demarcated by the conventional devices of explanatory prefaces, chapter-headings and titles, but in the experience of reading they are more drastically intermingled and resistant to systematic unravelling, like the interwoven 'braid' or 'topos' of different voices and codes which Roland Barthes identifies at work within Balzac's story in S/Z. [9]

After identifying the different and competing stories within a metafiction, Umberto Eco goes on to discuss the specialised and highly sophisticated procedures of reading which such writing demands. He claims that the metafiction 'must be read twice: it asks for both a naive and a critical reading, the latter being the interpretation of the former'. Eco thus seems to demand almost as much self-consciousness from the competent reader of such fiction as from the writer, and requires the audience for any metafictional text to be constantly astute, weighing up and reflecting on what they are being offered, comparing their imagined 'naive' responses with their more carefully attuned critical ones. Eco's competent reader seems to be a highly trained figure, constantly reassessing what is happening in a text, continually oscillating between the twin poles of the naive and the critical, developing two different readings simultaneously, one of which interprets and perhaps ironises the other.

As we might expect, Henry Fielding does not share Umberto Eco's confidence in the availability of such an astute audience, although he would clearly yearn for the ironic community that these adept and intellectually nimble readers would provide. In fact, the earlier novelist seems deeply sceptical about the ability of the existent novel-reading public of the 1740s to develop any such sophistication. For, amid all the uncertainties about who actually reads books, there remains the widespread hostility to re-reading, so central to Eco's argument. As Barthes puts it:

> Rereading, an operation contrary to the commercial and ideological habits of our society, which would have us 'throw away' the story once it has been consumed ('devoured'), so that we can then move on to another story, buy another book, and which is only tolerated in certain marginal categories of readers (children, old people, professors) . . .[10]

Aware of the problems of creating a book only appreciable by such economically inactive groups as the very young, the very old or the very wise, Fielding tries to make his book at once readable and complex, at once triumphant and aware of its own folly.

When Fielding directly addresses the person he assumes to be his reader in the various prefatory chapters of Tom Jones, he demands the strictest vigilance and deference, but also subtly infiltrates doubt about the possibility of any second, more critical reading being achieved by the kind of naive consumers with whom he normally has to deal. These rather hapless creatures (always assumed to be male, incidentally) are voracious rather than fastidious in their use of narrative, and in all ways remarkably unlike both the quick-witted volatile postmodern creatures envisaged by Eco and the careful scrutineers of texts identified by Barthes. In the opening chapter, for instance, Fielding immediately anticipates the language chosen by Barthes in the passage above when he presents his book as nothing more than a 'Feast', something to be joyously consumed ('devoured'), not seriously contemplated, and the possibility that the reader might both eat his cake and still have it (as Eco seems to require) is made to seem highly unlikely.

Interestingly, such scepticism about the perceptiveness of the public is not confined to the prefatory comments, and it infiltrates the main narrative time and again. After all, given the constant failures of acumen and worldliness exemplified by the wholly undiscerning and short-sighted male characters in the 'main' narrative, including the good-natured Allworthy, their persistent obtuseness in 'reading' their own experience in the face of more quick-witted deceivers like Blifil, what confidence can there be that the book's male readers are likely to be any more astute or sensitive to nuance, especially when they are confronted by the domineering and crafty intelligence of Henry Fielding?

But exactly who is the author speaking to? Fielding's addressee in Tom Jones is at first generously interpellated as 'my sensible Reader' (TJ, p. 31), and such apparent politeness and deference is just about maintained for much of the time. However, the courteous expression is quickly seen to be no more than a formality, a conventional civility generated by the complex economic relation involved in finding an audience for a novel and based on the interdependency of the provider and his customers. Although the terms of reference between author and audience are occasionally flattering and polite, the reader of *Tom Jones* is persistently hailed as no more than a customer or a consumer, a belittling and restrictive position, requiring little intelligence, discernment or imagination, and one which confers few rights and virtually no dignity. Similarly, the relation between reader and writer is constantly described in terms of buying and selling, in terms of commodities and their market value. For the first time in the book, but by no means for the last, the introductory chapter to Book I shows how the real motive behind a conversation can be disguised by a diverting reliance on form, and indicates how only the acute or critical reader (not the naive reader apparently being addressed) may see beyond what is actually said and find out what is really meant.

Reluctantly acknowledging that he is putting his work before the undiscriminating general public rather than a select few friends, no longer even with the security of the known audience for the *Miscellanies*, and recognising that, for better or for worse, the customer is always right, Fielding tries to articulate his own position. He starts the long narrative of his book with an extended metaphor in which his role as an author working within the recently established market economy of publishing is developed by means of an analogy with what he pretends to see as a parallel trade:

> An Author ought to consider himself, not as a Gentleman who gives a private or eleemosynary Treat, but rather as one who keeps a public Ordinary, at which all Persons are welcome for their Money. In the former Case, it is well known, that the Entertainer provides what Fare he pleases; and tho' this should be very indifferent, and utterly disagreeable to the Taste of his Company, they must not find any Fault; nay, on the contrary, Good-Breeding forces them outwardly to approve and to commend whatever is set before them. Now the contrary of this happens to the Master of an Ordinary. Men who pay for what they eat, will insist on gratifying their Palates, however nice and whimsical these may prove; and if every Thing is not agreeable to their Taste, will challenge a Right to censure, to abuse, and to d—n their Dinner without Controul.   (*TJ*, p. 31)

In terms of this heavily ironic account, the contemporary author is no longer in the privileged position of addressing invited guests or humble pensioners, from whom certain standards of polite behaviour and courtesy might reasonably be expected. Instead, he is running a kind of public house, where anyone with appropriate amounts of cash can enter, irrespective of their possession of 'Good-Breeding', and where people may do more or less as they please, regardless of what the landlord/author might prefer, and where the customers, not the providers, retain the time-honoured satirist's right to censure and abuse. At this stage of the book, the fragile etiquette between host and guests is maintained, but it never looks wholly secure, and Fielding's politeness already shows signs of strain.

Ironically and self-deprecatingly seeing himself as working alongside other 'honest Victuallers', Fielding then lays a menu before his customers, so that they will not be misled about the nature of the entertainment to come. The provision on offer in *Tom Jones* is to be nothing other than 'HUMAN NATURE', a single item perhaps, but one containing a number of exquisite delicacies and subtle tastes, as full of culinary possibilities as a succulent turtle, as long as it is prepared by the right hands. Finally, lest the prospective purchaser think the menu on offer too mundane, Fielding asserts that it is of the highest quality, most rare, and highly suitable even for the most discerning gourmet tastes – 'true Nature is as difficult to be met with in Authors, as the *Bayonne* Ham or *Bologna* Sausage is to be found in the Shops' (*TJ*, p. 32).

The humiliating and belittling (mis)representation of the novel as no more than a superior sausage – as *mortadella* rather than *Morte d'Arthur*, perhaps – is part of the paradoxical treatment of the relative positions of the reader and the writer which goes on throughout the book. While apparently pandering to the reader's tastes by speaking to him in a comprehensible and courteous language about things he may be expected to understand (inns, menus, sausages and so on), Fielding is simultaneously signalling his distance from the audience by his own obvious urbanity and by the deft incorporation of a barely comprehensible word like the splendid 'eleemosynary' into the sales pitch. And by means of this metaphor of the book as a public house the acknowledged desires of the readership are made wholly carnal rather than cerebral, suggesting, contrary to the ostentatious display of deference, that the customers in question are in possession of little nobility and less intelligence. So the question remains: in the

transaction of the novel, who is really patronising whom? Who is
really treating whom with disdain or contempt?

At the beginning of Book II, Fielding gleefully changes from civil
host to benevolent despot, and, gratefully leaving the sausages aside,
takes upon himself the more elevated role of patriarch and law-giver:

> For as I am, in reality, the Founder of a new Province of Writing, so I
> am at liberty to make what Laws I please therein. And these Laws, my
> Readers, whom I consider as my Subjects, are bound to believe in and
> to obey; with which that they may readily and cheerfully comply, I do
> hereby assure them that I shall principally regard their Ease and
> Advantage in all such Institutions: For I do not, like a *jure divino*
> Tyrant, imagine that they are my Slaves or my Commodity. I am,
> indeed, set over them for their own Good only, and was created for
> their Use, and not they for mine. Nor do I doubt, while I make their
> Interest the general Rule of my Writings, they will unanimously concur
> in supporting my Dignity, and in rendering me all the Honour I shall
> deserve or desire.   (*TJ*, pp. 77–8)

As Fielding plays with the possibilities of absolute power here, we see
once again the complex ramifications of his ironies and
self-projections. The position of '*jure divino* tyrant', sole monarch of
not just this book but of a whole 'Province of Writing', which he
momentarily assumes, only to shrug off, reflects a kind of Jacobite
absolutism which, as we shall see later, is also subjected to critical
ironies within the main text, in the treatment of the high Tory Squire
Western and in the episode with the King of the Gypsies. While
seeming to reject this possibility of complete dictatorial control,
however, Fielding yet retains the legislative power and the heightened
authority it confers, promising only to exercise that authority properly.
But as he protests his earnest desire to serve the reader/subject in any
way possible, his language takes on a further layer of irony, in its
unconvincing humility and deference, undercut by the yearning for
'Dignity' and 'Honour' at the end, and in the ostentatious (and rather
desperate sounding) confidence in the reader's good nature.

These elaborate and amusing self-projections are only the first part
of the extended disorientating dialogue between author and reader. As
Fielding constantly interjects, cajoles, and reprimands, the reader is
put in a position to be trained and nurtured throughout the book, his
abilities simultaneously flattered and belittled, his competence never
really assumed to be adequate to the complex demands of sophis-

ticated reading. To take one early example, after the death of Captain John Blifil at the end of Book II, Allworthy's grief is signalled, but not developed, and at the beginning of Book III the 'judicious Reader' is given space to imagine the subsequent events for himself:

> The Reader will be pleased to remember, that at the Beginning of the Second Book of this History, we gave him a Hint of our Intention to pass over several large Periods of Time, in which nothing happened worthy of being recorded in a Chronicle of this Kind.
>
> In so doing, we do not only consult our own Dignity and Ease; but the Good and Advantage of the Reader: For besides, that by these Means we prevent him from throwing away his Time in reading either without Pleasure or Emolument, we give him at all such Seasons an Opportunity of employing that wonderful Sagacity of which he is Master, by filling up these vacant Spaces of Time with his own Conjectures; for which Purpose, we have taken care to qualify him in the preceding Pages.   (TJ, p. 116)

Fielding here claims to be liberating and empowering the reader by creating this interpretive space, in which the reader may place his own 'Conjectures'. But the pretence of liberality remains unconvincing while, by his own admission, Fielding is retaining all the narrative authority for himself, with due concern for his own 'Ease'. He flatters 'that wonderful Sagacity' of the reader, duly trained by the preceding narrative, and leaves a gap in the text for it to operate within, so as to save himself the trouble of doing it. In a more restrained version of the flagrant gaps and blank spaces in *Tristram Shandy*, Fielding creates the illusion of interpretive freedom, of reader power, while actively seeking to make life easier for himself.

As the passage goes on, the narrator's apparent confidence in the reader's native or trained sagacity clearly begins to dwindle. The narrator draws suitable moral lessons from the episode while challenging his reader to admit that they are no more than commonplaces:

> . . . what Reader but knows what Mr. *Allworthy* felt at first for the Loss of his Friend, those emotions of Grief, which on such Occasions enter into all Men whose Hearts are not composed of Flint, or their Heads of as Solid Materials? Again, what Reader doth not know that Philosophy and Religion, in time, moderated, and at last extinguished this Grief? The former of these, teaching the Folly and Vanity of it, and

the latter, correcting it, as unlawful, and at the same time assuaging it by raising future Hopes and Assurances which enable a strong and religious Mind to take leave of a Friend on his Deathbed with little less Indifference than if he was preparing for a long Journey; and indeed with little less Hope of seeing him again.   (*TJ*, pp. 116–17)

The moral homily expressed here echoes the more straightforward version of the theme of consolation found in Fielding's 1743 essay 'Of the Remedy of Affliction for the Loss of our Friends', published in the first volume of the *Miscellanies*. But the terms of address here are significantly different, less clearly expository, and beset by uncertainties about the competence of readers to feel what they are supposed to feel. At first, Fielding pretends that the preliminary question 'what Reader but knows . . .?'is purely rhetorical. The implied assumption must be that surely *everybody* knows this stuff. But if so, why does he even include it? Behind the veneer of confidence, there lies the hidden suspicion that at least part of the audience for *Tom Jones* cannot be relied upon to know anything at all, and that leaving them gaps to fill correctly is a highly risky business.

Fielding immediately acknowledges that such pedestrian guidance has to be given to 'Readers of the lowest Class', and that perhaps when dealing with 'the upper Graduates of Criticism' it is possible to be more demanding, to assume that they are capable of engaging in the right kind of interpretation without such extensive instruction. And as he goes on to express his confidence that 'much the greatest Part of our Readers are very eminently possessed of this Quality' (*TJ*, pp. 117–18), it may be that the narrator overcomes his anxieties, and finds security in the knowledge of his well-qualified customers. But even within that confident statement, there remains the shred of doubt – if 'the greatest Part' are sophisticated, by definition there must remain lesser parts who are not. In short, the novel simply cannot address itself to a homogeneous audience, cannot make assumptions about the talents and capacities of its readers, and, like so many human actions within the main narrative plot of *Tom Jones*, it must always be in danger of misinterpretation. The naive and critical readings of the book, thought to be achieved simultaneously by Umberto Eco's sophisticated reader, are here seen to be polarised between different reading communities, and Fielding cannot confidently find terms of address which will effectively communicate the same thing to all members of such a heterogeneous crowd. In losing confidence in his ability to communicate, the narrator is thus drifting towards solipsism, and he knows it.

In the prefatory remarks to Book X (the beginning of the second half of the novel), Fielding directly faces the question of just who is out there:

> Reader, it is impossible we should know what Sort of Person thou wilt be: For, perhaps, thou may'st be as learned in human Nature as *Shakespear* himself was, and, perhaps, thou may'st be no wiser than some of his Editors. Now lest this latter should be the Case, we think proper, before we go any farther together, to give thee a few wholesome Admonitions; that thou may'st not as grosly misunder-stand and misrepresent us, as some of the said Editors have misunderstood and misrepresented their Author.   (*TJ*, p. 523)

As well as returning to the original target for Pope's *Dunciad* and denigrating the talents of Shakespeare's eighteenth-century editors – the Augustan satirist's equivalent of shooting fish in a barrel – Fielding slyly identifies himself with the acknowledged great author of the past, at once venerated and abused by commentators. By seeing himself alongside Shakespeare, and by seeing some correspondence between his own inarticulate readership and Shakespeare's dunce-like editors, Fielding sets highly challenging and disparaging terms of reference for his audience. Unlike Shakespeare, however, Fielding can attempt to take control of the situation, and he can offer strict guidance to his readers about how they ought to proceed, which they may or may not choose to follow.

The concerns with form in *Tom Jones* are thus more than simply decorative. Faced with what he assumes to be an unsympathetic and insensitive reading public, unsure of the status of authorship, Fielding strives to build a structure sufficiently robust to withstand the onslaughts of even the most cretinous audience. Yet the book invites multiple perspectives, and, like a piece of modern architecture, it lays bare its mechanisms and its internal systems of organisation. Fielding's prime commitment throughout this book is to the principle of organisation, as an aesthetic goal in the first place, but as an aesthetic concept which increasingly reveals political and moral implications.

As Fielding strives to control and organise his writing, that writing in its turn discusses the organisation and control of society and of individual conduct, and so the presentation and the substance of the narrative become fascinatingly intertwined and entangled. The ideological implications of his metafictional enterprise need more consideration, and without reproducing any crude distinctions between 'form' and 'content', it is now time to turn from the self-reflexive features of *Tom Jones* to the even more contested questions of its representations of the volatile and, occasionally, indecipherable world beyond its pages.

Human nature

Besides displaying that Beauty of Virtue which may attract the Admiration of Mankind, I have attempted to engage a stronger Motive to Human Action in her Favour, by convincing Men, that their true Interest directs them to a Pursuit of her. For this Purpose I have shewn, that no Acquisitions of Guilt can compensate the Loss of that solid inward Comfort of Mind, which is the sure Companion of Innocence and Virtue; nor can in the least balance the Evil of that Horror and Anxiety which, in their Room, Guilt introduces into our Bosoms. And again, that as these Acquisitions are in themselves generally worthless, so are the Means to attain them not only base and infamous, but at least incertain, and always full of Danger. Lastly, I have endeavoured strongly to inculcate, that Virtue and Innocence can scarce ever be injured but by Indiscretion; and that it is this alone which often betrays them into the Snares that Deceit and Villainy spread for them. A Moral which I have the more industriously laboured, as the teaching it is, of all others, the likeliest to be attended with Success; since, I believe, it is much easier to make good Men wise, than to make bad Men good.   (*TJ*, pp. 7–8)

After seeing all the narrator's uncertainties about the composition of the audience for *Tom Jones* and the scepticism repeatedly expressed about their aptitudes and sensitivity, it is refreshing to find a preliminary passage in the book where the writer clearly identifies both himself and his addressee, where Fielding talks directly to someone he calls 'the candid Reader' with at least the illusion of frankness. For once in his novel at least, the novelist seems to discover a space beyond irony, and locates a community of his peers within which an intelligent dialogue can be maintained. Speaking man to man, as it were, Fielding then takes the opportunity to provide his well-qualified reader with a frame of reference by means of which the ensuing text may be interpreted.

The passage quoted above comes from the signed dedication to Fielding's patron and sponsor George Lyttelton, who, like Fielding himself, had been part of the oppositional alliance against Robert Walpole in the 1730s and who had since become 'One of the Lords Commissioners of the TREASURY' in the subsequent Pelham administration of the second half of the 1740s. Later the first Baron Lyttelton, the dedicatee of *Tom Jones* was by the time of its publication a well-known and well-connected politician, one of a number of eminent figures (also including Ralph Allen and the Duke of Bedford) who helped the novelist considerably in his energetic, not to say undignified, search for remunerative and authoritative public offices in the legal service.

As well as being involved with the Treasury, Lyttelton was a minor writer and acknowledged patron of the arts to whom Fielding paid effusive tribute in the poems 'Of True Greatness' and 'Liberty', both collected in the *Miscellanies*. Lyttelton's involvement with *Tom Jones* does not end with the dedication – along with the philanthropic Ralph Allen, he is often seen as forming part of the model for Squire Allworthy in the main body of the novel, with Allworthy's country house, Paradise Hall, closely resembling Lyttelton's own Hagley Hall. A close reading of the text might suggest that the link with Allworthy is not perhaps as flattering as the terms of reference in the dedication seem to require – the squire, although generous of spirit and supremely well-intentioned, makes error after error in his judgements throughout the tale – but there is further external evidence that Fielding was very eager to represent his patron in as favourable a light as possible. In *The Jacobite's Journal* in 1748, at a time when Lyttelton himself was alleged to be the victim of widespread misunderstanding, Fielding hailed his sponsor as 'almost the only Patron which the Muses at present can boast among the Great', and Lyttelton's generous support for the poet James Thomson provided Fielding with an enviable model of effective patronage, a wholly desirable contrast to the material and commercial predicaments he found himself in as a practising novelist.[11]

The aristocratic and urbane George Lyttelton was thus an attractive addressee or audience for Fielding, for two main reasons. Firstly, he represented the possibilities of enlightened and influential patronage in a period where such a system was in rapid decline. Secondly, Lyttelton fancied himself as a fellow-author, and so he could plausibly be spoken to by the novelist as an equal. Signing himself as 'Your most Obliged, Obedient Humble Servant', Fielding's remarks about his patron are highly generous, not to say fawning and obsequious, and have none of the comic exasperation and irony we saw in his many addresses to less easily identifiable readers which are dispersed through the main narrative.

The confident tone of voice and the formal vocabulary used in conversation with Lyttelton resemble those employed elsewhere by Fielding at this time when speaking in his official capacity as a magistrate, addressing literate and responsible people about serious matters, as in his pamphlets *The True State of the Case of Bosavern Penlez* (1749) and *A Charge Delivered to the Grand Jury* (1749). Yet even although his greater confidence in the receptiveness of his audience (or at least of this particular member of his audience) is emphasised in the dedication, Fielding still seems remarkably eager to spell out his meaning and intentions in the most painstaking manner possible, in apparent anticipation of his book being misunderstood or misrepresented, if not by Lyttelton himself then by its anonymous purchasers and readers.

The interpretation of *Tom Jones* which the author lays before Lyttelton is of a particular and specific kind. In the passage quoted, Fielding seems to be encouraging Lyttelton to look beyond the incidental farce and comedy of the plot in all its intricacies, and to attribute a generalised serious and moralistic significance to his novel. Above all, the writer seems to be drawing on the traditional moral defence of comedy and inviting the well-qualified 'good' reader to recognise the universally applicable wisdom that the book displays and endorses, advising him to seek a coherent reading far removed from the ludic and paradoxical demands of irony or metafiction, and nearer to the sermonising of the essays on topics like 'greatness' or 'good nature' contained in the *Miscellanies*.

From this authorially endorsed point of view, the 'meaning' of the book lies in its capacity to encourage the acquisition of even greater wisdom and virtue in its more elevated audience, while at the same time persuading less astute readers of the need to improve their own lives and their personal conduct. As it is presented here, the plot of *Tom Jones* dramatises a particular moral view of human affairs, describing the pitfalls of naivety or imprudence, in order that a socially elevated audience may be reminded of what it knows already, and a more popular audience made to confront what it has forgotten.

Fielding thus splits his audience into two unequal sections, and represents the text differently for each of them. He addresses, first, a small group of his peers, exemplified and epitomised by Lyttelton, for whom the narrative is a diverting yet wholesome spectacle designed to confirm their convictions about the indiscipline of the lower orders and the professional classes, to provide some recognisable satiric types, and to heighten the awareness of universal moral complexities. The author then addresses a much wider class of general readers, for whom the narrative is more broadly didactic and educative, designed to provide a gallery of positive and negative models from which they should learn suitable and much-needed lessons. And if these initial remarks can be taken, seriously, as anything other than a conventional courtesy between author and patron, they show Fielding's own position, aligning himself with the therapeutic project of the high-minded moral satirist, earlier endorsed by Swift and many others – 'I have endeavoured to laugh Mankind out of their favourite Follies and Vices' (*TJ*, p. 8) – distancing himself from the more experimental literary concerns with the possibilities of communication and the status of the novel described in the last chapter.

Identifying themselves with the intelligent superior addressee like Lyttelton rather than with the popular audience so regularly reprimanded and chastened throughout the text, many subsequent critics have sought to read the novel doctrinally, in terms of its capacity to convey useful moral lessons to a largely recalcitrant general audience (an audience which presumably does not include these literary critics themselves). Within the eighteenth century, the morality of novels and fiction in general was a highly controversial issue, first raised by the sensationalist 'scandalous' chronicles of Mary Manley and Eliza Haywood early in the century, and later dramatised by the commercial success of what were seen as morally unorthodox books like *Roderick Random* and *Tom Jones* in the 1740s and 1750s. As different readers responded to the complex mixture of qualities in Fielding's characters differently, and appreciated or deplored the book's engagement with broad sexual comedy, the author was occasionally taken on his own stated terms and applauded for his encouragement of virtue, for his appropriation of the novel as a means of conveying moral lessons. However, that approval was by no means unanimous, and in the hands of his immediate contemporaries Fielding was more often castigated for his apparent endorsement of immorality and licentiousness than he was commended for his probity or high-mindedness.

Of course, not all of the earliest readers' responses to the book were articulated and only a few have survived. Nonetheless, there are a number of available examples of contemporary tributes to Fielding's didactic powers. In a letter written in 1749, for instance, a 'common reader' by the name of Captain Lewis Thomas described how he found *Tom Jones* a most salutary and elevating text:

> I am just got up from a very Amazing entertainment; to use a Metaphor in the Foundling, I have been these four or five days last past a fellow traveller of Harry Fieldings, & a very agreeable Journey I have had. Character, Painting, Reflexion, Humour, excellent each in its Kind . . . If my design had been to propagate virtue by appearing publickly in its defence, I should rather have been ye Author of Tom Jones than of Five Folio Volumes of sermons. [12]

Thomas's approval of the book's 'entertainment' – a term which at this time described both hospitality and amusement – and his endorsement of the agreeability of its defence of virtue was echoed by many, and those features he comments on were widely seen as the most praiseworthy. However, by no means all early readers accepted the wholesomeness of the book's provision quite as enthusiastically as Thomas, and many found themselves reproving the author for allowing the narrative to advertise and apparently to endorse various moral failings.

Also writing in 1749, for instance, in a letter to Astraea and Minerva Hill, the daughters of Fielding's friend Aaron Hill, Samuel Richardson summed up the more hostile view of the novel prevailing in certain circles at that time, with which he felt himself intuitively in agreement:

> . . . I must confess, that I have been prejudiced by the opinion of several judicious friends against the truly coarse-titled *Tom Jones*; and so have been discouraged from reading it – I was told, that it was a rambling collection of waking dreams, in which probability was not observed; and that it had a very bad tendency. And I had reason to think that the author had intended for his second view (His *first*, to fill his pocket, by accommodating it to the reigning taste) in writing it, to whiten a vicious character, and to make morality bend to his practices . . . But, perhaps, I think the worse of the piece because I know the writer and dislike his principles, both public and private, though I wish well to the *man* and love four worthy sisters of his, with whom I am well acquainted. [13]

In advance of reading the book for himself, Richardson sees it surrounded by a quickly established reputation for moral confusion and for propagating 'a very bad tendency', which he attributes to the author's desire to please the public and thereby 'fill his pocket'. Although Fielding the *man* may have been above such things, suggests Richardson, drawing an interesting and suggestive distinction, Fielding the commercially motivated *writer* was inevitably in complicity with the lowest elements of the reading public, and the squalid and shabby morality of his book reflects *their* low standards rather than his own, although that still does not excuse it.

Other eighteenth-century commentators also found Fielding's professions of morality particularly hard to swallow, for various reasons. In a famous essay in *The Rambler* in 1750, for instance, Samuel Johnson took exception to the contemporary novel's failure to be sufficiently exemplary. Within a generalised account of the moral responsibilities of the writer, especially the writer of works likely to be read by the young and inexperienced, and naming no names, Johnson placed great emphasis on the need to convey clear and uncomplicated lessons. Implicitly contrasting the graphic frankness of the recently successful *Roderick Random* and *Tom Jones*, in which the world is 'promiscuously described', with what he took to be the more acceptably serious and consistent novels of Samuel Richardson, Johnson discounted Fielding's pretensions to pedagogic authority:

> Many writers, for the sake of following nature, so mingle good and bad qualities in their principal personages, that they are both equally conspicuous; and as we accompany them through their adventures with delight, and are led by degrees to interest ourselves in their favour, we lose the abhorrence of their faults, because they do not hinder our pleasure, or, perhaps, regard them with some kindness for being united with so much merit. [14]

According to Johnson, the novel's commitment to rendering accurately and in detail all the complexities of human life served to undermine any authority it might have to comment on those complexities, leaving readers (and writers) inevitably confused. Put simply, the extreme particularity of the novel hindered its abilities to reach towards general moral truths, whatever its authors might claim, and so the novelist failed to live up to the writer's responsibility to strive to make the world a better place. Elsewhere, Johnson dismissed

Fielding as a 'blockhead', denied ever having read *Joseph Andrews*, and angrily protested that admitting to an acquaintance with *Tom Jones* was 'a confession which no modest lady should ever make'.[15] In sum, he seems to have shared Richardson's suspicion of the deleterious effects of the mercenary motives behind Fielding's writing, which he saw as lying behind the writing of *all* novels, and as a result he vehemently refused to take seriously the novelist's claims to high-mindedness and moral seriousness.

For many later eighteenth-century readers, sharing Johnson's severity or Richardson's suspicions some time after the heat might have been expected to die down, *Tom Jones* was still nothing more than a scandalous catchpenny endorsement of a pernicious libertine morality. For Sir John Hawkins in 1787, for instance, Fielding's work not only failed to live up to the elevated moral standards its author endorsed in the book's preface, it actively inculcated vice and immorality. Pulling no punches, Hawkins described *Tom Jones* as:

> . . . a book seemingly intended to sap the foundation of that morality which it is the duty of parents and all public instructors to inculcate in the minds of young people, by teaching that virtue upon principle is imposture, that generous qualities alone constitute true worth, and that a young man may love and be loved, and at the same time associate with the loosest women. His morality, in respect that it resolves virtue into good affections, in contradiction to moral obligations and a sense of duty, is that of Lord Shaftesbury vulgarized, and is an excellent system in palliating the vices most injurious to society. He was the inventor of that cant phrase, 'goodness of heart,' which is every day used as a symbol for probity, and means little more than the virtue of a horse or a dog; in short, he has done more towards corrupting the rising generation than any writer we know of.[16]

The extravagance of Hawkins's revulsion is remarkable, and it shows the intensity of the controversy continuing to surround Fielding's work nearly forty years after its first publication. Concentrating upon Tom's encounters with the 'loosest of women' like Molly Seagrim, Mrs Waters and Lady Bellaston, Hawkins refused to accept any declarations of high-minded intent on the author's behalf, and he saw in its place a feeble reliance on some vague emotionalism called 'goodness of heart,' which could only appeal to dissolute and lazy people. Responding to Fielding's own stated demand that the book be taken seriously, Johnson and Hawkins and a number of others came up with the conclusion that it was indeed serious, but that, alas, it was seriously wicked.

It is always interesting to try to recapture the immediate shocking impact of any book on its contemporary and near-contemporary readers, especially one that now seems as respectable and uncontroversial as *Tom Jones*. However, although it would be highly surprising to find any recent commentator as hostile to Fielding's work as Johnson or Hawkins were, the legacy of this debate about the novelist's professed integrity and the moral basis of the novel continues to this day. For many twentieth-century critics, the true meaning and significance of *Tom Jones* lie not in its self-referential playfulness or in its dialogue about the nature of fiction, as I have so far been suggesting, but remain instead in the area of what might be called its doctrine or its 'moral thesis', its concerns with assessing and evaluating the conduct of its characters.

For some critics, the huge intricate machinery of the plot and the overlapping ironies it conveys only serve as means to articulate its author's developed moral consciousness. As William Empson argued in 1958:

> What nobody will recognize, I feel, is that Fielding set out to preach a doctrine in *Tom Jones* (1749), and said so, a high-minded though perhaps abstruse one . . . he is expressing a theory about ethics, and the ironies are made to interlock with the progress of the demonstration. The titanic plot, which has been praised or found tiresome taken alone, was devised to illustrate the theory, and the screws of the engine of his style are engaging the sea. . . . Modern critics seem unable to feel this, apparently because it is forbidden by their aesthetic principles, even when Fielding tells them he is doing it; whereas Dr Johnson and Sir John Hawkins, for example, took it seriously at once, and complained bitterly that the book had an immoral purpose. It certainly becomes much more interesting if you attend to its thesis; even if the thesis retains the shimmering mystery of a mirage. [17]

Empson puts his case strongly, but he was clearly wrong to think that 'nobody will recognize' that Fielding was preaching a doctrine. In fact, the reverse was (and is) true, and many discussions of Fielding's novel over the last thirty years or so have chosen to debate the origins and nature of an alleged doctrine, to articulate or contest various versions of this 'theory about ethics', not always recognising that any such theory will be mediated and inflected by its localised and individuated presentation in a novel.

As we saw with M.C. Battestin's account of *Joseph Andrews*, the notion that Fielding's fiction articulates a body of religious or philosophical ideas is tenacious. Yet what remains impressive and intriguing is the way the 'theory' which seems to be so clearly stated in the books manages to keep evading final definition. As anyone who has completed (or examined) post-graduate work must know, to talk of the 'shimmering mystery of a mirage' in something purporting to be a thesis, as Empson does, is not normally thought to be complimentary. Fielding's statements of the moral thesis underlying *Tom Jones* as offered initially to Lyttelton and his peer group readers may look reassuringly easy to grasp and programmatic, but, as they are subsequently dramatised and problematised through the ensuing narrative, they nonetheless give rise to a host of variously inflected readings.

According to Empson, the doctrine put forward in the book is thus:

'If good by nature, you can imagine other people's feelings so directly that you have an impulse to act on them as if they were your own; and this is the source of your greatest pleasures as well as of your own genuinely unselfish actions.'[18]

Empson offers what looks like a reasonably accurate, if heavily reductive, interpretation of the eponymous hero's own behaviour throughout the book, claiming that Tom's intrinsic 'good nature' is given centrality and defended despite his occasional lapses. Tom's behaviour is schematically dramatised in contrast to the hypocrisy of Blifil or the various alternative models of conduct and belief represented by, for example, Thwackum and Square or Sophia Western or the Man of the Hill, all of whom are said by some critics to *stand for* something in what amounts to Fielding's detailed and localised version of the morality play.

In keeping with Battestin's account of the latitudinarian basis of Fielding's moral beliefs, this version of the novel emphasises the moral psychology and the religious affiliations of the protagonists, identifying Tom as the naturally virtuous man in a religious context, his honesty forming a challenging contrast to the procession of frauds and hypocrites who surround him. Then again, as Irvin Ehrenpreis sees it, the book draws more heavily on classical traditions of ethics and inquires more philosophically into the essential property of a good man, 'for Fielding considered that the deepest problem in human relations is to recognise the good-natured man and distinguish him from his opposite'.[19] Ehrenpreis's overtly masculinist reading of Fielding – seeing the author as a man writing to other men about the morality and conduct of men – has been properly challenged by a more recent writer, who finds in the whole of Fielding's creative writing, and at the heart of his doctrine, 'an active debate about the social position of women, and about sexual difference and gender roles in eighteenth-century society'.[20] The relative emphases of these readings may need greater clarification, but for Bernard Harrison, author of the most carefully developed study of Fielding's moral philosophy, the central issue in the book is not gendered, but a universally applicable moral conundrum, best expressed as a problematic: 'How can generous impulse be educated into virtue without becoming corrupted by the very prudence which it must learn?'[21]

Each of these accounts plausibly identifies an important area of the compendious book's concerns, and there is no reason to assume that Fielding would have wished to pass up the opportunity to pontificate or engage in moral instruction whenever it arose. Yet if the book is to be seen as a kind of parable, it surely has to be seen as a very self-conscious one, intermittently flaunting deep hesitations and uncertainties about its own didacticism. Within the text there are a number of ironic subversions of overtly directive and moralistic story-telling, parodic treatments of the narrative as extended moral fable, and they show Fielding's characteristically heightened awareness of the ridiculousness of his own position. Not only does the narrator take the appropriate opportunities to offer numerous examples of his conventional down-market 'wisdom' throughout the tale – as in the title to Book V, Chapter ix, 'Which, among other Things, may serve as a Comment on that Saying of AEschines, that DRUNKENNESS SHEWS THE MIND OF A MAN, AS A MIRROUR REFLECTS HIS PERSON' (TJ, p. 250) – he also incorporates teasing images of the futility of offering moral advice, however clearly stated, to a volatile and unpredictable audience, unlikely to respond in the appropriate way.

In Book III, for example, recounting yet another example of the easy success of the hypocritical Blifil in deceiving the benevolent but naive Allworthy, 'the Author himself makes his Appearance on the Stage':

. . . we shall, if rightly understood, afford a very useful Lesson to those well-disposed Youths, who shall hereafter be our Readers . . . Let this, my young Readers, be your constant Maxim, That no Man can be good enough to enable him to neglect the Rules of Prudence; nor will Virtue herself look beautiful, unless she be bedecked with the outward Ornaments of Decency and Decorum. And this Precept, my worthy Disciples, if you read with due Attention, you will, I hope find sufficiently enforced by Examples in the following Pages. (*TJ*, p. 141)

The message about the need for prudence drawn from the dramatised encounter between the deceiver and the deceived looks clear enough, and the narrator intervenes in order to reinforce it, to point the moral and adorn the tale for those 'well-disposed Youths' who form his readership, promising that similar situations will recur throughout the remainder of the book, to be recognised and turned to useful account by the public, with the assistance of the benevolent guiding figure of the narrator.

The brief summary discussion of the complex relation of goodness and prudence offered to Fielding's 'worthy Disciples' may seem to confirm Bernard Harrison's account of the book as an illustrated and dramatised exercise in instructive moral philosophy. However, although it is given prominence and apparent authorial support, the moral instruction seems to be surrounded by uncertainties about the receptiveness of the audience – 'if rightly understood', 'if you read with due Attention' – and subverted by doubts about the adequacy of the vehicle of narrative to convey the message effectively to the inattentive readership in question. After all, the narrator is asking his readers to display greater penetration and acumen than are seen in any of the characters, without offering any convincing evidence that they are capable of achieving this. And as the tale goes on, it is these doubts about the receptiveness and perceptiveness of the audience which are repeatedly confirmed, not the validity of the message offered to them.

Such hesitations about the possibility of communication not only dominate the dialogic form of the novel, they also infiltrate its action, which is beset by failures of communication, cross-purposes, and insensitivities of response. For Fielding, the most potent image of the communicative document within the narrative is the letter written by Dowling to Allworthy in which the true state of affairs concerning Tom's parentage is clearly expressed, a fragile and unreliable attempt at conveying meaning, easily intercepted and side-tracked by Blifil in a world where confusion reigns. Even the clearest and simplest message, it seems, can all too easily go astray if those involved in the process of communication are not uniformly benevolent and scrupulous. And it is worth remembering that in contrast to the use of apparently similar difficulties of epistolary communication in Richardson's *Clarissa*, the vital letter in Fielding's novel is withheld from the readers as well as from the participants.

The problems of narrative as a vehicle for the communication of any message become important within the main text as well as in the simultaneous running commentary. The most striking example of extended story-telling within the narrative comes in Book VIII, when Jones and and his new companion Partridge encounter the Man of the Hill, another comic and self-mocking image of the authorial figure. As Tom encounters him, the Man is being assailed by ruffians. Our hero characteristically rushes to his aid, without a moment's thought for his own safety, and rescues him. There then follows a long section where the curiously dressed and reclusive old misanthrope recounts the history of his own life, occasionally interrupted by that most credulous of audiences, Partridge – who, after a performance of *Hamlet* in Book XVI, cannot sleep for days for fear of the ghost – and that most generous and patient of listeners, Tom Jones.

Like the tale of Mr Wilson in *Joseph Andrews*, the tale of the Man of the Hill is a sombre account of wasted opportunities and betrayals, much of it set in the London to which Jones and Partridge are soon bound, relating bitter personal experiences from which its narrator has drawn what he considers to be suitable lessons about the characteristic and universal depravity of mankind. In contrast to Fielding, then, this story-teller has a number of advantanges: he is immediately aware of his audience and can assess their reactions to his tale as he recounts it; he is drawing directly on the events of his own life; and he is in an unquestionably authoritative position to speculate about their significance. However, as we shall see, his narrative authority does not go unquestioned.

Sickened by the false glamour of the world through which he has travelled extensively, the Man has retired to a life of contemplation and study, replacing human contact with a taste for abstraction:

> Shall the trifling Amusements, the palling Pleasures, the silly Business of the World, roll away our Hours too swiftly from us; and shall the Pace of Time seem sluggish to a Mind exercised in Studies so high, so

important, and so glorious! And as no time is sufficient, so neither is any Place improper for this great Concern. On what Object can we cast our eyes, which may not inspire us with Ideas of his Power, of his Wisdom, and of his Goodness?   (TJ, p. 484)

The account of contemporary life offered is powerful, the revealed depravity of the world balanced by the recluse's philosophic consolations. Yet the response of the listeners is unexpected and unpredictable, not at all consonant with the story-teller's requirements.

Each listener responds in the way he thinks appropriate, not in the way the story-teller requires. Partridge, having previously interrupted the tale to recite a foolish and inconsequential ghost story, has fallen asleep by the end – the horrors of deeply felt personal betrayal and city life seeming to disturb him less than David Garrick's powerful acting would do. Jones, although alert to the significance of what he has been told, also fails to defer to the story-teller's version of events. Instead, he takes the opportunity to challenge the narrator's authority, and denies the accuracy of his interpretation of his own experience:

'In the former Part of what you said,' replied *Jones*, 'I most heartily and readily concur; but I believe, as well as hope, that the Abhorrence which you express for Mankind, in the Conclusion, is much too general. Indeed, you here fall into an Error, which, in my little Experience, I have observed to be a very common one, by taking the Character of Mankind from the worst and basest among them; whereas indeed, as an excellent Writer observes, nothing should be esteemed as characteristical of a Species, but what is found among the best and most perfect Individuals of that Species. This Error, I believe, is generally committed by those who, from Want of proper Caution in the Choice of their Friends and Acquaintance, have suffered Injuries from bad and worthless Men; two or three Instances of which are very unjustly charged on all the human Race.'   (TJ, p. 485)

As Jones sees it, the world is not nearly as bad as the Man of the Hill understands it to be, and, in place of the interlocutor's misanthropy, he offers a less disturbing way of interpreting the Man's narrative. Drawing on his own 'little Experience', and rather surprisingly quoting Cicero (perhaps the teaching of the philosophic Square has worked after all!), Tom gives his own less jaundiced analysis of the events.

The Man of the Hill scoffs at Jones's optimism, saying that he too once laboured under such delusions:

'You might have remained so still,' replies *Jones*, 'if you had not been unfortunate, I will venture to say incautious in the placing of your Affections. If there was indeed much more Wickedness in the World than there is, it would not prove such general Assertions against human Nature, since much of this arrives by mere Accident, and many a Man who commits Evil, is not totally bad and corrupt in his Heart. In truth, none seem to have any Title to assert Human Nature to be necessarily and universally evil, but those whose own Minds afford them one Instance of this natural Depravity; which is not, I am convinced, your Case.'   (*TJ*, pp. 485–6)

So in the dialogue between them, neither Tom nor the Man of the Hill achieves full narrative authority. Jones's attack on the story-teller's belief in contemporary Hobbesian or Calvinist notions of the natural depravity of humans (as previously seen in *Jonathan Wild*) may be consistent with Fielding's broadly 'benevolist' view of human nature, as described initially to Lyttelton. However, as it is dramatised within the tale, Jones's voice does not survive intact, supported by full authorial endorsement, but remains only one argument among many, all of them contending for attention. And if Partridge represents the popular audience, then the various arguments seem to command little enough attention.

Jones contests the authority of one story-teller, but his own advocacy of the need to be circumspect in forming relationships also lacks persuasiveness. After all, this figure who accuses the Man of having been 'incautious in the placing of your Affections' has already had a problematic affair with Molly Seagrim in Books IV and V, and within the next twenty-four hours will find himself in bed with Mrs Waters. Later, Tom becomes part of the retinue of the unattractive Lady Bellaston, re-enacting the squalid standards of London life which he has at this point been explicitly warned against. The contrast between what Tom Jones does and what he says is made very obvious, and is part of the novel's overall comic conception of human flexibility. Fielding makes traditional comic play out of the rigidity and predictability of some characters (notably those associated with the Western household), but also out of the gap between protestation and action, showing that conduct is a better guide to people's true character than any testimony they might offer.

So the authority of the Man as story-teller is contested by Tom, whose own authority is quickly undermined by his subsequent conduct, and by what we know of his earlier behaviour. Elsewhere in the book, the attempt to turn experience into effective exemplary narrative is shown to be attended with equally great difficulties. When Sophia Western listens to the tale of Harriet Fitzpatrick in Book XI, she feels obliged to interrupt, sometimes to interject emphatic agreement with what is being said, and sometimes to suggest an altogether different reading of the events based on her own limited reading and knowledge:

> 'And yet, my Dear, this Conduct is natural,' replied Mrs. *Fitzpatrick*; 'and when you have seen and read as much as myself, you will acknowledge it to be so.'
>   'I am sorry to hear it is natural,' returned *Sophia*; 'for I want neither Reading nor Experience, to convince me, that it is very dishonourable and very ill-natured: Nay, it is surely as ill-bred to tell a Husband or Wife of the Faults of each other, as to tell them of their own.'
>
> (*TJ*, p. 598)

The headstrong fugitive Sophia may lack the knowledge of the world displayed by Harriet, just as Tom lacks the wealth of experience available to the Man of the Hill. However, in each case, the addressee refuses to 'read' the story that is being told in the way the apparently authoritative narrator wishes. And if that dissident 'misreading' happens within the operation of the plot, even with the benefits of personal testimony and face-to-face communication, as it so regularly does, what chance has Fielding of conveying a set of agreed moral values to a heterogeneous and potentially dissident audience through the vehicle of his own much larger narrative?

This refusal to be coerced by a narrator into a particular view of events, taken alongside the parallel misreadings of experience which arise from depravity or from obtuseness or simply from being misguided (as in Allworthy's tribunals and the various other legal operations in the novel), forms small but persistent images of disorder and volatility throughout the book. Through its cumulative treatment of such instabilities, the narrative thus turns away from the definition of universal ethical qualities in the abstract or from the moral assessment of individual conduct towards more localised considerations of authority and control, and of government. The relationship between story-teller and audience is only one of many images of attempted control throughout the book, which is replete with many versions of the breakdown of order, always ironised within the overall covert architecture of the book. As the narrator recognises in the title of

Book XII, Chapter vi, 'it may be inferred, that the best Things are likely to be misunderstood and misinterpreted' (*TJ*, p. 640).

As well as distorting the author's hold over his potentially dissident or rebellious readers, the disorder in *Tom Jones* dominates its accounts of both domestic and public life, with the whole issue of misunderstanding and deliberate refusal to accept authority being simultaneously localised and historicised. The orderly rural system of the family and the parish is seen to be radically unstable, and the city is even worse. Tom is a foundling of uncertain (and misunderstood) parentage; Mrs Partridge attacks her husband; the women of Allworthy's parish brawl in the churchyard; Sophia Western refuses to accept parental authority and runs away from home; the Western's marriage is an arena of tension and combat; Allworthy makes distressing mistakes in his arbitrations as Justice of the Peace; Blifil succeeds in cheating almost everybody; and, in London, adultery and deception and outbreaks of violence are rife, and the good-natured Tom even lands in jail. The social panorama of the novel reproduces a breakdown of order between those in authority and those subject to it, and heightens the sense of hopeless confusion and disorganisation surreptitiously running through the apparently organised and coherent book.

What I have said so far treats the book as a remote and timeless text, but that is by no means all it is. From this distance, it is easy to forget how topical and up-to-the-minute the novel must originally have seemed to its first readers. After all, the book was described by its author as being a 'History,' and however ambivalent that term might have been, it suggests links between the private lives of its characters and a wider public context. When *Tom Jones* first appeared in 1748/9, it was at least in part an extended commentary on the disturbing events of only three years previously, recording a private history lived out amid the bizarre and turbulent events of 1745, disturbingly fresh and controversial in the minds of the book's earliest readers.

Put briefly, the crisis of the 'Forty-Five', a period when Britain's on-going war with France seemed more than usually unsuccessful, became intense when Charles Edward Stuart, known as 'Bonnie Prince Charlie', the Scottish Pretender to the throne of Great Britain, landed in the Western Isles of Scotland in July, and led a Jacobite rebellion against the incumbent Hanoverian monarchy. Drawing support mainly from the disenfranchised (and Catholic) Scottish

Highlands, Charles assembled an army under the command of Lord George Murray, and quickly took Perth and Edinburgh with little bloodshed. Turning south, the Jacobite army invaded England and soon induced near panic in London by advancing as far as Derby. At that point, for reasons which remain unclear, and which still give the more romantic Scot many a sleepless night, they turned back. As the army gradually dispersed, dispirited by the non-appearance of the promised French troops and supplies, they were hounded by the Hanoverian forces under the direction of the ruthless Duke of Cumberland, culminating in the bloody rout at Culloden, which ended the Jacobite and Roman Catholic challenge to the Protestant succession once and for all. The defeated Charles Edward Stuart fled, first to Skye, and then to the Continent, where he fell into a gradual but terminal decline. By the end of April 1746 the immediate political and military crisis was over, but the shock to the British political system was severe, and the lessons remained to be learned. [22]

Amid the very bleak and troubled winter of 1745, Fielding had written a number of commentaries on the rebellion, notably his pamphlets *A Serious Address to the People of Great Britain*, *The History of the Present Rebellion in Scotland* and *A Dialogue Between the Devil, the Pope, and the Pretender* as well as his weekly periodical of 1745–6, *The True Patriot: And, The History of Our Own Times*. In all of these, conscious of the urgencies of the moment, he analyses the political significance of the rebellion, and looks to consolidate the opposition to resurgent Jacobitism. Although much of his writing is understandably highly charged, he represents himself as a temperate and moderate figure, aligned against the zealots of both sides. As he puts it in the first number of *The True Patriot*:

> The Rebellion is at present so seriously the Concern of every sensible Man, who wishes well to the Religion and Liberties of his Country, and the Zeal which all the different Sects of Protestants have discovered on this Occasion, is so hearty and unanimous, that it would be lost Labour to endeavour at inflaming the Minds of my Countrymen on this Occasion.
>
> On the contrary, it is rather the Business of a good Public Writer, in some Measure, to moderate and direct this Spirit, which now so gloriously animates us. Cool and temperate Councils will be of singular Use at this Time, when the Rashness of inconsiderate, tho' well-meaning Men, may do Injury to that Cause which they desire to support with their All, and on which their ALL depends. [23]

Seeing himself at this point as a 'good Public Writer', Fielding offers a sustained commentary on events, within the descriptive paradigms of contemporary political journalism. Even if he was, as some scholars think, also active in composing much of *Tom Jones* at the same time, the more reflective and comic version of the rebellion offered there is very different, and inflected towards radically different ends.

Scathing references to the events of 1745 recur constantly through the novel. The flagrantly incompetent domestic tyrant Squire Western, with his expostulatory outbursts against 'Hanover Rats' and his regular toasts to 'the King over the Water', is an obvious caricature of those high 'Country' Tories holding views close to outright Jacobitism, antithetical to those expressed in Fielding's pamphlets and in *The True Patriot*. In Western's case, commitment to the Jacobite cause consists almost entirely of empty ideological flourishes, with his own immediate self-interest gaining supremacy whenever any conflict arises.

Elsewhere, the credulous Partridge believes in dark 'mysteries', aligning himself thereby with the superstitious end of Jacobite ideology, which he openly endorses on a couple of occasions. In Book XI, Sophia Western is mistakenly identified at an inn as Jenny Cameron, the best-known of the 'Rebel Ladies', a collection of early groupies said to have accompanied the Pretender on his march south. Needless to say, Sophia's personal charms are such that the landlady 'became in a Moment a staunch *Jacobite*, and wished heartily well to the young Pretender's cause' (*TJ*, p. 580).

As well as appearing through these satiric portraits, none of them flattering either to the Jacobites or to the general public, the wider context of events infiltrates the action of the narrative to create a climate of enormous apprehension and an air of crisis. In Book VII, following his expulsion from Paradise Hall, Tom meets some soldiers preparing to head north to face the rebels:

> The Serjeant informed Mr. *Jones*, that they were marching against the Rebels, and expected to be commanded by the glorious Duke of *Cumberland*. By which the Reader may perceive (a Circumstance which we have not thought necessary to communicate before) that this was the very Time when the late Rebellion was at its highest; and indeed the Banditti were now marched into *England*, intending, as it was thought, to fight the King's Forces, and to attempt pushing forward to the Metropolis. (*TJ*, pp. 367–8)

By Books X and XI, persistent rumours that the rebels were nearing London cause great upheaval and confusion in the inn at Upton which temporarily houses Jones, Mrs Waters, Partridge, Mrs Fitzpatrick and Sophia, and at other points in the book the remarkable events taking place further north cast a shadow over the immediate proceedings.

As expressed through the novel, the whole social context of the rebellion is one of disorder and chaos, creating a world of virtual absurdity. When Tom discusses the two Jacobite risings of 1715 and 1745 with the Man of the Hill, he presents the events as so extraordinary as to confound belief:

> '. . . it has often struck me, as the most wonderful thing I ever read of in History, that so soon after this convincing Experience, which brought our whole Nation to join so unanimously in expelling King *James*, for the Preservation of our Religion and Liberties, there should be a Party among us mad enough to desire the placing of his Family again on the Throne.' 'You are not in Earnest!' answered the old Man; 'there can be no such Party. As bad an Opinion as I have of Mankind, I cannot believe them infatuated to such a Degree! There may be some hot-headed Papists led by their Priests to engage in this desparate Cause, and think it a Holy War; but that Protestants, that Members of the Church of *England* should be such Apostates, such *Felos de se*, I cannot believe it; no, no, young Man, unacquainted as I am with what has past in the World for these last thirty Years, I cannot be so imposed upon as to credit so foolish a Tale: But I see you have a Mind to sport with my Ignorance.' 'Can it be possible,' replied *Jones*, 'that you have lived so much out of the World as not to know, that during that Time there have been two Rebellions in favour of the Son of King *James*, one of which is now actually raging in the very Heart of this Kingdom?' At these Words the old Gentleman started up, and, in a most solemn Tone of Voice conjured *Jones* by his Maker to tell him, if what he said was really true: Which the other as solemnly affirming, he walked several Turns about the Room, in a profound Silence, then cried, then laughed, and, at last, fell down on his Knees, and blessed God, in a loud Thanksgiving-Prayer, from having delivered him from all Society with Human Nature, which could be capable of such monstrous Extravagances.   (*TJ*, pp. 477–8)

The reclusive Man of the Hill, unlike Jones, unlike Fielding, and unlike the novel's first readers, has lived 'out of the World' for some time, and may thus be excused his comic and disturbing Parson

Adams-like astonishment. However, for those less sheltered story-
tellers and auditors who have lived *in* the world, the whole affair of
the Jacobite rebellion remains no less baffling, leaving Fielding with
the opportunity to exploit the disruptions it creates for comic purposes
while at the same time trying to get them under some kind of
ideological control.

The key to the issue as Fielding addresses it is once more the
question of the legitimate limits of authority. For him, the Jacobite
cause venerated a despotic absolutism, epitomised by the charismatic
and egotistic charlatan Charles Edward Stuart, and its ideology was
hostile to the complex balance of interests he saw as essential to the
proper exercise of political power. Within the novel, these questions
are at once developed and ironised in Book XII, through a discussion
between Tom and the King of the Gypsies, an absolute monarch in
miniature, who can command absolute obedience from his subjects.

The two meet as Jones comes upon a riotous gypsy wedding:

> While he was looking every where round him with Astonishment, a
> venerable Person approached him with many friendly Salutations,
> rather of too hearty a Kind to be called courtly. This was none other
> than the King of the *Gypsies* himself. He was very little distinguished in
> Dress from his Subjects, nor had he any *Regalia* of Majesty to support
> his Dignity; and yet there seemed (as Mr. *Jones* said) to be somewhat in
> his Air which denoted Authority, and Inspired the Beholders with an
> Idea of Awe and Respect; tho' all this was perhaps imaginary in *Jones*,
> and the Truth may be, that such Ideas are incident to Power, and
> almost inseparable from it.   (*TJ*, p. 667)

The connections made here between power and authority are
suggestive, reminiscent of the alienated stance of earlier Augustan
satirists – power lends an air of (often spurious) authority to those
who wield it, whereas the possession of authority does not
automatically convey the right to power. Fittingly, these hints are laid
out by the narrator, and not by Jones, whose customary impulsiveness
of judgement has been further befuddled by his enjoyment of a few
strange gypsy drinks, and who is acknowledged in this extract to be a
habitually unreliable audience, once again misinterpreting virtually
everything he has been told.

It is also the main narrator who intrudes to comment on the King's
account of gypsy culture, appraising it first as a commendable example
of effective political organisation, at least in theory, before drawing

attention to its manifest drawbacks. The King talks (in comically stylised broken English) of a community based on mutual respect and dignity:

> Me have Honour, as me say, to be deir King, and no Monarch can do boast of more dutiful Subject, ne no more affectionate. How far me deserve deir Goodwill, me no say, but dis me can say, dat me never design any Ting but to do dem Good. Me sall no do boast of dat neider: For what can me do oderwise dan consider of de Good of dose poor People who go about all Day to give me always de best of what dey get. Dey love and honour me darefore, because me do love and take Care of dem; dat is all, me know no oder Reason.   (*TJ*, p. 668)

Creating a community of trust, affection and respect, the benevolent despot represented in this episode, however ironically miniaturised, looks like the most successful community leader to appear anywhere in the narrative, much more successful than Allworthy, Western, or any of the others. When called upon to deal with a wrong-doer, the King imposes a punishment based on shaming the individual, on making him look ridiculous, reinforcing thereby the power of the integrated gypsy community to act in unison, a possibility far removed from the internally divided community outside – 'My People rob your People, and your People rob one anoder' (*TJ*, p. 671).

At first, the narrator seems so impressed by this happy picture of sovereignty in action that he sees reasons in it to embrace the possibilities of political absolutism on a larger scale:

> Indeed their Happiness appears to have been so compleat, that we are aware lest some Advocate for arbitrary Power should hereafter quote the Case of these People, as an Instance of the great Advantages which attend that Government above all others.
>
> And here we will make a Concession, which would not perhaps have been expected of us, That no limited Form of Government is capable of rising to the same Degree of Perfection, or of producing the same Benefits to Society with this. Mankind have never been so happy, as when the greatest Part of the then known World was under the Dominion of a single Master . . .   (*TJ*, p. 671)

The blissful period of living contentedly 'under the Dominion of a single Master' referred to here is long gone – Fielding identifies it as the 'Golden Age' of the later Roman emperors running from AD 96 to AD 180 – and the narrator goes on to distance himself from any possibility of such contentment reappearing. Drawing on a famous and frequently reprinted sermon by the latitudinarian bishop Benjamin Hoadly, *The Happiness of the Present Establishment, and the Unhappiness of Absolute Monarchy* (1708), Fielding digresses at some length in order to bring out all the practical problems of absolutism in the contemporary world.[24]

Put simply, the basic problem with absolute monarchy lies in the opportunities it offers to the absolute monarch:

> In reality, I know but of one solid Objection to absolute Monarchy. The only Defect in which excellent Constitution seems to be the Difficulty of finding any Man adequate to the Office of an absolute Monarch: For this indispensably requires three Qualities very difficult, as it appears from History, to be found in princely Natures: first, a sufficient Quantity of Moderation in the Prince, to be contented with all the Power which is possible for him to have. 2dly, Enough of Wisdom to know his own Happiness. And, 3dly, Goodness sufficient to support the Happiness of others, when not only compatible with, but instrumental to his own.   (*TJ*, p. 672)

Clearly, the temptations of absolute power call for extraordinary restraint and diplomacy in the sovereign, and under a corrupt or incompetent master, the system of a single all-powerful monarch is taken to resemble Hell. The fact that such a method of government works for the gypsies must not be taken as evidence of any more wide-spread applicability, according to the narrator, since their culture differs from others in one very important respect – 'they look on Shame as the most grievous Punishment in the World' (*TJ*, p. 673).

Once again, Fielding's apparently clear account of the issue of absolutism becomes encrusted with ironies and self-conscious confusions. His hostility to Jacobitism is not in doubt, and the satiric attacks on the incompetence of Squire Western and the superstitiousness of Partridge are undiminished. However, the closing remark about the power of shame is intriguing. Shame, after all, is the operating principle of satire – the satirist wishes to make his victims feel ashamed of their conduct, humiliated by their own ridiculousness. Fielding himself sets out in his novel to laugh people out of their follies and vices, while simultaneously acknowledging that the efficacy of shame may have dwindled beyond recognition. In *A Charge Delivered to the Grand Jury* (1749), for instance, he shows the distinction between his own world and that of the gypsies – 'the Rod of the Law, Gentlemen, must restrain those within the Bounds of Decency, who are deaf to the Voice of Reason, and superior to the Fear of Shame'.[25] Clearly, as novelist and as magistrate, Fielding was losing confidence in the power of shame to rectify matters, and as a result he was seeking more authoritarian methods of control.

The paradox here is that Fielding himself takes the liberty to act as absolute monarch of his fictional world. Despite his promise at the opening of Book II, that he will not behave like a 'jure divino Tyrant' in the government of his 'new Province of Writing' (TJ, p. 77), he arbitrates and regulates entirely as he thinks fit, ruling his possibly dissident and rebellious readership with all the power he can assemble, in the faint hope that they, like the gypsies, are not impervious to the workings of shame. Not only does he reinforce his own authorial power by springing various surprises (Square falling out of Molly's bed, for instance, or the unexpected encounter between Tom and Sophia at Upton) and by contriving a relocation of Tom's class position at the end of the book, he constantly tries to maintain order throughout a rumbustious narrative, and stave off the imminence of mayhem, while recognising all the difficulties of such a task.

Like the King of the Gypsies, Fielding can maintain order only within the confines of his own little demesne – in this case, the enclosed system of the book. As we have seen, it has its own shape, and its events are eventually shown to follow a coherent pattern, subject to a plan and a design. Within that enclosed world, questions of order and regulation emerge both as literary and moral problems. The formal discipline of the book is mirrored in the quest of the characters after self-discipline, and there are, as Fielding suggested to Lyttelton, recognisable moral issues under discussion. But the most interesting complexities arise in the points of contact and abrasion between the book and its context. As it attaches itself to questions of individual ethics, such as Tom's sexual morality or Western's patriarchal family structure, and to more immediate political issues, such as the 1745 rebellion or the contemporary status of women, the book uncovers a world which has made itself ridiculous, without needing any help from the authoritative writer. The fiction may be orderly and systematic, but the reality it encounters is most definitely not.

So whereas Fielding may have absolute power over the internal workings of his book, and is able to emphasise what he wants and to exert control, that power is meaningless as soon as the book makes contact with its potentially dissident readership. In the dialogic relationship between the book and its readers, Fielding seeks the satirist's authority in the absence of the legislator's power. Unable to impose direct control over his audience, he relies on exuberant displays of learning and literary sleight-of-hand to impress readers with his erudition and cultural sway. But, as the internal images of story-telling confirm, the narrator eventually has no real hold over his audience, and, much to his exasperation, he is forced to recognise that the real power to interpret, judge and assess lies in their hands.

Rather than seeing *Tom Jones* either entirely as a metafiction, or entirely as a way of putting forward a body of doctrine, I prefer to see it as an argumentative and disputatious text, negotiating between its internal order and the disorder of human behaviour at large, sexually, politically and in all other ways, with the developed figure of the narrator carrying out these negotiations before an ill-equipped general readership. That is not to say, of course, that it is ideologically neutral or disinterested – Fielding's representations of individuals and society betray once again the system of allegiances and affiliations which marked his earlier work, and as an *auteur* he finds ways of bringing them close to the surface of material which is not always congenial. Rather, it is to recognise that the literary debate about the status of the novel and the proper role of authors which sustains the comedy of *Tom Jones* is in itself an ideological and doctrinal one, carrying in its midst a series of judgements about government, responsibility and regulation.

The vibrant comedy of *Tom Jones* is thus based as much on the deliberately adversarial relationship established between narrator and reader as it is on the internal mayhem and accidents of the plot. The intertextual energy which makes it a book about other books also makes it a book about the readers of other books, and thereby enters a whole series of opportunities for the author to reach out to make contact with the world at large. In his final novel, *Amelia*, Fielding cast aside these self-referential features, stepped back from his prominent role as comic or satiric author/narrator and experimented with a much less explosive literary form, addressed specifically to a number of contemporary social issues. After acting as parodist or mimic in *Shamela*, Lucianic satirist in *A Journey from This World to the Next*, master puppeteer in *Jonathan Wild*, and master of ceremonies, 'jure divino Tyrant' and King of the Gypsies in *Tom Jones*, Fielding eventually turns more serious, and addresses his readers from the magistratical bench.

Notes and references

1. Henry Fielding, *The History of Tom Jones, a Foundling* (1749), ed. Fredson Bowers, 2 vols (Oxford, 1974), I, 75–6.   Further references will be incorporated in the text.

2. Alexander Pope, *An Essay on Man*, Twickenham edn (III, i), ed. Maynard Mack (London and New York, 1950), p. 11.

3. See the discussion of the argument from 'design' in Martin C. Battestin, *The Providence of Wit: Aspects of Form in Augustan Literature and the Arts* (Oxford, 1974), pp. 143–50.

4. Samuel Taylor Coleridge, *Table Talk*, 5 July 1834, quoted in C.J. Rawson, *Henry Fielding: A Critical Anthology* (Harmondsworth, 1973), p. 259.

5. See Roland Barthes, 'Introduction to the Structural Analysis of Narratives' (1966), in *Image-Music-Text*, trans. by Stephen Heath (Glasgow, 1977), pp. 93–4.

6. Patricia Waugh, *Metafiction: The Theory and Practice of Self-conscious Fiction* (London, 1984), p. 2.   For Genette's use of the phrase 'metanarrative', see his *Narrative Discourse*, trans. Jane E. Lewin (Oxford, 1980), p. 228.

7. Victor Shklovsky, 'Sterne's *Tristram Shandy*: Stylistic Commentary', (1921), in *Russian Formalist Criticism: Four Essays*, trans. by Lee T. Lemon and Marion J. Reis (Nebraska, 1965), p. 57.

8. Umberto Eco, '*Lector in Fabula*: Pragmatic Strategy in a Metanarrative Text', in *The Role of the Reader: Explorations in the Semiotics of Texts* (London, 1981), p. 205.

9. See Roland Barthes, *S/Z*, trans. by Richard Miller (Oxford, 1974), pp. 20–2.

10. Barthes, *S/Z*, pp. 16–17.

11. Henry Fielding, *The Jacobite's Journal and Related Writings*, ed. W.B. Coley (Oxford, 1974), p. 346.   For further information about Lyttelton, see M.C. Battestin with Ruthe R. Battestin, *Henry Fielding: A Life* (London, 1989), pp. 453–6.

12. See *Henry Fielding: The Critical Heritage*, ed. Ronald Paulson and Thomas Lockwood (London and New York, 1969), p. 162.

13. Samuel Richardson, letter to Astraea and Minerva Hill, 4 August 1749, in *Selected Letters of Samuel Richardson*, ed. John Carroll (Oxford, 1964), p. 127.

14. Samuel Johnson, *The Rambler* 4, 31 March 1750, in *The Yale Edition of the Works of Samuel Johnson*, ed. W.J. Bate and Albrecht B. Strauss (New Haven and London, 1969), III, i, 23.

15. From Hannah More, letter to a sister, 1780, quoted in *Henry Fielding: The Critical Heritage*, ed. Ronald Paulson and Thomas Lockwood (London and New York, 1969), p. 443.

16. Sir John Hawkins, *The Life of Samuel Johnson LL.D.* (1787), ed. Bertram H. Davis (London, 1962), p. 95.

17. William Empson, 'Tom Jones', *Kenyon Review*, 20 (1958), 217, 220.

18. Empson, *op. cit.*, p. 225.

19. Irvin Ehrenpreis, *Fielding: Tom Jones* (London, 1964), p. 25.

20. Angela Smallwood, *Fielding and the Woman Question* (Hemel Hempstead, 1991), p. 1.

21. Bernard Harrison, *Henry Fielding's 'Tom Jones': The Novelist as Moral Philosopher* (Sussex, 1975), p. 69.

22. There are more books about the '45', the Jacobite cause, Bonnie Prince Charlie, and Culloden than you can shake a stick at, and for many of them that might be the most appropriate critical response. However, a good recent survey is Jeremy Black, *Culloden and the '45* (London, 1990).

23. Henry Fielding, *The True Patriot*, ed. W.B. Coley (Oxford, 1987), p. 113.

24. See Martin C. Battestin, 'Tom Jones and 'His Egyptian Majesty': Fielding's Parable of Government', *PMLA*, lxxxii (1967), 68–77.

25. Henry Fielding, *A Charge Delivered to the Grand Jury* (1749), in *An Enquiry into the Causes of the Late Increase of Robbers and Related Writings*, ed. Malvin R. Zirker (Oxford, 1988), p. 25. See also the discussion of shame and satire in my *Literature and Crime in Augustan England* (London, 1991), pp. 159–83.

CHAPTER 6
Marriage prospects

Living together

Most private histories, as well as comedies, end at this period, the historian and the poet both concluding they have done enough for their hero when they have married him; or intimating rather that the rest of his life must be a dull calm of happiness, very delightful indeed to pass through, but somewhat insipid to relate, and matrimony in general must, I believe, without any dispute, be allowed to be this state of tranquil felicity, including so little variety, that, like Salisbury Plain, it affords only one prospect, a very pleasant one it must be confessed, but the same.   (JW, pp. 142–3)

MARRIAGE. A kind of traffic carried on between the two sexes, in which both are constantly endeavouring to cheat each other, and both are commonly losers in the end.   (CGJ, p. 37)

Embedded amid all the exuberant rhetorical playfulness of *Tom Jones* there lay a number of intensely contested issues which gave the whole novel its intermittent points of contact with the lives and experiences of its heterogeneous audience. Although openly a fantasy about fiction and an exploration of the status of the novel and the author, that book was nonetheless at the same time an attempt at a running commentary on recent affairs, and an engagement with the 'real' public world inhabited by its readers, whoever they might be. By treating the recent rebellion of 1745 (which only someone as remote from ordinary life as the Man of the Hill could possibly have failed to notice or have views about) to sustained satiric commentary and by subjecting a host of familiar questions about sexual morality, honour, civic responsibility and family conduct to his own sceptical interrogation, Fielding introduced a representational and overtly ideological dimension to his formal extravaganza. In the context of the comic novel, however, these issues of order and authority were explored through disorientating paradox and irony, leaving those frequently berated and humiliated general readers confused and perplexed about what exactly they were being told, about what exactly was being recommended and what disparaged, in consequence saddling the author with the reputation of libertine and trifler.

However, alongside the persistent and at times anarchic strain of frivolity in Fielding's fiction, there has always been a vestigial (if suppressed) yearning after a version of seriousness, also recognisable at other points in his non-literary career. The distinction set up at the beginning of this study between the twin poles of the 'serious' and the 'rhetorical', borrowed from Stanley Fish, has been used so far to legitimise a predominantly ironic reading of Fielding. The author has been seen operating from *Shamela* onwards as a quintessentially 'rhetorical' figure, as one who 'manipulates reality, establishing through his words the imperatives and urgencies to which he and his fellows must respond . . . [who] manipulates and fabricates himself'.[1] Such reinventive 'fabrication' has until now lain at the heart of my version of Henry Fielding, as he appears both as narrator and as a pervasive presence through the narratives, with his various self-projections and his uncertainty about the terms of his dialogue with readers opposing the clear presentation of any developed certainties in his writing.

What Fish goes on to say about the activities of 'rhetorical' man also has a bearing on my presentation of Fielding: 'by exploring the available means of persuasion in a particular situation, he tries them on, and as they begin to suit him, he becomes them' (Fish, *op. cit.*, p. 208). The consequence of this instability of identity or versatility is that Fielding becomes an altogether more mercurial and inconsistent figure, more Swiftian, than many of the more traditional critical accounts (like Battestin's in particular) make him out to be. As he positions himself through prefaces and interruptions of the narrative, he becomes both jocund and abrasive, constantly engaged in one-sided rhetorical combat with his slower-witted counterparts in the reading public. Thus, instead of being seen to use fiction as a convenient vehicle for the articulation of an identifiable body of doctrine, recommended and endorsed by the stable controlling figure of the narrator, the author can be represented as essentially problematising and destabilising any such confidence. In short, as I read and re-read Fielding I see him inhabiting the fictions as a game-player rather than as a truth-teller, as often ludic as didactic, as exuberant and subversive *auteur* rather than as old-style author.

Yet to see Fielding as being exclusively concerned with these rhetorical jousts and stylistic inflections is obviously inadequate. In as much as the project behind his comic novels and the *Miscellanies* texts was a satiric one, the author was perforce required to attempt to establish some points of contact, however tentative, with the world beyond the printed page. When, for instance, Fielding uses the unpleasant figure of Lord Fellamar in Book XV of *Tom Jones* to stigmatise and deconstruct the notion of the 'gentleman' thought to be prevailing in contemporary Augustan high society, the episode is only given meaning if people recognised the fittingness of the portrait. If that were not to happen, Fellamar would simply be seen as a grotesque or a gargoyle within the text, serving certain internal dramatic purposes only and no more real or recognisable or threatening than the villain of a pantomime or a fairytale (or Wile E. Coyote). On a more general level, while there is no reason to assume that the 'London' represented in the second half of *Tom Jones* is an entirely accurate and reliable picture of the metropolis as it was in the later 1740s, it must still maintain *some* identifiable connection with that place, however tangential or mediated, if the book is to be available to its readers as anything other than a self-contained system of internal cross-references.

The perennially problematic relationship between 'fiction' and 'reality' in Fielding's writing changed throughout his career, and it became particularly complex in his last novel. Whereas the earlier comic and satiric works seemed to enjoy the use of fiction as a window on the world, at times transparent and at other times opaque, there is a corresponding body of writing in Fielding's journalism and his pamphlets which simply lays these literary problems aside. By the time of his final novel, *Amelia*, first published in December 1751, the author seemed to have publicly turned his back on the volatility and the adversarial game-playing of his earlier drama and fiction, and seemed to have set himself up as a more serious cultural arbiter, a graver and more responsible figure who could be expected to offer authoritative commentary on the more controversial issues of the day, both private and public.

Significantly, the book was dedicated to Ralph Allen, the philanthropic figure praised by Pope in *The First Satire of the Second Book of Horace Imitated* (1733) and hailed in *Tom Jones* (VIII, i) as a man good almost beyond belief. Like the earlier addressee George Lyttelton, Allen was a well-connected patron of the arts, but the terms of reference between author and dedicatee and the general readership established in Fielding's final novel are considerably more austere and less obviously self-seeking than any we have seen before:

> The following Book is sincerely designed to promote the Cause of Virtue, and to expose some of the most glaring Evils, as well public as private, which at present infest the Country; tho' there is scarce, as I remember, a single Stroke of Satire aimed at any one Person throughout the whole. [2]

Whereas Fielding spoke to his patron at the equivalent point in *Tom Jones* as someone who could do him a good turn, he seems to be addressing Allen as an equal, as a man who will be as concerned as he is about the problems of the day, forcefully laying bare the bones of his novel as an analysis of contemporary society and its ills, 'sincerely designed to promote the Cause of Virtue'. The point about the connectedness of the 'private' and the 'public' is vital – unlike the sexual misadventures of Tom Jones, the stressful marriage of William and Amelia Booth is seen to be put under great pressure not only by their individual strengths and weaknesses, but by the flawed institutions which they (and Allen and Fielding and the general public) inhabit.

The shift in emphasis from the comic and more experimental fiction is obvious already. By centralising problems and issues, by analysing the private marital and financial problems of William and Amelia Booth and drawing out their broader social and political significances, the novel thus becomes immediately less concerned with its capacity for self-reflection, and more single-mindedly involved with its contemporary social referents and contexts. The concerns with sex and money which were intermittently exploited in the earlier fictions for mainly comic purposes here assume a greater gravity, and their capacity to distort the lives of the feckless or the innocent are subjected to detailed exegesis. The key word in the dedication is thus 'expose' – Fielding here seems to be promising an unmediated, frank revelation of the workings of the world, rather than a playful or metafictional revelation of the workings of a novel.

Indeed, on a first reading, it is the differences between this later book and the earlier ones which are noticeable, not any points of continuity. Unlike the peripatetic comic novels, *Amelia* is predominantly domestic, and mainly (though not exclusively) restricted in its setting to one or two rather down-at-heel parts of London. In dealing with the private lives of its married participants – 'the various Accidents which befel a very worthy Couple, after their uniting in the State of Matrimony, will be the Subject of the following History' (*Amelia*, p. 15) – Fielding tries to contextualise individual experiences in a very local and intensely realised social scene, showing the particularity of its institutions (law courts, sponging houses, Newgate, the army, Haymarket masquerades, etc.) and drawing out what he sees as the general human significance of these episodes.

Such an engagement with immediate and pressing social problems and with the world of the contemporary reader not only anticipates many of the formal procedures and the motivating ideology of the nineteenth-century 'realist' novel, it also aligns Fielding more firmly with 'serious' man than we have previously seen him to be. As Richard Lanham defines that figure, he 'possesses a central self, an irreducible identity. These selves combine into a single, homogeneously real society which constitutes a referent reality for the men living in it. This referent society is in turn contained in a physical nature itself referential, standing "out there" independent of man.'[3]

As the newly serious Fielding introduces *Amelia*, he feels more able directly to address his audience about the world they all inhabit together – to 'expose' it – speaking clearly in a personal testimony and with at least the illusion of authority, leaving aside his earlier embattled and defensive reliance on paradox. The men (and, despite Lanham's reluctance to include them in the category of the 'serious', presumably the women) who read the book are assumed to be capable of making appropriate and provocative connections between the fiction they individually peruse and the reality they collectively inhabit, enabling them to recognise, and perhaps even to attempt to rectify, those 'most glaring Evils, as well public as private, which at present infest the Country'. As he goes beyond the comic literary conventions of poetic justice and festive matrimony to look at the public world of the law and the private world of marriage, Fielding initially seems to put aside the ironic destabilising zest of earlier works in favour of a more flagrantly and ostentatiously well-motivated concern for the well-being of his public.

Readers of *Amelia* are thus promised an expository and revelatory social analysis based round the pathetic figures of the suffering female heroine and the irresponsible male hero, the narrative beginning after their marriage, at the point where the comic fictions conventionally drew to a conclusion. The book is thus presented as an activist and admonitory text conducted through some means other than the more boisterous and exuberant satire of the earlier work. The sombre tone of address is continued in the opening 'Exordium', where the novelist, in one of his very few obtrusive appearances on this particular scene, continues the analogies between the intricacies of the world and the construction of a coherent work of art, a conventional comparison already discussed in several of the prefatory chapters in *Tom Jones*. In this case, however, the focus of attention is on the meaning of the novel, not on the author's skill in manipulating and orchestrating the plot.

The new novel is put before its readers as an exemplary text from which they may gain instruction, its principles of construction showing how the larger catastrophes in the lives of the protagonists are built up from a fabric of numerous tiny and individually insignificant episodes. As the narrator reminds us several times, the text demonstrates 'how capable the most insignificant Accident is of disturbing human Happiness, and of producing the most unexpected and dreadful Events. A Reflection that may serve to many moral and Religious Uses' (*Amelia*, p. 184).

By reassessing the importance of apparently trivial episodes, the whole narrative looks for the larger meaning or plan behind the unstructured lives of its participants, and the moral and religious significance of the episodes is much more prominent here than hitherto. At the beginning of his book, the 'serious' or didactic novelist emphasises the ease of transferring meaning from the words on the page to the world outside the text, and insists that there is a message enclosed in the narrative:

> Life may as properly be called an Art as any other; and the great Incidents in it are no more to be considered as mere Accidents, than the several Members of a fine Statue, or a noble Poem. The Critics in all these are not content with seeing any Thing to be great, without knowing why and how it came to be so. By examining very carefully the several Gradations which conduce to bring every Model to Perfection, we learn truly to know that Science in which the Model is formed: As Histories of this Kind, therefore, may properly be called Models of HUMAN LIFE; so by observing minutely the several Incidents which tend to the Catastrophe or Completion of the whole, and the

minute Causes whence those Incidents are produced, we shall best be
instructed in this most useful of all Arts, which I call the ART OF LIFE.

(Amelia, p.17)

Where 'Art' and 'Life' seemed to be clearly demarcated and even
polarised in the comic novels – the novelist there being able to solve
by literary sleight-of-hand social and personal problems which would
be intractable or insoluble outside the confines of a book – here the
two categories are elided. In this passage, Fielding invites his readers
to read closely and scrupulously, and promises them tangible rewards
for doing so. By paying attention to his book, readers will be
instructed in the 'Art of Life', becoming wiser in the process, if also a
little sadder. In contrast to the previous addresses to the audience
dispersed throughout the comic novels, the narrator of *Amelia* seems
unusually confident at this point that a homogeneous and inquisitive
readership for serious fiction can be found, and that his audience is
capable of the kind of forensic closeness of attention he requires.

However, despite the widespread previous criticisms of his levity
and trifling, and irrespective of the optimism of the publisher Andrew
Millar, who printed five thousand copies of the novel as soon as he
had it, Fielding's new serious turn of mind was not conspicuously
successful with his immediate audience. In fact, the book was thought
by many of its first readers to be astonishingly dull, describing in
inordinate detail the predicaments of an insipid heroine with very
little nose and a weak hero with equally little character, slackly
narrated through a series of improbable and 'low' scenes involving
unglamorous criminals and uninteresting low-life figures.[4]

Whereas Fielding had anticipated a hostile reaction to his comic
novels and had got his retaliation in first, as it were, by means of the
adversarial prefaces, he responded to these adverse readings of *Amelia*
outwith the text itself, using a playful satiric device which is wholly
unlike the predominantly sombre voicing of the novel. Through the
pages of *The Covent-Garden Journal* in January and February 1752,
within six weeks of the book's first appearance, he brought his novel
up before the regular session of the 'Court of Censorial Enquiry',
charged with 'Dulness', and he himself made a startling personal
appearance in its defence. Like the similar 'Court of Criticism' in *The
Jacobite's Journal*, this farcical tribunal shadows the court proceedings
described in the novel, and, of course, those which had become
increasingly prominent in Fielding's active working life.

The strongest case against the book is summarised by 'Counsellor Town', appearing before 'Mr. Censor' for the prosecution:

> We shall prove then, to you, Sir, that the Book now at the Bar, is *very sad Stuff*; that Amelia herself is a *low* Character, a *Fool*, and a *Milksop*; that she is very apt to faint, and apt to *drink Water*, to prevent it. That she once *taps a Bottle of Wine, and drinks two Glasses*. That she *shews too much Kindness for her Children*, and is too apt to *forgive the Faults of her Husband*. That she exerts *no Manner of Spirit*, unless, perhaps, in supporting Afflictions. That *her concealing the* Knowledge of her Husband's Amour, when she knew he had discontinued it, was *low and poor*. That *her not abusing him*, for having lost his Money at Play, when she saw his Heart was already almost broke by it, *was contemptible Meanness.* . . . Lastly, That she is a Beauty WITHOUT A NOSE, I say again, WITHOUT A NOSE. All this we shall prove by many Witnesses.
>
> We shall likewise prove that Dr. Harrison is a very *low, dull, unnatural* Character, and that his arresting Booth, *only because he had all imaginable Reason to think he was a Villain*, is unpardonable.
>
> That Colonel Bath is a *foolish Character, very low, and ill-drawn*.
>
> That the Scene of the Gaol is *low and unmeaning*, and brought in by Head and Shoulders, without any Reason, or Design.
>
> That the Abbé is supposed to *wear a Sword*; in short, not to descend to too many Particulars, which you will hear from the Mouths of the Witnesses, that the whole Book is a Heap of *sad Stuff, Dulness, and Nonsense*, that it contains no Wit, Humour, Knowledge of human Nature, or of the World; indeed, that the Fable, moral Characters, Manners, Sentiments, and diction, are all alike bad and contemptible.
>
> All these Matters, Sir, we doubt not to prove to your Satisfaction, and then we doubt not but that you will do exemplary Justice to such intolerable sad Stuff, and, will pass such a Sentence as may be a dreadful Example to all future Books, how they dare stand up in Opposition to the Humour of the Age.   (CGJ, pp. 58–9)

Although it passes over the problematic figure of William Booth and the outright improbability of the book's slickly contrived happy ending, the accusation includes many individual points actually made against the novel in its earliest reviews. The characterisations of poor Amelia herself, Booth, Miss Mathews, Dr Harrison and the Colonels James and Bath came in for some very unfriendly treatment in contemporary reviews. In particular, the ostentatious Richardsonian sensibility of the heroine (swooning, weeping, fainting, and constantly waiting upon the more decisive activities of others) and the persistent weakness of the hero (imprisoned, unfaithful, gambling, feeling that he cannot be held responsible for his actions) were not generally well received.

In response, Fielding covertly belittles his accusers in this mock-trial by mixing the serious points with the more trivial. Placing hostility to the book's structure and to the passivity of its central characters alongside equally fierce denunciation of the author's possible inaccuracies in describing clerical dress and waxing indignant over the vexed question of poor Amelia's damaged nose (happily repaired in later editions) introduces a kind of absurdity by association into the prosecution's case, and it is clear that the whole project mounted in *The Covent-Garden Journal* amounts to a paradoxical defence of Fielding's work. Just like Justice Thrasher's courtroom in the first scene of the novel itself, this trial is rigged from the start.

However, the sly mockery and undercutting of the accusers is not enough on its own, and in the next issue of the journal, a week later, a more vociferous defence of the book is offered by 'a grave Man' – none other than the author himself in his most serious guise:

> 'If you, Mr. Censor, are yourself a Parent, you will view me with Compassion when I declare I am the Father of this poor Girl the Prisoner at the Bar; nay, when I go farther, and avow, that of all my Offspring she is my favourite Child. I can truly say that I bestowed a more than ordinary Pains in her Education; in which I will venture to affirm, I followed the Rules of all those who are acknowledged to have writ best on the Subject; and if her Conduct be fairly examined, she will be found to deviate very little from the strictest Observation of all those Rules; neither Homer nor Virgil pursued them with greater Care than myself, and the candid and learned Reader will see that the latter was the noble model, which I made use of on this Occasion.
>
> 'I do not think my Child is entirely free from Faults. I know nothing human that is so; but surely she doth not deserve the Rancour with which she hath been treated by the Public. However, it is not my Intention, at present, to make my Defence; but shall submit to a Compromise, which hath been always allowed in this Court in all Prosecutions for Dulness. I do, therefore, solemnly declare to you, Mr. Censor, that I will trouble the World no more with any Children of mine by the same Muse.'   (CGJ, pp. 65–6)

This offer is greeted with 'a loud Huzza' and the tender Amelia is publicly reconciled to her caring parent. Despite Fielding's suggestion that his full defence is only deferred to a later date, the case is over, and when the Court reconvened the following week, it was to put on trial the Irish actor Henry Mossop, charged with unlawfully impersonating Macbeth, whom only David Garrick could properly represent. The issue of 'Dulness' only reappears some time later, when Eliza Haywood's 'Grub Street' novel, *The History of Miss Betty Thoughtless*, is arraigned.

It is thus clear that the 'Court of Censorial Enquiry' is not an entirely serious forensic tribunal. However, amid this knock-about tomfoolery, Fielding does not want to surrender entirely, and his closing remarks in the *Amelia* case indicate that the author has only made a tactical and temporary retreat:

> Then Amelia was delivered to her Parent, and a Scene of great Tenderness passed between them, which gave much Satisfaction to many present; some of whom, however, blamed the old Gentleman for putting an End to the Cause, and several very grave and well-looking Men, who knew the whole Merits, asserted, that the Lady ought to have been honourably acquitted.   (CGJ, p. 66)

Fielding's defence of his own book is thus conducted in suitably grave terms, addressed to the 'candid and learned Reader', citing the austere (if rather implausible) classical precedents of Homer and Virgil, and vouchsafing his own integrity. For once, though, the author seeks to avoid confrontation with the unresponsive reading public, and chooses not to pursue his line of argument at all costs. Instead, he rather meekly accepts the verdict of his peers with only that unobtrusive minority report from 'several very grave and well-looking Men' tucked away in these final lines to indicate his most deeply held views about the value of his book. The real problem, it seems, lies not so much with the book itself, as with the public who misunderstand it.

It looks, then, as though Fielding's public display of contrition and repentance and his revelation of his emotional vulnerability associated with *Amelia* are at best conditional, at worst self-advertising. Although he did in fact carry out his promise not to repeat his offence, the irony of the final remarks introduces greater ambiguity and expresses dissidence from the main view. As he repudiates his novel, another of his many voices repudiates this repudiation.

In fact, this remarkable refusal to stand out strongly or aggressively in defence of his own work in public, however much he may value it privately, is only one of a series of complex public repudiations offered by Fielding at this time. In his new and secure capacity as a magistrate – assisted by the patronage of the Duke of Bedford, he was elected as Chairman of the Middlesex Sessions in May 1749 – he took the opportunity to recreate his own identity in a much more serious and less playful form than we have seen previously. Conscious that his authorial and magisterial role was now the site of strongly contending pressures, he strove to stand up for a very emphatic version of order and authority, far removed from the licence of authorship he had previously enjoyed, although, as his self-presentation as the embattled author of Amelia and his uncertain representation therein of William Booth clearly show, the conflicts between the two never entirely disappeared.

As one contemporary commentator put it, accurately identifying the emerging conflict after reading the first volume of Amelia, 'the Justice has spoiled the Author'.[5] The voice of the 'Justice' does indeed become stiflingly prominent in many of Fielding's later non-fictional works (An Enquiry into the Causes of the Late Increase of Robbers, and A Proposal for Making an Effectual Provision for the Poor), as he deconstructs his own earlier role as volatile and disruptive satirist and seeks to replace it with his new stable and socially integrated identity as official censor. Indeed, within this context Amelia is very much a transitional text, the author uneasily oscillating between his two opposing roles of apparently non-aligned social commentator and established conservative social legislator. We have already seen the complexities and paradoxes of his satiric identity, orchestrating the mayhem of Joseph Andrews and Tom Jones, but after 1749, the sober and censorious voice begins to drown out the more boisterous alternatives. In some respects, it is as though the author, who ironically represented himself through the pugnacious Parson Adams, has now turned into the high-minded and grave Dr Harrison, a process which involves both gain and loss.

The development of a more authoritative method of address around this time can be seen in other texts. In A Charge Delivered to the Grand Jury (1749), Fielding seems to dramatise his new role as cultural arbiter. Addressing an audience which is now identifiable as comprising his more fortunate fellow-citizens, prosperous males involved in the regulation of society and anxious about the behaviour of the 'mob', Fielding enacts his new sobriety, ceremonially intoning the liturgy of conservative legislative practice, railing against the twin iniquities of 'Luxury' and 'Pleasure':

> This Fury after licentious Pleasures is grown to so enormous a Height, that it may be called the Characteristic of the present Age. And it is an Evil, Gentleman, of which it is neither easy nor pleasant to foresee all the Consequences. Many of them, however, are obvious; and these are so dreadful, that they will, I doubt not, induce you to use your best Endeavours to check the further Encrease of this growing Mischief; for the Rod of the Law, Gentlemen, must restrain those within the Bounds of Decency and Sobriety, who are deaf to the Voice of Reason, and superior to the Fear of Shame.[6]

As Fielding speaks from the bench to his fellow-citizens, he lays aside what he sees as the ineffective rod of satire and gratefully takes up the stricter rod of law, accepting the conflicts which may attend a significantly more authoritarian position in return for the increased authority it allows him. The 'Voice of Reason' and the 'Fear of Shame' which were the legitimising bases for comedy are now to be replaced by legislative authority and the executive power to carry out projects of amendment.

In this pamphlet, even more than in the subscribed *Miscellanies*, the author is engaging in dialogue with a known community of listeners or readers, on the subject of shared concerns about the workings of their own society. And indeed, perhaps it is even going too far to talk of dialogue here, since the speaker's role does not countenance the possibilities of interruption or dissidence, presenting him instead as the final spokesman on the matters under inspection. Unlike the novelist, the 'Justice' really could command the full and undivided attention of his listeners, and he had genuine sanctions in his power should they prove inattentive.

Unsurprisingly, the views Fielding put forward as a magistrate were radically discontinuous with positions voiced earlier. The most striking example occurs when the newly appointed legislator coldly repudiates the theatre, with which an earlier incarnation of Fielding had been previously so greatly involved. Rather than embracing the stage's opportunity for stimulating political commentary and satire, the magistrate sees it from his privileged position on the bench as a deplorable part of the contemporary 'Fury after licentious Pleasures':

> But, Gentlemen, so immoderate are the Desires of many, so hungry is their Appetite for Pleasure, that they may be said to have a Fury after it; and Diversion is no longer the Recreation or Amusement, but the whole Business of their Lives. They are not content with three

> Theatres, they must have a fourth; where the Exhibitions are not only
> contrary to Law, but contrary to Good-Manners, and where the Stage is
> reduced back again to that Degree of Licentiousness which was too
> enormous for the corrupt State of *Athens* to bear.   (*Charge*, pp. 23–4)

Although the argument is couched in generalities, and the oddity of
the notorious ex-playwright denouncing the wickedness of the theatre
is not allowed to gain prominence in the text, there is nonetheless a
real about-turn here, perhaps hard to understand in terms of personal
psychology, but easy to recognise politically and rhetorically. Just as in
The True State of the Case of Bosavern Penlez (1749), *An Enquiry into
the Causes of the Late Increase of Robbers* (1751) and *A Proposal for
Making Effectual Provision for the Poor* (1753), Fielding is here
addressing an audience which requires the speaker to display at least
the appearance of solutions to disturbing social problems, and Fielding
the magistrate does not disappoint them – paradoxically, his climactic
performance as 'rhetorical' man is to reinvent himself as a born-again
'serious' figure.

In his fiction, however, he is able to leave this pragmatic
imperative aside, and, as he does in *Amelia*, the novelist can still dwell
on the apparent intractability of those very issues which the
magistratical pamphlets seek to solve, to explore the human side of
problems which the magistrate has to obliterate. The contrast
between Fielding's grave endorsement of the legal world as magistrate
and his scepticism about it as novelist can be seen immediately in the
dramatic opening of his last novel:

> On the first of April, in the Year ——, the Watchman of a certain
> Parish (I know not particularly which) within the Liberty of *Westminster*,
> brought several Persons whom they had apprehended the preceding
> Night, before *Jonathan Thrasher*, Esq; one of the Justices of the Peace for
> that Liberty.   (*Amelia*, pp. 17–18)

The teasing combinations of omniscience and ignorance in the
author's narration of this episode create the illusion of its unmediated
authenticity. He knows the date (April Fool's Day!), but does not
divulge the year (from internal evidence it can be identified as 1733),
and he is to some extent uncertain about the location. To the best of
his abilities, it seems, the narrator assures us that he is telling it
factually – merely recording a state of affairs, not intervening in it.
The author acts as a witness to these events rather than as their

instigator or controller, and we are reliant on his ability to recall what he knew. When he operated as an omniscient narrator elsewhere, Fielding felt able to orchestrate the scenes he presented in any way he thought fit, but by introducing some purely conventional recognition of his limited access – 'I know not particularly which' – he grounds this narrative in a real world of which he claims to learn only by report.

Of course, as the episode goes on, we can see vestigial traces of the more prominent narrator of the earlier novels, and the significance of the trading justice's tribunal becomes clearer through just such a stealthy intervention:

> The second Criminal was a poor Woman, who was taken up by the Watch as a Street-walker. It was alledged against her that she was found walking the Streets after Twelve o'Clock, and the Watchman declared he believed her to be a common Strumpet. She pleaded in her Defence (as was really the Truth) that she was a Servant, and was sent by her Mistress, who was a little Shopkeeper, and upon the Point of Delivery, to fetch a Midwife; which she offered to prove by several of the Neighbours, if she be allowed to send for them. The Justice asked her why she had not done it before. To which she answered, she had no Money, and could get no Messenger. The Justice then called her several scurrilous Names; and declaring she was guilty within the Statute of Street-walking, ordered her to *Bridewell* for a Month.
> (*Amelia*, p. 22)

The presiding justice and the presiding narrator find themselves in interestingly similar and interestingly different positions in this episode. With the breezy disregard for proper procedure seen in the tribunals run by Squire Western in *Tom Jones*, Thrasher takes upon himself the absolute authority to allocate punishments and rewards at will, without feeling under any obligation to establish all the relevant facts, thereby abusing the system within which he operates. His aggressive and unjust treatment of this woman is typical of his judgements, and the episode as a whole seems to be preparing us dramatically for the introduction of Booth, while at the same time moving the book more generally towards a satiric exposure of the failings of a corrupt system carried out by a well-informed but unobtrusive narrator.

As an example of the system's corruption, the previous defendant has been confined, despite all the evidence to the contrary, on the grounds of his nationality: 'Sirrah, your Tongue betrays your Guilt.

You are an *Irishman*, and that is always sufficient Evidence with me'
(*Amelia*, p. 22). The narrative seems to be making a clear satiric point
here: the aptly named Thrasher is not responsible for the articulation
of justice but for the expression of reactionary personal prejudices.
Yet, if we remember the ridiculous caricature of Fitzpatrick from *Tom
Jones*, we may suspect that the anti-Irish prejudice was not exclusively
the property of the English bench, then or now. And we might go
further and begin to see odd resemblances between the justice and the
narrator – their prejudices may be different, but they act with equal
briskness and finality. The narrative is as judgemental as Thrasher,
and, at least as far as his courtroom is concerned, not much more
tolerant. Thoughout this novel, prejudice is not set up in opposition
to tolerance, but to other prejudices, closer to the heart of the
narrator.

However, the key phrase here is the narrator's brief parenthetical
interjection '(as was really the Truth)', which changes the whole
perspective of the narrative. After the disavowal of authority at the
beginning, the narrator here assumes full power to inform readers of
relevant material available only to him. The intervention makes very
graphic the injustice of the proceedings, but also changes the role of
the narrator in his chronicle. To put it in the terms used by Gerard
Genette, the point of narration here seems to start out as 'external
focalization', where some important information might be withheld
from the reader through the narrator's partial ignorance of events: 'I
know not particularly which.' Then, as the story unfolds the narration
moves towards the 'zero focalization' associated with omniscient
narrators who know everything about a world of their own creation –
'as was really the Truth'.[7] These two positions are simply conventions,
and neither is a guarantee of authenticity. After all, nothing in this
narrative is *really* the truth, just as there can be no part of the story
unknown to its inventor. Fielding's uncertainty over narrative here
hints at some of the paradoxes exploited in the comic novels, but
betrays a deeper uncertainty about the possibilities of verisimilitude
and of contacting the world beyond the page.

The point about the story-teller's protestations of ignorance and
knowledge is small and rather technical, but it indicates deep
underlying uncertainties about the narrator's role in *Amelia*, and
indeed about the function of the novel as a whole. Sensitive to his
own complicity in the legal system, Fielding at first offers the book
simply as imperfect testimony to particular abuses. But uncertain of

his reader's acumen, Fielding feels the need to spell things out every so often, within the overall context of a mystery novel in which certain relevant facts are withheld. More importantly, his insecure narrative position leaves the whole book suspended between the poles of the public and the private, between agitation towards creating a better world and consolation for living in an imperfect one. It remains unclear throughout *Amelia* whether the narrative is designed to stir its readers into demanding reform, so that such problems as they see exposed in the plot will not be repeated, or whether it is meant to reinforce their notions of the essential imperfections of human nature, which can only be dealt with by the philosophic resignation of a Dr Harrison. In as much as the book is the first of these, it articulates the novelist's authority to cry out for reform of the 'real' world. In as much as it is the second of these, it projects the justice's willingness to work within an imperfect system, illustrated through an exemplary literary world created by the author.

In fact, the treatment of the legal system in *Amelia* is a case where this division is obvious. Talking of the wrongful imprisonment of Booth, the narrator seems to reach for a very radical social analysis:

> It will probably be objected, that the small Imperfections which I am about to produce, do not lie in the Laws themselves, but in the ill Execution of them; but, with Submission, this appears to me to be no less an Absurdity, than to say of any Machine that it is excellently made, tho' incapable of performing its Functions. Good Laws should execute themselves in a well regulated State; at least, if the same Legislature which provides the Laws, doth not provide for the Execution of them, they act as *Graham* would do, if he should form all the Parts of a Clock in the most exquisite Manner, yet put them so together that the Clock could not go. In this Case, surely we might say that there was a small Defect in the Constitution of the Clock.
>
> (*Amelia*, p. 19)

By comparing the defects of the law to those of a clock, even one constructed by as famous and reliable a horologist as George Graham, Fielding may be inviting cries for the most sweeping and radical reform of the constitution. This statement looks as though it is asking readers to consider whether the law is formulated as it should be, and whether the eradication of incompetent or corrupt individuals would be sufficient to improve its operations. By moving towards an institutional critique of the legal system, Fielding may be returning to the distinction between attacking the individual and describing the species which he used to legitimise some of his comic writing. In that case, the awful Thrasher is not just a peculiar grotesque, but a more representative figure, representing a species rather than an individual – the species being the darker shadow of the grave and serious Justice Henry Fielding. To put the case diagrammatically: Fielding's own representation in the book is thus as both a more authoritative version of Thrasher and a more lively version of Harrison.

Throughout this book, Fielding oscillates between an apparent plea for legal reform and a more individualised and domestic case history, where the moral status of individuals is seen as the main motivating force in the tale. Newgate, for instance, the setting of the first three books, is portrayed as an infernal region of misunderstandings and suffering, but also as a discrete working community of its own. In contrast to the pitiful scenes in Bondum's sponging house (VIII, x; XII, ii, v) where debtors and their helpless families are held, Newgate is seen as accommodating genuine villains of many varieties as well as the imprudent and maligned Booth. Fielding represents the prison as a truly vile place, full of utterly impenitent criminals such as 'Blear-Eyed Moll', confidence tricksters like Mr. Robinson, a few pathetic victims of circumstance, and only one or two displaced persons of real merit. Like the nether regions of A Journey from This World to the Next, Newgate is a heavily stylised image of the world beyond the pages of the book, with the author making no attempt to see it exclusively in its own terms, to call for prison reform or to agitate on behalf of the wrongfully incarcerated.

Frequently, the opportunity for direct social criticism made available by the tale is side-stepped by the narrator in favour of a more limited commitment to reforming the laws covering the treatment of debtors and a plea for clear-sightedness about the personal integrity of individuals, whatever their social standing. Furthermore, the responsibility for conducting the narrative is regularly passed over to one of the characters – we hear the histories of Miss Mathews (I, vii–ix), Booth (II, III), Mrs Bennet (VII, ii–ix), Mr Trent (XI, iii), amid the running commentary offered by Dr Harrison. By using this technique of 'multiple focalization' again, Fielding thus disengages from the authorised institutional analysis his narrative seems to set up, and creates in its place a detailed fable about individual morality, presented in a vividly realised contemporary setting.

The attack on the pretentions of 'rank' in episodes like the
stagecoach scene in *Joseph Andrews* is here intensified, but it is not
inflected towards any radical questioning of authority. As Booth
himself tells Miss Mathews:

> . . . yet I know not, on a more strict Examination into the Matter,
> why we should be more surprised to see Greatness of Mind discover
> itself in one Degree, or Rank of Life, than in another. Love,
> Benevolence, or what you will please to call it, may be the reigning
> Passion in a Beggar as well as in a Prince; and wherever it is, its
> Energies will be the same.   (*Amelia*, pp. 123–4)

Throughout the novel, this disparity of status and merit is reinforced
by the mismatch of rank and integrity seen in the characters of, say,
the good Serjeant Atkinson, the ridiculous Major Bath and the
untrustworthy Colonel James. But the radical potential of this
disparity is not as strongly pressed in this book as it was in
Richardson's *Pamela*, being instead surrounded by ironic
misunderstandings, such as the confusion of the eligibility of Serjeant
Atkinson as a marriage partner for Mrs Ellison, and naturalised as no
more than the inevitable and irreversible way of the world.

Some of the conflicts raised by the discrepancies between merit
and status are dramatised in this novel through the institution of
marriage. The rewarding of true merit is seen increasingly as
something to be carried on by enlightened individuals in their private
lives rather than as a political project falling within the
responsibilities of the state and its officers. A true marriage, it is
suggested, shows the superiority of brotherhood over rank:

> 'How monstrous then,' cries *Amelia*, 'is the Opinion of those, who
> consider our matching ourselves the least below us in Degree, as a kind
> of Contamination!'
> 'A most absurd and preposterous Sentiment,' answered Mrs. *Bennet*
> warmly, 'how abhorrent from Justice, from common Sense, and from
> Humanity – but how extremely incongruous with a Religion, which
> professes to know no Difference of Degree, but ranks all Mankind on
> the footing of Brethren!'   (*Amelia*, p. 305)

This endorsement of brotherhood (underlined later by Dr Harrison)
infiltrates the novel through the recurrent conflict between
characters' public roles and their contending private desires. Through

Fielding's increasingly omniscient narration in the second half of the book, hidden motives are discovered, secrets are disclosed, leading us into constant suspicion that the public performances of any individuals may not properly represent their real moral character.

The analysis of hypocrisy is by now familiar, and once again Fielding is reluctant to find a fully coherent scheme of values beyond the broader encouragement of honesty and decency, preferring to expose problems and paradoxes for their own sakes. He articulates the complexities of everyday domestic life through the confusions of supporting characters like Mrs Bennet, who at various points is noble, pathetic, snobbish, tipsy, helpful, and naive, showing again how challenging it must always be to seek to be definite about anyone's character. And as dramatised particularly in the extraordinary masquerade (X, ii–v), the world of the text is one of inconsistency, confusion and duplicity, in which it is once again virtually impossible to convey even a simple message effectively. Within this complex world, Fielding chooses to investigate questions of private morality. Through the figure of William Booth he examines the difficulties encountered by a man presented as basically good, if weak, as he tries to live a decent life in a hostile world. The impediments before him are obvious: Booth lacks a private income and spends most of the narrative in prison or in debt, pursued by the corrupt attorney Murphy. As an unfortunate officer, and an impractical farmer, he retains the standards and responsibilities of a gentleman, but these are seen as unreliable without the necessary material resources.

Booth is presented as a challenge for the discernment of readers. After his prolonged 'criminal Conversation' in Newgate with Miss Mathews, he is metaphorically brought before the reader's court of conscience, where his conduct is defended by the narrator in some startling terms:

> We desire that the good-natured and candid Reader will be pleased to weigh attentively the several unlucky Circumstances which concurred so critically, that Fortune seemed to have used her utmost Endeavours to ensnare poor *Booth's* Constancy. Let the Reader set before his Eyes a fine young Woman, in a manner a first Love, conferring Obligations, and using every Art to soften, to allure, to win, and to enflame; let him consider the Time and the Place; let him remember that Mr. *Booth* was a young Fellow, in the highest Vigour of Life; and lastly, let him add one single Circumstance, that the Parties were alone together; and then

if he will not acquit the Defendant, he must be convicted, for I have
nothing more to say in his Defence.   (*Amelia*, p. 154)

By personifying himself as a barrister acting on behalf of his
characters, Fielding recognises the interpretive freedom available to
readers and tries to put as much controlling pressure on it as possible.
The hostile contemporary response to the novel showed just how
necessary (and also how ineffective) this pressure was, and even here
it seems that the narrator is much happier talking to male readers
about male concerns than to anyone else.

As it concerns private life, the novel is inevitably entangled in
issues of gender. The passage above transforms male predators into
victims, in thrall to female fortune, and this is a message Booth
repeats several times – 'how little dost thou guess at the Art and
Falsehood of Women!' he tells his long-suffering wife (*Amelia*, p. 241).
Some contemporary commentators saw behind this a covert attempt
at self-justification on the author's part, at a time when his own
matrimonial entanglements were coming under scrutiny, but the
novel goes beyond the confines of the confessional, and problematises
sexual politics less specifically.[8] Throughout the narrative, different
versions of sexual entrapment are presented, and the complexities of
sexual attraction are made as prominent in the world of the novel as
the need for cash. Alongside Booth's infidelity, we see the pressures
put on Amelia during her husband's absence, the attempted seduction
of Mrs Bennet by a Lord and a host of other sexual stratagems at the
masquerade. Marriage might occasionally act as a private way to
rectify the anomalies of rank and merit, but within the tale sexual
desire is seen as a predominantly destructive and dangerous force,
disfiguring any stable and hierarchical model of society, beyond the
reach of legislators. Although this perception had also infiltrated the
comic and satiric novels, in the assaults on Mrs Heartfree, Sophia and
Fanny, it had been contained and accommodated within the overall
narrative. In this book, the sexual appetites and desires of the
characters have the capacity to cause much greater distress.

In *A Charge Delivered to the Grand Jury*, Fielding was very
authoritarian about what he saw as the increasingly necessary attempts
to regulate sexual behaviour in a licentious world, and the book
reinforces this conservative position on a number of occasions.
Speaking authorially, he discussed the significance of the passion felt
by Colonel James for Amelia:

Thus the Object of the Colonel's Lust very plainly appears; but the Object of his Envy may be more difficult to discover. Nature and Fortune had seemed to strive with a kind of Rivalship, which should bestow most on the Colonel. The former had given him Person, Parts, and Constitution, in all which he was superior to almost every other Man. The latter had given him Rank in Life, and Riches, both in a very eminent Degree. Whom should this happy Man envy? Here, lest Ambition should mislead the Reader to search the Palaces of the Great, we will direct him to *Gray's-Inn-Lane*; where in a miserable Bed, in a miserable Room, he will see a miserable broken Lieutenant, in a miserable Condition, with several heavy Debts on his Back, and without a Penny in his Pocket. This, and no other, was the Object of the Colonel's Envy. And why? because this Wretch was possessed of the Affections of a poor little Lamb; which all the vast Flocks that were within the Power and Reach of the Colonel, could not prevent that Colonel's longing for. And sure this Image of the Lamb is not improperly adduced on this Occasion: For what was the Colonel's Desire but to lead this poor Lamb, as it were, to the Slaughter, in order to purchase a Feast of a Few Days by her final Destruction, and to tear her away from the Arms of one where she was sure of being fondled and caressed all the Days of her Life.   (*Amelia*, p. 339)

The 'writerly' intrusion here, moving from realistic portraiture to allegory, is far from the portrayal of the alluring Miss Mathews, and it shows some of the ideological and formal uncertainties within this narrative. 'Lust' and 'Envy', as expressed by Colonel James and a great many other characters, do not respect social position, yet nor do they contribute towards any sense of brotherhood. The inability of either society or the narrator to contain these destructive impulses creates great points of stress and pressure within Fielding's narrative, which he seems helpless to resolve or exploit to controlled thematic ends. Ironically, and perhaps self-consciously, the actual author of the novel seems to become as helpless in the organisation of his own book as the feeble author who talks to Booth in the sponging-house (VIII, v).

As *Amelia* progresses, the certainties and confidence of the opening, with its unambiguous satiric portrait of Thrasher, get stealthily swallowed up by the developing confusions of sexual politics, personal character, money, the law and all the other imperfect systems of regulation the book uncovers. The recognisable satiric portrait of the unjust justice becomes beset and beleaguered by more complex formulations of disorder, culminating in the licensed chaos of the masquerade. The scenes at the Haymarket allow the plot to develop in a rather baffling way, but they also infiltrate a carnivalesque notion of disorder into the book, strictly opposed to the Harrisonian morality it seems to yearn to endorse. When the Doctor's letter to James goes astray (like Dowling's letter in *Tom Jones*) and is publicly performed, mockingly, by some young men in masquerade, the book offers an ironic reappraisal of its own meanings and its capacity to effect communication between author and public. Speaking in a less sombre and authoritative voice, *Amelia* suddenly parodies itself, and jeopardises its own pretentions to clarity and meaning.[9]

Time and again in this book, the operations of chance overcome the attempted exercise of control. Card games, dreams, sudden attacks, coincidences, physical collapses, disturbing propinquities, all serve to impede the progress of the narrative, and make it much less firmly on the track towards one clear meaning than at first appeared. Of course, the book *is* still an informed critique of the contemporary legal system, but it is intermittently an attack from a more extreme position than at first appears, and the twin poles of agitation and consolation are never fully organised into coherent shape. The darkness at the heart of the book is expressed by the heroine herself, when she says 'I have often wished . . . to hear you converse with Dr *Harrison* on this Subject; for I am sure he would convince you, though I can't, that there really are such Things as Religion and Virtue' (*Amelia*, p. 451).

Glimpsing the difficulty of being convinced of even the very existence of 'Religion' and 'Virtue', the plot begins to disintegrate, and the second half of the novel is full of interspersed anecdotes and tales. Only at the end does the narrator seize control of events, and, with the same dexerity with which he effected the sly re-orientation of the hero's class position in the two comic novels, he realigns the social and financial position of the Booths by means of a lost will, put into probate by a rather familiar-looking intelligent magistrate. In fact, despite some strident cries for reform from the narrator, the authority of the text is no longer made central. Fielding seems to endorse the melancholy position put forward near the end of the text by a Peer, for whom the nation is now in its third, terminal phase:

> In its Youth it rises by Arts and Arms to Power and Prosperity. This it enjoys and flourishes with a while; and then it may be said to be in the Vigour of its Age, enrich'd at home with all the Emoluments and

Blessings of Peace, and formidable abroad with all the Terrors of War. At length this very Prosperity introduces Corruption; and then comes on its old Age. Virtue and Learning, Art and Industry, decay by Degrees. The People sink into Sloth and Luxury, and Prostitution. It is enervated at Home, becomes contemptible abroad; and such indeed is its Misery and Wretchedness, that it resembles a Man in the last decrepit Stage of Life, who looks with unconcern at his approaching Dissolution.   (*Amelia*, p. 461)

Such a combination of resignation and erudition seems to have become Fielding's own ideological position at this time. In a similar passage in *An Enquiry into the Causes of the Late Increase of Robbers*, he draws connections between the state of Hanoverian England and the later days of the Roman Empire – comparisons of the relative stages of decline suffered by mighty civilisations requiring the vast narrative canvas of Edward Gibbon to explore.

In his final novel, then, Fielding seeks a narrative position from which he can explore or expose all the ills of his society – its endemic injustices, its venality, its intemperance, its fondness for luxury, its sexual improprieties and its inability to recognise true merit – while also producing a compelling account of a particular marriage. He offers himself as a historian, in two obvious senses. He anatomises his culture, and he tells a tale. However, what becomes increasingly apparent is the tension between the authoritarian magistrate and the abrasive narrator. By this novel, the various uncertainties we have seen developing earlier about the nature of the dialogue and the sensitivity of the audience have infiltrated the tale itself, and Fielding as narrator has nowhere to present himself. He offers himself as narrator as a kind of SuperFielding, at last able to arbitrate successfully amid the confusions of the world. But, alas, the more prominent he becomes, the more artificial and constructed becomes the world of his jurisdiction. The only solution to the problems exposed in *Amelia* lies in the realm of fantasy, and the author once again resorts to presiding over artifice when he is unable to intervene in reality.

Notes and references

1.   See Stanley Fish, 'Rhetoric', in *Critical Terms For Literary Study*, ed. Frank Lentricchia and Thomas McLaughlin (Chicago and London, 1990), p. 208.

2. Henry Fielding, *Amelia*, ed. Martin C. Battestin (Oxford, 1983), p. 3. Further references will be incorporated in the text.
3. Richard Lanham, *The Motives of Eloquence* (New Haven, 1976), p. 1.
4. For a series of early responses to the novel, predominantly hostile, see *Henry Fielding: The Critical Heritage*, ed. Ronald Paulson and Thomas Lockwood (London and New York, 1969), pp. 286–333.
5. Thomas Edwards, in a letter to Philip Yorke, 8 January 1752, quoted in *The Critical Heritage*, p. 287.
6. Henry Fielding, *A Charge Delivered to the Grand Jury* (1749), in *An Enquiry into the Causes of the Late Increase of Robbers and Related Writings*, ed. Malvin R. Zirker (Oxford, 1988), p. 25. Further references will be incorporated in the text.
7. See Gerard Genette, *Narrative Discourse*, trans. Jane E. Lewin (Ithaca, NY, 1980), pp. 190, 189.
8. For an account of the autobiographical elements in *Amelia*, see Battestin's 'General Introduction' to his edition of the text, pp. xvi–xxi.
9. See the excellent discussion of the masquerade in Terry Castle, *Masquerade and Civilisation: The Carnivalesque in Eighteenth-Century English Culture and Fiction* (Stanford, California, 1986), pp. 177–253.

CHAPTER 7
Conclusion

We are now, Reader, arrived at the last Stage of our long Journey. As we have therefore travelled together through so many Pages, let us behave to one another like Fellow-Travellers in a Stage-Coach, who have passed several Days in the Company of each other; and who, notwithstanding any Bickerings or little Animosities which may have occurred on the Road, generally make up all at last, and mount, for the last Time, into their Vehicle with Chearfulness and Good-Humour; since, after this one Stage, it may possibly happen to us, as it commonly happens to them, never to meet more. (*TJ*, p. 913)

The recurrent themes of this study have been the complex relationships and dialogues which Fielding establishes with his readers, with the existent materials of his contemporary literary culture, and with what he saw as the most pressing issues of the day, principally those involving order and disruption. In his dealings with readers, the narrator of a Fielding novel retains full control, and is often brusque and misleading, even deliberately adversarial – the 'Bickerings or little Animosities' of the journey through the narratives only turn to 'Chearfulness and Good-Humour' when the end of the relationship is in sight. These readers are interpellated as unimaginative and rather recalcitrant creatures through the author's revisionist re-reading of contemporary literary culture, where he articulates his contempt for the low standards of that culture at the very moment when he tries to enter it as a successful literary producer.

Alongside all his other interests, and made very prominent in the preceding remarks, there is a chronic niggling concern throughout Fielding's writing about whether he can really exert proper authority over his readers, or whether in the end the consumerist ideology of popular publishing means that they have the ultimate power over him. In short, is the author still the figure of authority, or is the customer always right? In Umberto Eco's terms, are the novels 'open' or 'closed'?[1] The paradoxes and uncertainties arising from this uneasy position inevitably put in some jeopardy Fielding's claims to authority as a commentator on the issues of the day and problematise his engagement with the novel. After all, to whom is he speaking? Are they listening? And how serviceable a vehicle is fiction as a way of representing the world?

Amid these paradoxical versions of authorship and authority, Fielding's novels are distinguished by the self-consciousness of their literary procedures. More than any eighteenth-century novelist writing before Laurence Sterne, Fielding displays and exploits the conventions and artifice of fiction in order both to establish his credentials as an author-creator and to undermine the growing hegemony of verisimilitude. In discussing *Tom Jones*, I claimed it as a 'metafiction', but on examination it is obvious that all of Fielding's writing embodies recurrent concerns with the nature of fiction and the creation of illusions. The parodic polyphony of *Shamela*, the mock-heroic and Cervantic form of *Joseph Andrews*, the allusiveness and material artificiality of *A Journey from This World to the Next*, the constant concern with the creation of illusions in *Jonathan Wild*, and even the complex internal story-telling and the abrupt ending to *Amelia* all evince Fielding's exploitation of the gap between fiction and reality. What makes the issue interesting is that this was a gap opened up at the same time as the writer was exploring the intermittent points of contact between the book and the world, questioning the nature of the reality inhabited by himself and his readers.

When he comes to conclude each novel, therefore, Fielding is uncomfortably split between a desire to finalise and isolate the shape of the constructed work of art and an equally powerful desire to emphasise the continuing contingency of life. In the words of Mikhail Bakhtin, the problem facing Fielding at the end of each of his texts is 'the fundamental unfinalizability of the polyphonic novel'.[2] In seeking to show both his own controlling hand behind the literary text and the persistent volatility of day-to-day life outside the covers of a book, Fielding exploits this 'unfinalizability' by offering a kind of coda, where the main plot is sketchily continued, where the ability to have the final say is disputed.

The closing words of *Shamela*, for instance, are used by Parson Tickletext to fill in that curious gap between the point of narration and the moment of reading:

> *P. S.* Since I writ, I have a certain Account, that Mr. *Booby* hath caught his Wife in bed with *Williams*; hath turned her off, and is prosecuting him in the spiritual Court.   (*JA*, p. 357)

The text may now be complete, but the moment of its conclusion is not the end of the story, and this particular narrator clearly does not know everything that has gone on. Closure is seen to be arbitrary, and the 'story' of Shamela Andrews is not to be easily confined within the pages of one book, to be told by one imperious author.

Such a distinction between the artifice of the book and the contingency of life is also used at the end of *Joseph Andrews*, where the narrator takes his leave by briefly filling in the subsequent careers of the main participants, after the climactic nuptials of Joseph and Fanny. We learn that at the point of writing, Fanny's life has changed:

> Mr. *Booby* hath with unprecedented Generosity given *Fanny* a Fortune of two thousand Pound, which *Joseph* hath laid out in a little Estate in the same Parish with his Father, which he now occupies, (his Father having stock'd it for him;) and *Fanny* presides, with most excellent management in his Dairy; where, however, she is not at present very able to bustle much, being, as Mr. *Wilson* informs me in his last Letter, extremely big with her first Child.   (*JA*, p. 311)

Suddenly, then, the grand narrator and orchestrator of the novel has left the stage, and in his place comes a mere correspondent, dependent on Mr Wilson of all people for his information about the later trajectory of the narrative. By the end of the book, the narrator has turned into a kind of package-holiday-maker, who has exchanged addresses with his characters and his readers at the end of his brief, but intense, acquaintance with them, and who receives the occasional letter from them.

This droll and self-conscious abnegation of the narrator's responsibilities is not the only jest at the end of *Joseph Andrews*. The final words of the text return to the original satiric project of the book, and sneer at the littleness of contemporary authors:

> *Joseph* remains blest with his *Fanny*, whom he doats on with the utmost Tenderness, which is all returned on her side. The Happiness of this Couple is a perpetual Fountain of Pleasure to their fond Parents; and what is particularly remarkable, he declares he will imitate them in

> their Retirement; nor will be prevailed upon by any Book-sellers, or
> their Authors, to make his Appearance in *High-Life*.   (JA, p. 312)

The very specific joke at the expense of Richardson's relatively
unsuccessful sequel to the original *Pamela* is widened out into an
enjoyably absurd image of literary characters being besieged by the
representatives of the press – the eighteenth-century *paparazzi* – eager to
sign up celebrities and ghost-write their lives for an eager and credulous
public. The confusions of illusion and reality deliberately created here
once again belittle the contemporary audience, but more forcefully
denigrate the booksellers and authors who cater to that market.

By leaving the text flagrantly incomplete, Fielding avoided this
problem in *A Journey from This World to the Next*, and his own
sardonic exercise in ghost-writing, *Jonathan Wild*, ends with a fairly
perfunctory summary of the eventual fates of the main participants,
and a simplification of the meaning of Wild's career. In *Tom Jones*,
the catalogue of fates is continued, after the narrator takes formal
leave of his readers:

> Thus, Reader, we have at length brought our History to a Conclusion,
> in which, to our great Pleasure, tho' contrary perhaps to thy
> Expectation, Mr. *Jones* appears to be the happiest of all human Kind:
> For what Happiness this World affords equal to the Possession of such a
> Woman as *Sophia*, I sincerely own I have never yet discovered.
>
> As to the other Persons who have made any considerable Figure in
> this History, as some may desire to know a little more concerning them,
> we will proceed in as few Words as possible, to satisfy their Curiosity.
>   (*TJ*, p. 979)

Casually offering 'as few Words as possible' at the end of an enormous
novel, the narrator then gives the briefest sketches of the subsequent
careers of Allworthy, Blifil, Square, Thwackum, Mrs Fitzpatrick, Mrs
Western, Lady Bellaston, Mr Nightingale, Mrs Miller, Mrs Waters,
Parson Supple, Black George, Molly Seagrim, Partridge, and, rather
surprisingly, none other than Parson Abraham Adams, who wanders
into this novel a few paragraphs from the end. The effect is at once
that of a conclusive curtain call, where actors celebrate their
performance before stepping back from their roles and returning to
the 'real' world, and that of a strange continuation of the fictional
world, where the distinctions between the novel and reality (and
between this novel and others) remain blurred.

The persistent negotiation between fiction and 'fact' is very prominent at the end of *Amelia*. Having brought the plot to conclusion by authorial sleight-of-hand, Fielding remembers his obligations to tidy up all the loose ends:

> Having brought our History to a Conclusion, as to those Points in which we presume our Reader was chiefly interested, in the foregoing Chapter; we shall in this by way of Epilogue, endeavour to satisfy his Curiosity, as to what happened to the principal Personages of whom we have treated in the foregoing Pages.   (*Amelia*, p. 531)

In this version, the conventional curtain call is preceded by an acknowledgement that the earlier narrative has been deliberately shaped, and that the narrator has some overall selective and interpretive strategy based on his assumptions about the audience – 'as to those Points in which we presume our Reader was chiefly interested'. However, the acknowledgement of the fiction and artifice lying behind the narrative is compromised by the last remarks made in the book:

> *Amelia* is still the finest Woman in *England* of her Age. *Booth* himself often avers she is as handsome as ever. Nothing can equal the Serenity of their Lives. *Amelia* declared to me the other Day, that she did not remember to have seen her Husband out of Humour these ten Years; and upon my insinuating to her, that he had the best of Wives, she answered with a Smile, that she ought to be so, for he had made her the happiest of Women.   (*Amelia*, p. 533)

Here again Fielding introduces an entirely spurious intimacy with his characters, suddenly investing them with a 'real' existence beyond the pages of the book at that very moment when their textual construction is most strongly acknowledged.

The difficulties of concluding novels are, of course, not exclusive to Fielding, and might need a larger theoretical inquiry to explore. But for the present purposes, they identify a particular dilemma in Fielding, and in the book you are holding in your hands. Would that I were able to conclude the present study in such a way as Fielding concludes his novels, vouchsafing my remarks by ensuring the reader that Fielding himself had cast an eye over them and expressed his approval. Of course, the idea is absurd. Yet, the Fielding who has been under examination in these pages has flitted from being a historical entity to a textual construction many times, just like a character in one of his own narratives, and the problem of how to make my farewell to him (and to you) remains complex.

The paradox that has both invigorated and beset my argument is that Fielding is made so prominent at the very moment when his insubstantiality is to be declared. And that is a paradox I do not wish to dispel or develop further. The ridiculousness of trying to have the final say on the dialogic nature of Fielding's texts is clear to me, and I thus take my leave merely by hoping that the debate continues. Since this study has been shadowed by Fielding's biography, the final words should be his, from his posthumously published travel narrative *The Journal of a Voyage to Lisbon* (1755). In his 'Author's Preface' he sets out some terms of reference, deigned to recommend his book to the public, and with these I leave you:

> Having thus endeavoured to obviate some censures, to which a man without the gift of foresight, or any fear of the imputation of being a conjurer, might conceive this work would be liable, I might now undertake a more pleasing task, and fall at once to the direct and positive praises of the work itself; of which, indeed, I could say a thousand good things; but the task is so very pleasant that I shall leave it wholly to the reader, and it is all the task that I impose on him. A moderation for which he may think himself obliged to me when he compares it with the conduct of authors, who often fill a whole sheet with their own praises, to which they sometimes set their own real names, and sometimes a fictitious one.[3]

Notes and References

1. Umberto Eco, *The Role of the Reader: Exploration in the Semiotics of Texts*, (London, 1979), pp. 47–67.
2. Mikhail Bakhtin, *Problems in Dostoyevsky's Poetics* (2nd edn), trans. R.W. Rotsel (no place of publication indicated, 1973), p. 34.
3. Henry Fielding, *The Journal of a Voyage to Lisbon* (1755), ed. A.R. Humphreys (London, 1964), p. 189.

Index